DOWN
42ND
STREET

ALSO BY MARC ELIOT

WARNER BOOKS

An AOL Time Warner Company

MARC ELIOT

DOWN 42ND STREET

Sex, Money, Culture,
and Politics at
the Crossroads
of the World

Warner Books, Inc., 1271 Avenue of the Americas, New York, NY 10020
Visit our Web site at *www.twbookmark.com*
For information on Time Warner Trade Publishing's online program,
visit www.ipublish.com.

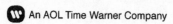 An AOL Time Warner Company

Printed in the United States of America
First Printing: November 2001
10 9 8 7 6 5 4 3 2 1

BOOK DESIGN BY RALPH FOWLER

Library of Congress Cataloging-in-Publication Data

Eliot, Marc.
    Down 42nd Street : sex, money, culture, and politics at the crossroads
of the world / Marc Eliot.
      p.   cm.
    Includes bibliographical references and index.
    ISBN 0-446-52571-5
    1. Forty-second Street (New York, N.Y.)—History.   2. New York
(N.Y.)—Social conditions.   3. New York (N.Y.)—Economic conditions.
4. New York (N.Y.)—Politics and government.   I. Title: Down Forty
Second Street.
    F128.67.F7 E44   2001
    974.7′1—dc21   2001026117

ILLUSTRATIONS. Page iii: *Aerial view of West 42nd Street and Times Square in the mid-1940s. The Hudson River is visible in the background and, beyond it, the shores of New Jersey.* (Courtesy of Fred Papert's Committee to Develop 42nd Street) Pages iv–v: *42nd Street between Seventh and Eighth Avenue in the mid-1960s. Hubert's Museum and Flea Circus was a favorite hangout of the fringe crowd. The once-elegant legitimate playhouses had turned the strip into a freewheeling cinematheque that charged a tenth the price of—and often outgrossed—the mainstream theaters sometimes playing the same films around the corner.* (Corbis-Bettman)

IN MEMORY OF KAREN HUBERT'S

WIT, TALENT, AND ETERNAL GRACE

CONTENTS

DRAMATIS PERSONAE

{in order of appearance}

Edward Koch: mayor of New York City, 1978–89. Koch helped in the fight to save Grand Central Terminal and, as mayor, favored corporate redevelopment of West 42nd Street.

Abe Beame: under-rated, single term (1974–77) mayor of New York City, who failed to effectively redevelop 42nd Street.

Mario Cuomo: governor of New York State, 1983–95. Mayor Koch's main adversary in the tug-of-war between the state and the city for political control of the redevelopment of 42nd Street.

John Lindsay: mayor of New York City, 1966–73. Introduced massive rezoning as a means to spur redevelopment of Midtown West.

Abram S. Hewitt: mayor of New York City, 1887–88.

William "Boss" Tweed: power broker, corrupt "boss" of nineteenth-century Tammany Hall political machine.

August Belmont: private developer. The son of German-Jewish immigrants, in 1902 he created the privately owned Rapid Transit Subway Construction Company, which struck a deal with the city to build the first underground subway system in New York City, the Interborough Rapid Transit Company, or IRT.

William Barclay Parsons: chief architect of Belmont's IRT subway.

George B. McClellan: mayor of New York City, 1904–9. Extremely popular mayor who helped transform the city into a modern metropolis. Although he had little to do with the planning or inception of

xi

the IRT, he became a populist hero in October 1904 when he rode in the first car of the subway's inaugural run.

William Randolph Hearst: newspaper publisher/mogul, a founder and leading practitioner of "yellow journalism." His morning *Journal* (with Joseph Pulitzer's *New York World*) was the chief competitor to Adolph Ochs and the *New York Times*.

Adolph Ochs: publisher of the *New York Times* from 1896 to 1935. With help from August Belmont, he built the Times Tower, which led to Long Acre Square being renamed Times Square.

Joseph Pulitzer: publisher of the *New York World*. An early competitor of Adolph Ochs and, with Hearst, one of the practitioners of late nineteenth- and early twentieth-century "yellow journalism."

James J. "Jimmy" Walker: mayor of New York City, 1926–32.

Al Smith: governor of New York State, 1919–20, 1923–28.

John F. Hylan: mayor of New York City, 1918–25.

Samuel Seabury: head of the investigation into corruption at City Hall that eventually led to Mayor Walker's resignation.

Franklin Delano Roosevelt: governor of New York State, 1929–33; president of the United States, 1933–45.

Walter P. Chrysler: automobile tycoon who in 1930 financed construction of the Chrysler Building.

Joseph V. McKee: acting mayor of New York City, 1932.

John P. O'Brien: mayor of New York City, 1933.

Fiorello H. La Guardia: mayor of New York City, 1934–45, who targeted 42nd Street as the moral sinkhole of the city.

Robert Moses: appointed by Mayor La Guardia in 1934 to serve as city parks commissioner, became a key player in the changing face of New York's physical layout.

William O'Dwyer: mayor of New York City, 1946–50.

Vincent Impellitteri: mayor of New York City, 1950–53.

Robert F. Wagner, Jr.: mayor of New York City, 1954–65, who considered West 42nd Street the city's moral leper colony.

Nelson Rockefeller: governor of New York State,1958–74; vice president of the United States under Gerald Ford, 1974–76. With his brother *David*, responsible, for convincing their father, *John D.*, to purchase and then donate land on the east side of 42nd Street on which the United Nations would build its headquarters.

William Zeckendorf: real estate developer who sold John D. Rockefeller the seventeen-acre parcel that was donated to the United Nations.

Gerald Ford: president of the United States, 1974–76. As New York

City neared bankruptcy during Beame's administration, the *Daily News* carried the front-page headline "Ford to City: DROP DEAD."

Frank Serpico: New York City police officer during the Lindsay administration whose revelations about corruption within the department led to the formation of the Knapp Commission.

George Washington: first president of the United States, 1789–97. As leader of the Continental Army, he fought a Revolutionary War battle that took place on 42nd Street.

De Witt Clinton: mayor of New York City, 1803–7, 1808–10, 1811–15.

Tommy "Paddy" Corcoran: notorious leader of the nineteenth-century "Roosters."

Cornelius "Commodore" Vanderbilt: shipping magnate and owner of the New York Central Railroad who completed construction of the first Grand Central Depot in 1871.

William H. Vanderbilt: son and partner to Cornelius.

Cornelius Vanderbilt II: grandson of Cornelius, son of William H., builder of the second and third Grand Central Terminals.

J. P. Morgan: banking mogul and partner of Cornelius II. He helped restructure the finances of Vanderbilt's rail company and participated in the building of the second Grand Central Terminal.

John Jacob Astor: (1763–1848) New York City real estate tycoon.

James Astor: son of John Jacob and one of the patrons of the Fifth Avenue New York Public Library.

Samuel J. Tilden: governor of New York State, 1875–76, and benefactor of the Fifth Avenue New York Public Library.

Andrew Carnegie: nineteenth-century steel magnate who helped finance several branches of the New York Public Library.

T. Henry French: son of play-publishing giant Samuel French. Built the American, the first legitimate theater on 42nd Street.

John Hamilton: Broadway producer arrested in 1896 for obscenity, following the opening-night performance of *Ten Minutes in the Latin Quartier, or, A Study in the Nude.*

Hope Booth: star of Hamilton's show, who was also arrested.

Klaw and Erlanger: turn-of-the-twentieth-century team of independent Broadway producers.

Hayman and Frohman: turn-of-the-nineteenth-century team of independent Broadway producers.

Nixon and Zimmerman: turn-of-the-nineteenth-century team of independent Broadway producers.

Oscar Hammerstein: turn-of-the-nineteenth-century theatrical entre-preneur. Called the father of Times Square after building several Broadway theaters, including the Olympic, the Republic, and the Victoria. Introduced electrical lighting in his theaters, source of the term "Great White Way." Introduced movies as curtain-raisers to Broadway audiences.

Robert A. Van Wyck: mayor of New York City, 1898–1901.

William J. Gaynor: mayor of New York City, 1910–13.

D. W. Griffith: groundbreaking film director whose 1915 *Birth of a Nation* premiered at the Liberty Theater on 42nd Street.

The Shuberts: show business producing and real estate partnership. Begun by Sam, J. J., and Lee Shubert with a single theater, the Lyric, on 42nd Street. Became Broadway's most powerful theatrical organi-zation.

Florenz Ziegfeld: creator of the *Ziegfeld Follies,* which, in one form or another, ran on 42nd Street for nearly thirty years.

Al Jolson: Broadway stage performer. Signed by Warner Bros. to star in the Hollywood's first commercial "talkie."

Busby Berkeley: Broadway and Hollywood choreographer.

Eugene O'Neill: American playwright.

Rodgers and Hammerstein: Broadway musical team that created 1943's groundbreaking *Oklahoma!* Oscar Hammerstein (II) was the grand-son of theater builder and producer Oscar Hammerstein.

Tennessee Williams: American playwright.

Arthur Miller: American playwright.

Edward Albee: American playwright.

Joe Franklin: Times Square-based radio and TV personality.

Andrew Sarris: film historian, educator, leading voice of American auteur school of film criticism.

Martin Scorsese: American filmmaker.

Irving Maidman: real estate developer and off-Broadway producer.

The Gambino family: one of New York City's so-called Five Familes of organized crime. Major presence on 42nd Street from the mid-1960s to the mid-1990s.

Gerald Schoenfeld: chairman of the board of the Shubert Organization.

Bernard "Bernie" Jacobs: longtime friend and associate of Gerald Schoenfeld.

Seymour Durst: real estate developer.

Kent Barwick: president of the Municipal Art Society from 1983 to 1985 and 1999–.

James Marcus: Mayor Lindsay's head of the Department of Buildings, Licenses and Traffic.

Louis Brandt: former owner of several commercial Times Square properties, including the Apollo and the Lyric Theaters.

Richard Weinstein: political aide to Mayor Lindsay. Member of the original team of developers for the City at 42nd Street project.

Gerald Minskoff: New York City real estate developer.

Harold Prince: Broadway director.

David Merrick: Broadway producer.

Bill Smith: head (1972) of the Theater Development Fund, a not-for-profit theater organization based in New York City.

John C. Portman, Jr.: Atlanta-based realestate developer.

Peter Sharpe: Mayor Lindsay's campaign finance manager.

Richard Ravitch: private developer involved with the Manhattan Plaza project in the 1970s. Later became chairman of the New York State Urban Development Corporation.

Bill Daly: head of the federally funded Midtown Enforcement Project.

John F. Ryan: police lieutenant whose beat in the 1970s was the Port Authority Bus Terminal.

Dick Oliver: reporter for the *Daily News*.

Richard Basciano: owner and operator of several porn-related businesses, including the Show World Palace.

Robert Morgenthau: Manhattan District Attorney.

Ludwig Mies van der Rohe: leading Bauhaus architect and one of the designers of the Seagram Building.

Philip Johnson: Highly influential post-Modernist architect. One of the designers, with Rohe, of the Seagram Building, he also worked on the "four corners" project with George Klein.

Robert R. Young: real estate speculator and majority owner during the 1970s of the New York Central Railroad.

Walter Gropius: Bauhaus-influenced designer involved in design of Pan Am Building.

Morris Saady: British real estate developer involved in the failed plan to tear down Grand Central Terminal.

Marcel Breuer: hired by Saady to design proposed skyscraper to replace Grand Central Terminal.

Hugh Carey: governor of New York State, 1974–81. In 1974, he granted Trump, his single largest campaign contributor, the right to rebuild the Commodore.

Donald Trump: real estate developer who rebuilt the old Commodore Hotel on 42nd Street.

Ada Louise Huxtable: former architecture critic—the first full-time architecture critic on any American newspaper—for the *New York Times* and winner of a Pulitzer Prize. Was Board member of the Municipal Art Society vehemently opposed to the attempted demolition of Grand Central Terminal.

Frederic Papert: former president of the Municipal Art Society, chairman of the Committee to Save New York City, key organizer in the successful fight to save Grand Central Terminal and a major player in the redevelopment of West 42nd Street.

Jacqueline Kennedy Onassis: former First Lady active in the battle to save Grand Central Terminal.

Roger Starr: the city's representative to the state-run Department of Housing and Urban Development (HUD) during the time of the Manhattan Plaza project.

Alexander Cohen: Broadway producer.

Bill Green: HUD city administrator in the 1970s.

Rodney Kirk: first managing director of Manhattan Plaza.

Joan Davidson: board member of the Municipal Art Society in the 1970s and 1980s.

Celeste Holm: Broadway and Hollywood actress active in the battle to save the Helen Hayes Theater.

Robert Brandt: senior vice president of the Brandt Organization, the family-owned theatrical real estate company with extensive holdings in Times Square. Son of Louis.

Roger Kennedy: former vice president of the Ford Foundation who helped raise initial funding for Fred Papert's 42nd Street Development Project and was extensively involved with the City at 42nd Street project.

Mark Finkelstein: former owner of the New Amsterdam Theater.

Don Elliot: deputy mayor during the Lindsay Administration, former chairman of the City Planning Commission, and member of the original team of developers for the City at 42nd Street project.

Paul Reichmann: part owner/operator (with his brothers Albert and Ralph) of Olympia and York, the giant Toronto-based real estate development corporation.

Harry Helmsley: head of the Helmsley-Spear Realty Corporation.

John Gutfreund: former investment banker for Salomon Brothers and chairman of the City at 42nd Street project.

Holloway and Schlager: real estate financial managers involved with the City at 42nd Street project.

Victor Riesel: labor leader, columnist, and broadcaster.

Herb Sturz: Mayor Koch's deputy mayor, former chairman of the New York City Planning Commission, and member of the editorial board of the *New York Times*.

George Klein: real estate developer involved in the planning of four high-rises for the corners of 42nd Street at Times Square (Broadway and Seventh Avenue). One of the founders of Manhattan's Holocaust Museum.

I. M. Pei: architect responsible for the design of several New York buildings, including George Klein's flagship Park Tower Realty headquarters on 59th Street and Park Avenue.

Trammel Crow: Dallas-based billionaire real estate developer.

Tishman-Speyer: New York City real estate development firm.

Larry Silverstein: 1970s real estate investor and developer.

Michael Lazar: member of Mayor Koch's City Council and former head of the Taxi and Limousine Commission. Involved with Koch administration's plan to redevelop 42nd Street. Indicted in 1986 for complicity in a scandal involving the city's Parking Violations Bureau and eventually convicted on several counts of racketeering.

The Morse family: upstate New York real estate developers.

Vince Tese: chairman of the state-supervised Urban Development Corporation.

John Burgee: architect who designed the AT&T Building.

Donald Manes: Queens borough president. Committed suicide in 1986.

Asa Griggs Candler: one of the founders of Coca-Cola and builder of the Candler building on 42nd Street, the original New York headquarters of the famous soft drink.

Carl Weisbrod: chairman of the City Planning Commission, 1987–91.

Edwin Meese: attorney general of the United States during the Reagan Administration who released the 1986 Reese Commission Report on Pornography.

John Gotti: godfather of the Gambino crime family. Once known as the Teflon Don, he is currently serving a life sentence for murder with no hope of parole.

Raymond Washington, aka Aussie "Beaver" Chandler: drug dealer whose 1987 death intensified the war on drugs.

David N. Dinkins: mayor of New York City, 1990–94.

Rudolph W. Giuliani: mayor of New York City, 1994–2002.

Reverend Al Sharpton: controversial Harlem-based minority spokesperson.

Rebecca Robertson: president of the New 42 involved with the campaign to bring Disney to 42nd Street.

Rocco Landesman: president of Jujamcyn Theaters, the third largest Broadway theater conglomerate in the country.

Arthur Ochs "Punch" Sulzberger: publisher of the *New York Times*, 1963–92, and Times Square community activist.

Marian Effie Sulzberger Dryfoos Heiskell: sister of Arthur Ochs Sulzberger; member of the board of the New 42. Instrumental in bringing Disney to 42nd Street.

Cora Cahan: chair of the New 42. Previously led the development of Lincoln Center.

Sammy "The Bull" Gravano: mob hit man whose testimony helped convict John Gotti.

Robert Di Bernardo: "made" mob member murdered by Gotti in 1987. Connected the Gambino crime family to porn on 42nd Street via part ownership of Richard Basciano's Show World Palace.

Michael Eisner: chairman of the Disney organization.

Robert Stern: architect and Disney board member.

David Malmuth: vice president and general manager of the Disney Development Company during the mid-1990s. Involved with the restoration of the New Amsterdam Theater.

Peter Rummel: president of the Disney Development Company.

John Dyson: deputy mayor during the Giuliani administration.

Garth Drabinsky: former head of the Canadian-based Livent Organization, former partner with the Ford Foundation in the restoration of the Apollo and Lyric Theaters, which later became the Ford Center for the Performing Arts.

Todd Haines: artistic director of the Roundabout Theater Company.

Mort Zuckerman: publisher of the *Daily News*.

Lew Rudin: real estate developer.

Milstein brothers: New York real estate developers.

Frank Sinatra: singer.

Jackie Gleason: comic actor.

DOWN 42ND STREET

Learning procures Preferment,
Preferment gains money, and
Money commands all things.

—*Allan Melvills' Book*

        I walked over to Lexington, and took the subway down to
Grand Central. My bags were there and all and I figured
I'd sleep in that crazy waiting room where all the benches
are. . . . It wasn't too nice. Don't ever try it. I mean it.
It'll depress you.

        —Holden Caulfield,
           from J. D. Salinger's *Catcher in the Rye*

Yeah, a movie house on 42nd Street
Ain't a very likely place for you and I to meet.

—The Rolling Stones

PART ONE

AT THE CROSSROADS

H

OW'M I DOIN'?"

It was one of those gorgeous January afternoons when the sidewalks of 42nd Street sparkle in the sunlight as if embedded with the dust of guaranteed genuine *would-I-kid-you?* diamonds. Edward Irving Koch had just embarked on a river-to-river victory walk, along the way asking passersby his signature campaign slogan, made to appear as if it were a real question by the high tone of his voice, the concerned shake of his head, the sheriff's squint in his eyes. Koch had become an expert at using exaggerated facial gestures to convey his concern for the public's welfare. That previous November he had been elected mayor of the city of New York.

He'd survived a long and difficult Democratic primary to beat no-nonsense (and no future) incumbent mayor Abe Beame and another Democrat he'd correctly perceived as his real threat, the fiery and popular favorite, Mario Cuomo. Things got more complicated when the mayoral election then unexpectedly turned into an old-fashioned four-man dog fight with Koch also finding himself up against relative unknown Republican Roy Goodman, who didn't stand a chance in the overwhelmingly Democratic city; Conservative Party talk show host Barry Farber—no way there either; and a still-unbowed Cuomo, who had somehow managed to wrest

"How'm I doin'?" Ed Koch, 109th mayor of the City of New York, campaigning for the job in the fall of 1977. (Corbis-Bettman)

the Liberal Party nomination from both Koch and Beame to mount a ferocious, if losing, campaign in the general election.*

Neither Koch, the self-proclaimed "reform Democrat" (for capital punishment, against municipal labor unions), nor Cuomo, the traditionalist (against capital punishment and for municipal labor unions), would soon forget this bitterly fought contest. Inevitably the politics of personality reduced the campaign to a single subjective-point-of-view issue: whether New Yorkers wanted to live in Koch's anything-goes, disco jam-till-dawn Joytown or Cuomo's joyless modern-day Jamestown. Koch won by convincing the voters they were better off trusting their future to his crinkled grin than Cuomo's furrowed brow. He reveled in victory, his Old World Yiddish-tinged hands held high, while his opponent smoldered with the Catholic-guilt humiliation of defeat.

A year later, Cuomo double-jumped Koch by snagging the governor's seat in Albany, a victory that resurrected his political career. The mayor appeared ready to publicly forgive if not privately forget any lingering bitterness toward the governor-elect, while Cuomo may have been willing to publicly forget, but those close to him knew he could never privately forgive the newly magnanimous mayor.

Before either left office, the simmering animosity between them would come to a boil over the single issue that most clearly represented the difference in their governing philosophies, the longstanding and problematic redemption of the west side of 42nd Street. By 1980, the city's fabled Manhattan crossroads had become ground zero for the manufacture, exhibition, and distribution of pornography, drug dealing, pedophilia, prostitution, and violent street crime. Like every major city and state politician before them, both Koch and Cuomo saw more than just urban blight on West 42nd Street. Each saw *political opportunity* in the ragged morality of the notorious boulevard. Each sensed the chance to create a higher national profile for himself as the moral savior of "the Deuce." And each wanted to be the star quarterback for this championship game

*Koch received 50 percent of the vote, Cuomo 42 percent. Goodman and Farber split the remaining 8 percent.

of political football, scoring the winning touchdown while knocking the other guy's team onto the permanent sidelines.

T HE PERSONAL FROST that coated the political relationship between Cuomo and Koch was not an unusual happenstance for either of these two politicians. Each had a tendency to over-personalize his professional battles. Their styles more closely resembled two tough neighborhood boys duking it out in the school yard rather than a couple of budding suburban intellects debating in the classroom. From the earliest days of his career in public office, Koch especially had displayed a special knack for making long-term personal enemies out of political foes, broadly depicting them as bad guys and placing himself in the role of the public's defender as a way of endearing himself to the electorate. Koch's sheriff-versus-gunfighter scenario paid off in 1973 when as a party-line reformer he first came up against Mayor John Vliet Lindsay, the Republican who'd captured City Hall in 1966, a time of particularly hard racial and fiscal unrest in New York City. Lindsay had won by running on the Liberal ticket (after being soundly defeated in his own party's primaries by conservative John Marchi). Koch was still largely unknown when, after Lindsay's successful run for mayor, he won the right to temporarily represent Lindsay's so-called Silk Stocking District (which, because of the peculiar zoning of the city, included part of the elite Upper East Side of the city and much of Greenwich Village). Although Koch had supported Lindsay for mayor, Lindsay still supported the Republican nominee for permanent election to the congressional seat.

A vengeful Koch waited for the right opportunity and then made the most of it when he came out against Lindsay in the last year of his second term. He vilified the mayor over the Forest Hills Project, a low-income ("scatter site") housing development, which would have moved mostly poor black and Puerto Rican New Yorkers into a solidly middle-class, white section of Queens. Lindsay's controversial plan managed to pull back the rock from the hitherto-hidden racist anthill that existed in the upper-middle-class outer boroughs of New York in the seventies. Supporters of the plan called their opponents racists, while those who fought against it claimed it would seriously depress property values. When the long-term, mostly Jewish residents of Forest Hills formally organized in angry protest against what they labeled "slum housing," Koch stepped in as their unofficial spokesman and used the subsequent media flurry to raise his own profile among the city's prominent Jewish population (and lower the patrician Lindsay's) by accusing the mayor of pandering to the black liberal vote in the upcoming elections. By doing so, Koch created a campaign issue to position himself for his first, unsuccessful, run for City Hall. For his part, Lindsay chose a mediator to try to settle the Forest Hills situation, a little-known Queens-born-and-bred community lawyer by the name of Mario Cuomo. Cuomo was able to get everyone to agree to a modified plan that would turn one half of the projects into public housing and the other half into luxury cooperative apartments.* And, although Koch's campaign lasted a total of forty-five days before he was forced to drop out for lack of funds, he still felt a measure of victory when Lindsay, due at least in part to his clumsy handling of the Queens housing controversy, lost his bid for a third term to old-line Democrat Abe Beame.

In 1974 a defeated but vindicated Koch returned to his duties as a congressman. Two years later he found his next front-page cause, the campaign to save 42nd Street's Grand Central Terminal from being torn down by real estate developers who wanted to replace it with a skyscraper. His participation in that battle, during which he was often photographed with one of the city's most revered and unassailable citizens, Jacqueline Kennedy Onassis, returned his name to the newspaper headlines and the lead story of the local news telecasts, making his peculiar facial expression—the one that made him look as if he were smiling and frowning at the same time—instantly recognizable to every New Yorker. This time he used his exposure to buy a first-class ticket on the express train to City Hall.

---

*The middle-income development would go on to become one of the most successful in the city's history, what one long-term resident referred to as "the jewel of public housing."

KOCH HAD THE SPRINGY STEP of success in his feet, the rhythmic stride of a winner, as he briskly walked river-to-river across the two and a half miles of 42nd Street. He began his one-man march in front of the United Nations Secretariat Building, jogged the steps up to the oddly aloof residential outpost of Tudor City, then continued west past the Chrysler, Chanin, Lincoln, and Daily News Buildings, to the majestic facade of the great Grand Central Terminal. Here on the East Side of 42nd Street, it was business as usual. The sidewalks were filled with executives wearing open overcoats, carrying attaché cases and going somewhere too fast; salesgirls wearing boots, chewing gum, and window-shopping on their lunch hour; vendors, in need of a shave and a clean shirt, hawking hot dogs with ingredients of suspicious origin; green corner kiosks selling newspapers, magazines, and panty hose; and a honking herd of cabs, cars, buses, and bikes moving slower than the pedestrians. Jammed nine to five, every night and all weekend long, like a special-effects shot from some end-of-mankind movie, this nonresidential stretch of city street would become eerily deserted.

Immediately to the west of the venerable Times Square everything changed. Whereas on the East Side, big business seemed sexy on 42nd Street, to the west, seamy sex was big business. This was where the air stank, a turgid waft of human sweat and canned Lysol that hung tough around the nostrils. Civilians' eyes on West 42nd bugged out like those on the heads of deep-fried fish, the "bookstores" sold "dirty" movies and magazines, and the peeps offered "stars" having live sex with each other *eight times a day!* Young boys, young girls, grown men dressed as women, old men dressed as young boys—all openly hustled themselves out on street corners, while drug dealers sold nickel bags and instant skin-pops in doorways without any apparent fear of a police force nowhere to be seen.

West of Seventh, Koch passed under an isosceles marquee whose flashing daytime lights and alternating horizontal tubes of blue, red, and yellow neon offered "TODAY ONLY" a triple-feature XXX movie marathon and a "NAKED AND HOT" live show. A thick blue wood arrow pointed *"Right This Way"* to a staircase next to the tiny glass-enclosed box office. Across the street a hooker in wedding-gown drag with a bright yellow wig and bloodred lips smiled, waved, and called out in a pleasant southern accent, "How y'all doin' there, Mr. Mayah?" Koch tucked his upper lip into his thrust jaw and looked the other way. He was nothing if not media savvy, and he slow-burned until he was sure the cameraman who'd been filming him had caught his full facial reaction. Koch knew his moral consternation transferred well to the small screen. It was his money shot, a look he could produce on cue.

"Forty-second Street and the Statue of Liberty are what tourists want to see when they come to New York City," he said as he stared with watery eyes directly into the TV camera. One reporter asked what his immigrant parents would have thought about his campaign promise to save the street, and Koch's face wrinkled into a silent billboard of distressed melancholia. His micro-veined cheeks became rounded and pale, his face a rough approximation of a plate of matzo balls as he recalled his dear mother's words. "'Sonny,'" he murmured, deliberately wistful, or wistfully deliberate, as he gazed through the camera's portable spot lamps in the direction of the past to an imagined apartment up in the Bronx where he'd lived some fifty years ago, "'that was *very smart of you* to save 42nd Street!'" Smothered in and dripping with tasty if greasy self-aggrandizement, this last line was not unlike a city street-corner Sabrett's with relish, mustard, and onions. It was full of fat, filler, and flavor, if notably lacking in actual food for thought. In other words, for the mayor it was the way it had always been in city politics for the last hundred years. Business as usual.

I N 1898, for those living in the five boroughs, no single act more clearly defined the end of one century and the start of the next than the Charter of Incorporation and Consolidation that united them as the Greater New York, more commonly known as New York City, one of the largest, richest, and most powerful ports in the world.

Despite the glorious economic promise of incorporation, the move was not particularly welcomed by the clique of wealthy farmers and successful industrialists. These were the privileged Manhattanites, the island's social elite who went into a collective morning-after malaise from the decades-old soirée they had thrown for and among themselves since the end of the Civil War. The rest of the world would remember the final years before incorporation as the Gay Nineties. To Manhattanites grown wealthy from various real estate and shipping enterprises, it was a bittersweet ending to a long, private, and prosperous affair.

The ending had not come peacefully. Organized, hostile anti-consolidation protests had turned into riots on both sides, beginning a decade before Tammany Hall finally restored peace and united the boroughs. Conceived as a private club in the years immediately following the American Revolution by the officers of George Washington's army to look after the widows of fallen patriots, by the dawn of the nineteenth century the original Lodge of Tammany, so named in honor of a friendly Delaware Indian chief who'd sacrificed his life for the new nation, was commonly referred to as Tammany Hall. By 1850 the Hall's goals had shifted from paternal benevolence to political power. Tammany became the political link between the growing elitist power base of the industrialists and a powerful electoral body of mostly Irish immigrant workers. It also became the city's collective voice of liberalism, the first organized voice of the working class, an increasingly influential power base for those disenfranchised New Yorkers without land, money, or political representation.

Into the second half of the nineteenth century, Tammany Hall was led by William Magear "Boss" Tweed.* Tweed, a former chairman of the Democratic Central Committee of New York County, was the undisputed leader of the so-called Tweed Ring, which controlled all aspects of New York City's financial lifelines. More powerful than any of the eighteen Democratic mayors he helped elect, Tweed prided himself on "getting things done" by keeping an iron grip on virtually every aspect of the municipality and amply rewarding himself for it. Eventually convicted on a number of charges having to do with the theft of city funds, bribery, and other extracurricular activities, Tweed was sent to jail in 1873, and except for a brief escape to Spain, where he was captured and

---

*Although often stated incorrectly as Marcy, Tweed's middle name was actually Magear. See *The Encyclopedia of New York City* (1995).

deported back to New York City, he never regained either freedom or power. Five years later, in 1878, he died penniless in prison.

However, the machine he left behind remained the most influential Democratic organization in the city. Although Tweed was Protestant, he had led a mostly Irish Catholic working-class constituency, which emerged for the first time during the 1880s as a dominant force in New York politics. This demographic tilt complicated the increasingly tense relations between the city's Old World Catholics and staid New World Puritans.

In 1887 Tammany produced a peace and unity candidate, Abram S. Hewitt, who won the mayoral election, thus preserving the Democratic Party's ironclad grip on the city, unbroken since before the Civil War. It was, however, a decision the party would quickly come to regret. Once in power, the wealthy Hewitt revealed himself to be more divisive than anyone suspected when he became an outspoken supporter of the city's old-line Protestant aristocracy. He detested the ever-increasing influx of Irish immigrants, and in open defiance of the Catholic contingent of his party and Tammany Hall, two months after his inauguration in a move that would eventually destroy his political career, he banned the flying of the Irish flag over City Hall on St. Patrick's Day. This so outraged the Hall that they pulled all further machine support from the new mayor. Unbowed, Hewitt supported the continuation of low wages for workers and high profits for landlords and manufacturers, and imposed heavy restrictions on those he referred to as "ethnics"—i.e., the Irish—who wanted to go into business, receive an education, or acquire property.

He also began a police crackdown against what he considered their sinful pleasures: the numerous saloons, dance halls, brothels, movie nickelodeons, gambling dens, sport halls, street-corner dice, or "craps," and two-dollar whorehouses located in the city's so-called Tenderloin district, which ran from 23rd to 39th Streets and from Fifth to Ninth Avenues, what was then the northwestern fringe of developed Manhattan.

To the mind and spirit of the city's capitalist Puritans who enthusiastically supported Hewitt, the working class's collective love for all things loose and leisurely was not only wasteful, tasteless, and ungodly, but, they quickly learned, unstoppable. To get rid of the daily flow of immigrants into the city, Hewitt devised a plan to ship them off every evening en masse to the raw Siberia of the outer boroughs, where he insisted they belonged and hoped they would stay.

By 1890 Manhattan already had the largest and most comprehensive mass-transit system in the world. In use for many years at the time of Hewitt's election were 94 miles of elevated railways that extended from one end of the island to the other, along with 265 miles of horse-drawn railways and 137 miles of surface omnibuses, also horse-drawn, that congested the city's main thoroughfares and left a fetid aroma in the air from the endless piles of fresh, hot dung. The main problem with Manhattan's "elevateds" was inefficiency and lack of range. Besides being unconnected to eath other, slow, outmoded, under-routed, and overcrowded, the deafening overhead rail systems that lumbered along fifty feet above the street thrust the streets below them—Second, Third, Sixth, and Ninth Avenues—into the grinding screech and dreary gray of endlessly sunless days. It was estimated at one point that citizens living beneath or adjacent to the "elevateds" put up with as much as nineteen hours of rumbling and roaring every day, seven days a week.

Still, by 1890 the rails had played a key role in helping to bring Manhattan's population farther northward, which in turn helped speculators develop raw land into livable real estate, so much so that by the end of that year, the average Manhattanite was clocking almost three hundred mass-transit trips a year. However, the lack of direct service to the outer boroughs, the relatively slow speed, and the horrid noise and chronic overcrowding left much to be desired.

What the city needed, Hewitt insisted, was an interborough underground, or subway, an interconnected rail system modeled after those in Europe, which could move great numbers of workers in and out of the city on a daily basis. In fact, just such a system might have been in place in New York much earlier, before London, Paris, Glasgow, Budapest, Boston, and even Berlin, all of which had operating underground systems by 1861, if not for three major forces of opposition. The first was John Jacob Astor II, the son of New York's great real estate baron, who feared that widespread underground excavation would physically jeopardize or financially devalue his extensive Manhattan surface land holdings, as well as create the chance for workers to move to less expensive competitive housing. The second was shipping magnate, railroad builder, and legendary robber baron Cornelius "Commodore" Vanderbilt, owner and operator of the New York Central Railroad. Vanderbilt believed a mass transit system would cut into the profits of his own surface passenger and freight city rail lines, the last stops on his statewide transport line that connected the city's seaports to upstate and then, via the Erie Canal, to the rest of the country. The third, ironically, hit much closer to home. Hewitt's former mentor, Boss Tweed, while still alive and in power, had received considerable kickbacks from the predominant horse and carriage trade that operated out of the Great Kill barnyard on 42nd Street and Broadway, situated just above an east-west cattle and sheep path that ran from river to river. The barnyard sat on the northern end of Long Acre Square, an island twenty feet wide at one end and sixty feet wide at the other, the southern half of the so-called bow-tie islands created by the traffic-defined intersections of Broadway and Seventh Avenue.*

Across from the Square was the Vanderbilt-owned American Horse Exchange of the Long Acre Farm, where people from all over the city traveled to buy everything from horses and buggys to fresh milk. Tweed had always opposed anything that might cut into this rich source of tribute, regardless of whatever benefit it might provide to the city. Although his demise removed one long-standing obstacle to Hewitt's plan, by the time he became mayor, his abandonment of Tammany left him with no political machine to help

---

*Broadway (Heere Street to the Dutch, Great George Street to the British) is so named because of its width. It is the longest uninterrupted boulevard in the city, and it follows the natural contours of the land from the tip of Manhattan all the way up to the Bronx. Officially named Broadway on February 14, 1899, it was previously called Broadway only up to 59th, where it then became the Boulevard; from 155th to 157th the Boulevard Lafayette; from 157th to 170th Eleventh Avenue or the Boulevard again; and from 170th Street to Spuyten Duyvil Kingsbridge Road. Manhattan viewed from above at Times Square, looking north to south, reveals that Broadway is, in fact, unbroken at 42nd Street, while Seventh Avenue, a much narrower street that runs almost directly north and south, is slashed at a northwest to southeast angle (rather than criss-crossing into an X with the big boulevard). The southern bow-tie islands, the two triangles of land between 42nd Street and 49th that resemble a man's neckwear, were created to preserve the unbroken flow of horse-and-buggy traffic on the city's major thoroughfare of commerce.

convince anyone at City Hall to invest in a new, public, interborough underground rail system.

The idea looked dead until the notorious Blizzard of '88 paralyzed the city and finally made clear the need for a new and better way than foot, horse, "el," or surface vehicle to transport the people of New York City. To Hewitt, the snowstorm was nothing less than a vote of confidence from God for underground rapid transit.

Unfortunately the Lord wasn't a reform Democrat. By the end of 1888, Hewitt, even using the blizzard as his exhibit A, not only failed to convince the city of the need to build a subway system, he lost his bid for reelection. His defeat permanently removed him from elective political power, although he did remain something of an effective backroom dealer, and he waged a three-year battle to push through the Rapid Transit Act of 1891, which, when passed, officially mapped out the routes for what was intended to be New York City's first subway system. Due in part to Hewitt's divisive politics, the plan crawled through the bureaucracy, and in 1901, with primary routes stalled in the planning stages, two new privately funded proposals for an underground subway system came before the City Council. One had its cars running off gigantic fans that would "blow" them in one direction and "suck" them back in the other. The other and far more practical design, which utilized electric power, was presented by August Belmont, a private developer motivated by the industrial profit to be made from social progress, and his was the one the city went with.

August Belmont was the son of German Jewish immigrant August Schönberg, who had journeyed to the New World to find his fortune. Born in 1816 in the Rhineland-Palatinate, Schönberg at the age of thirteen got a job sweeping floors for the Rothschilds, the leading Jewish banking family in Europe at the time. In 1837 he was sent by them to represent their sugar holdings in Cuba. En route, his ship docked in New York City and Schönberg decided to do some sight-seeing. So charmed was he by Manhattan, he never returned to the ship.

Eager to make a name in finance, he rejected any opportunity to join the so-called segregated, or parallel, aristocracy of the prominent Jewish families of New York, which included the Seligmans, the Kuhns, the Loebs, and the Guggenheims, all of whom had banded together to protect their interests from the midcentury spi-raling of virulent anti-Semitism that had spread through the then still Protestant-dominated city. Schönberg did not want to be asso-ciated with the Jewish fringe, no matter how well made the cloth. He believed the opportunities for success remained too narrow. A young, aggressive man with heady dreams, he reinvented his name, his heritage, and his past as a way to gain entry into what he per-ceived as a highly restricted island of opportunity and wealth. In 1849, shortly before his thirty-third birthday, Schönberg changed his last name to Belmont and his religion to Episcopalian, wooed and married the daughter of the great and celebrated Commodore Matthew Perry (who in 1854 would go on to "open" Japan to the West), and entered a new phase of his career.

The marriage produced a son, also named August Belmont, who grew up in a world of enormous American privilege. He attended both Phillips Exeter Academy and Harvard, after which he entered the family's banking empire. He quickly developed close personal and business relationships with many of the most promi-nent names in New York City, including J. P. Morgan, John D. Rockefeller, and William C. Whitney. Belmont, an avid athlete all his life, by 1902 was chairman of the Jockey Club and had built what was considered at the time the most luxurious horse racing facility in the country, New York's Belmont Park racetrack.

For all his wealth and success, the younger Belmont remained an extremely unpopular figure in New York's social life. Short, fat, arrogant, and mean-spirited, he felt haunted by the Jewish ancestry he shunned and was forever sensitive to the point of paranoia about anyone who treated him with less than the respect he believed a successful Protestant of his standing deserved. In his late forties he began to consider what, besides a racetrack, his lasting legacy to the city might be and began to search for a project that would embel-lish his reputation with a fitting benevolence. He found it in Hewitt's dream of a citywide underground mass transit.

In 1904 Belmont broke ground on the first leg of the Interbor-ough Rapid Transit (IRT). He planned a dig through twenty-three square miles of Manhattan's subterranean geology, which proved far more difficult than he imagined due to the uneven rock formations just below the borough's surface. To help solve the problem, Bel-

The 1904 conversion of Long Acre Square included excavation for both the IRT subway and the Times Building. (Museum of the City of New York)

mont chose William Barclay Parsons, a young man of like privilege with political connections to Abram Hewitt. Parsons developed a plan of shallow excavation he called "cut and cover" that allowed progressive sections the length of a city block to be completed and filled in, the surface of one section repaved before ground was broken on the next.

After two years of continuous digging that saw the city's streets uprooted in wormlike eruptions and that caused dozens of worker deaths, the IRT finally opened to the public with great fanfare. Thousands turned out on October 27, 1904, for its inaugural run. The new mayor, George B. McClellan, Jr., grandly took the controls of an eight-car train for the inaugural nine-mile, twenty-six-minute trip below Manhattan. This ride brought out huge crowds, who stood at the street-level subway stops and cheered when they heard the rumble of the train. Thousands gathered at the only place to see it aboveground, at the viaduct over Manhattan Valley, from 100th to 110th Streets. That same day, more than 100,000 people bought tickets to ride the subway. Two days later the number reached 350,000, and a New York institution had arrived.

Its instant success provided Belmont his legacy and turned the mayor into a New York City folk hero.

McClellan, a liberal with a clean record, the son of a Civil War general and a veteran of Tammany Hall politics, had run on a plat-

Construction of the West 42nd Street headquarters of the New York Times *during the spring of 1904.* (Corbis-Bettman)

form of anti-Tammany reform. His overwhelming popularity was primarily due to his support for the right of all adult working citizens to drink freely (his puritanical opponent had sought more prohibitive nighttime and weekend restrictions on the consumption of alcohol).

Among McClellan's many achievements during his six-year term were reorganization of the city's traffic grids to adjust for the arrival of automobiles and the removal of horsecars, a general clean-sweeping of the police, health, and street-cleaning departments, expansion of the park and playground systems, completion of the Queensboro and Manhattan Bridges, expansion of the Croton reservoir system into the Catskill Mountains, significant harbor improvements, and supervision of the enormous influx of millions of European immigrants (by far the greatest numbers being Russian Jews), which by the end of his tenure had seen the city's population rise to an unprecedented 41 percent foreign-born. The mayor's achievements in controlling the outbreak of violence caused by the resentment of native New Yorkers for the immigrants, in particular the still surging anti-Semitism, led the social reformer Jacob Riis to call McClellan "the best organization mayor" New York ever had. Indeed, McClellan ruled the city during one of its most challenging and exciting times and guided it headlong into the twentieth century.

Everything he accomplished, however, took a backseat among the citizens of the city to his being the mayor who "gave" them a subway.

The IRT quickly redefined not just the physical movement but the social direction of its riders, integrating the ethnic working class and thus helping to spiritually liberate it. By providing literal and symbolic deliverance from the isolation and limitation of the city's various ethnic ghettos, the subway became the public's essential link to education, recreation, housing, and commercial opportunity.

It also created the city's first twentieth-century social and cultural center. The opening of the IRT stop at 42nd Street between Broadway and Seventh Avenue coincided with the *New York Times*'s breaking ground on construction of its highly anticipated skyscraper headquarters. The two events combined to reconfigure Manhattan's midtown boulevard into a crossroads of recreation and commerce the likes of which had never before been seen in America. High-ticket entertainment, fabulous restaurants, luxury hotels such as the Knickerbocker on Broadway and 42nd Street, which both opera great Enrico Caruso and the reigning theatrical "superstar" of his day, James O'Neill, called their New York City home, modern underground transportation, and the newest northern border of the notorious Tenderloin with its well-equipped houses of prostitution—all shared space on the streets that immediately surrounded the *Times*'s new headquarters.

The planned convergence of the great newspaper with the grand subway seemed far too much a coincidence to competing news publisher William Randolph Hearst, who was resolutely against either and who had the money and power to try to stop both. For all of Belmont's newfound status, the success of his subway and his "hidden" past created convenient targets for Hearst's tainted "yellow" journalism practices. When in his recently acquired *New York Journal* the publisher headlined stories of a "Jewish conspiracy" between the subway builder and *Times* publisher Adolph Ochs, the accusation touched Belmont in the most haunted recesses of his lifelong insecurities.

Hearst had discovered that the surest way to boost circulation in his newspapers was by headlining sex, crime, and scandal. His main competition for circulation in New York City at the time was Joseph Pulitzer's ravamped *New York World,* a once-prestigious newspaper that, in an attempt to increase circulation in the city's increasingly crowded field of thirty-five daily newspapers, was turned by its owner into the same type of scurrilous gossip- and scandalmongering rag as the *Journal.*

Hearst's notions of a conspiracy were based on what he considered the underhanded dealings of two prominent Manhattan Jews. The first was Belmont, whose Jewish background and Schönberg family name Hearst "revealed" in his paper. The second was Ochs, the publisher of the *New York Times,* who happened to be Hearst's newest and potentially most formidable competitor. The son of a Talmudic scholar and successful diamond dealer, Ochs had gone into publishing and first established offices for his newly purchased journal on the ground floor of Printing House Square, the center of what was then the city's unofficial newspaper publishing district, Park Row, opposite City Hall. Although occupying quarters that bumped up against Hearst's, the *New York Times* stood apart from the *Journal* and all the other newspapers of the day precisely because of its marked lack of sensationalism. So much so that by the time Ochs decided to buy the financially failing paper, it was considered the dullard of the daily pack (a situation not helped by its inability to print clear photographs).

In July 1902 Ochs, realizing his newspaper had physically outgrown its downtown address, began to search for a new location. His first choice was a site a few doors up the street, but when the offered rents were suddenly and, to him, suspiciously jacked up, he made a bold and, to some, incomprehensibly risky decision to move uptown to Long Acre Square, what was then the northern end of the city's business district.

While to many it might have seemed an odd place to want to relocate, to Ochs and Belmont it looked like a bargain. With every neighborhood in Manhattan changing so rapidly—the brothels and the businessmen having already squeezed the first-generation middle-class residents out of the streets to the west of Long Acre Square—the entire city had become a paradise for real estate speculators. Throughout the lower part of the island, the undeveloped hills and valleys along the riverbanks that had been temporary dwellings for the homeless were quickly converted to high-end brownstones, and just as quickly collapsed back into slum dwellings, as working New Yorkers moved in league-boot jumps to find suitable housing close enough to where they could commute by trolley, elevated train, or rapid transit, yet far enough away, usually in the outer boroughs, to feel as if they lived in what was then considered the distanced safety of the sleepy suburbs.

In 1904, the year midtown subway service began and Ochs moved the *Times* to its new location, Long Acre had in just the last decade already economically yo-yoed twice, with prices for property in the area now low enough for Ochs to be able to buy. The initial cost was no problem. It was the building of his tower that almost ruined him.

The construction budget was $250,000, which was considered at the time enough to build a twenty-five-story, 363-foot-tall structure. Ochs intended his to be the tallest building in the city, an ornate reach-for-the-sky tower, with the first three floors made of Indiana limestone surmounted by sixteen stories of white brick, elaborate ornamental Gothic-styled balconies and cornices cast from terra-cotta, topped off by a six-story tower.

The actual cost at completion of his new headquarters ballooned to an astonishing $1.7 million in turn-of-the-century dollars. Ochs had hoped that his primary outside tenant, the Equitable Life Assurance Society—which had already loaned him $150,000 to use as seed money against a security interest of 51 percent of the newspaper's stock—would make up the difference. Equitable, however, turned him down at the last minute over a dispute involving access to exterior advertising signage (it wanted more than Ochs was willing to give), approval rights regarding other tenants, and, for safety reasons, elimination of the six-story tower (due to foundation problems). The tower proved the breaking point for Equitable when Ochs refused to eliminate it from his building plan. Uncertainty remains as to where his completion money finally came from, although there is some evidence to suggest that mining magnate Daniel Guggenheim may have loaned Ochs an additional quarter of a million dollars (the original estimate of the entire cost of construction) he now so desperately needed.

With his new financing at last in place, Ochs scheduled the ceremonial cornerstone inset for 3 P.M. on January 18, 1904. It was a quiet event on an unusually cold day, and limited to a one-sentence speech by Ochs's daughter, curly-haired eleven-year-old Iphigene Bertha Ochs, who spoke softly into a megaphone, to "declare this stone to be laid plumb, level and square." The crowd then quickly dispersed.

Despite Adolph Ochs's best efforts, at its completion his magnificent building, which was visible on a clear day from as far as twelve miles away—all the way up in the Bronx, and in Queens, Brooklyn, and New Jersey as well—was considered by many to be only the *second* tallest in the city. He had wanted his tower to surpass his competitor's Pulitzer office building on Park Row, home to the *New York World* (which, at *its* completion in 1892, had replaced Wall Street's 284-foot Trinity Church spire, erected in 1846, as New York's tallest structure). Ochs nevertheless insisted for years that, when measured from its lowest subbasement to the tip of the tower, his building was, in fact, taller than Pulitzer's.

What had finally prevented Ochs from soaring well past the *World* and straight into the heavens, was not being able to dig deep enough to support the heights to which he aspired. As it turned out, much of the subterranean rights directly under and surrounding his new tower belonged to August Belmont, whose new IRT subway ran too close to the building's center of gravity to safely allow any further excavation. The deepest the *Times* could go was fifty-five feet, which, in addition to limiting the height of the tower, made for an incredibly crowded and ultimately inadequate operating space for the paper's presses.

Mayor George B. McClellan, Jr. (seated, right), with several officials from the newly formed Interborough Rapid Transit Company and workers in the cab of the first IRT train, on the occasion of its inaugural run, October 27, 1904. (Museum of the City of New York)

Why, then, Hearst inquired in print, would Ochs acquire such an impractical site? The answer also came from Hearst, whose two New York Park Row organs, the morning *American* and evening *Journal,* published the same front-page story two days before the *Times* cornerstone was laid, "revealing new evidence of the Jewish conspiracy" afoot to make 42nd Street the "Jewish" cultural center of the city.

Hearst's "scoop," published during the height of a particularly hot anti-Semitic backlash resulting from the immigration explosion, gained new life when, on April 8, 1904, just three months after the cornerstone ceremony, the New York City Board of Aldermen renamed Long Acre "Times Square," a moniker that just so happened to have been suggested to them by none other than August Belmont. The move infuriated not only Hearst and Pulitzer, but also James Gordon Bennett, Jr., another powerful city publisher whose highly respected *New York Herald,* located eight blocks to the south of the new Times Tower, continued to refer to the square in his papers as Long Acre (Herald Square, another Broadway criss-cross, had been so named with much fanfare just a few years earlier to honor the relocation of Bennett's newspaper to the triangular plot of land on 34th Street across from Macy's department store).

The day of the renaming, Hearst signed yet another angry editorial that appeared in both the *American* and the *Journal* aimed at the so-called Jewish conspiracy. Headlined "Mr. August Belmont and His Tame Ochs," the piece suggested that Ochs was financially indebted to and therefore controlled by Belmont and so viciously attacked the physical features of both with such blatant language it brought an immediate libel suit from Ochs. Hearst's description of the publisher of the *New York Times* included such terminology as "uneducated . . . oily . . . [with] obsequiously curved shoulders," imagery that became the paradigm for the new century's anti-Semite caricature of the American Jew.

Buried somewhere beneath the avalanche of Hearst's racist attacks lay the untold truth behind what was, in fact, the less-than-coincidental relationship between Ochs and Belmont. Not known at the time to Hearst, whose hatemongering had lockstepped his own journalists' investigative abilities into a campaign of racist propaganda, Belmont was in fact a major stockholder in the *New York Times* and had disguised his holdings by what appeared to be but in fact was not a blind trust managed by one E. Mora Davison, a politically influential business associate. Belmont was also on Equitable's board of directors, and although Equitable did not become a tenant and refused to put any more money toward construction of the top of the Times Tower, it still held a controlling interest of stock in the *Times* against its initial $150,000 investment. Later on, Equitable was rumored but never proved to be the grantor of an additional million-dollar mortgage to Ochs, against even more stock, and also (and also never proved) the source of an early $75,000 loan young Adolph had used to originally purchase the *Times* in 1896, just one day before the paper was to land in bankruptcy.

Belmont's Subway Realty Corporation, the company he had created to build the IRT, also happened to have brokered the sale to Ochs of the raw land upon which he built his tower. As soon as the deal had been finalized and even before the cornerstone had been laid or plans for the new 42nd Street subway stop made public, Belmont and Davison quietly began lobbying the Board of Aldermen to rename Long Acre "Times Square."

If any reason were needed as to why Ochs and Belmont wanted to keep these dealings private, if not secret, Hearst's ongoing and brutal anti-Semitic attacks on every motive, interest, dealing, and the integrity of both men provided excellent ones. Hearst's loud and angry insistence of the extent of the veiled relationship between Ochs and Belmont (although apparently he did not know all the details) and his running accusations of a Jewish conspiracy sufficiently intimidated Ochs, who downplayed the occasion of the renamed square in his own *New York Times.* Rather than splashing it on the front page, which in those days carried dozens of stories, he placed it several pages inside the newspaper.

Nor did Ochs ever fully acknowledge the facts of the many and complex connections he had with Belmont and Equitable directly linked to the new subway station being built at his corporate front door, which, while it hindered the operations of the *Times*'s presses, in a relatively short period increased the real estate value of both the station and the *Times*'s headquarters nearly tenfold.*

When the new station opened, it soon transformed the cultural map of 42nd Street and the neighborhoods that surrounded it. Shortly after the IRT began making its regular Times Square stop, middle to high-end residential housing became available from 44th and Broadway up to 47th Street and all the way to the Hudson River, a plot of land on which the Astors quickly built two hundred additional town houses and several hotels, including the family's newest crown jewel, the Astor Hotel, on the west side of Broadway at 44th Street. Because of it, 43rd Street, the single block between the new commercial center of Times Square and the neighborhood's burgeoning upscale residents to the north, became an unintentional

---

*The turn-of-the-century assessment of 42nd Street between Broadway and Eighth Avenue for city taxes was less than half a million dollars. By 1919 it was more than $5.5 million, and by 1930 it had risen to $7.35 million. Adjacent properties increased in similar amounts. The single block to the west of the Times Tower between Seventh and Eighth Avenues, where many of the new theaters were located, had been assessed in 1919 for $18.5 million, in 1930 for more than $41 million.

buffer zone that filled with the increasingly crowded Tenderloin's pretty young prostitutes.

As for West 42nd Street itself, the subway station effected a tidal change. Hewitt's original mass transit plan to keep the working-class people out of Manhattan, had delivered precisely the opposite. Midtown was now accessible twenty-four hours a day to anyone in the city who could spare a nickel to ride the subway. Ironically it was this surge of endlessly coming-and-going visitors that helped transform the all-but-deserted-after-dark stretch of sex and crime into a round-the-clock commercial boulevard of naughty gentility where every type of family entertainment conducted business alongside the hottest and most infamous brothels this side of Paris.

THE NEW *Times* headquarters officially opened on New Year's Eve 1904. To celebrate the occasion, Ochs threw an all-day street party that concluded with a fireworks display set off from the base of the tower. Much to Hearst's anger and disappointment, the promotion proved so successful that Times Square immediately replaced City Hall Park as the favorite gathering site for New Yorkers to ring in the new year. By 1906 the crowds had grown so large that the *Times,* by now fully integrated into the new social and economic scene that had blossomed around its namesake square, began a holiday custom that soon became recognizable around the world as the official time and place America noted the arrival of the new year. To mark the annual occasion, Ochs arranged to have a large illuminated four-hundred-pound glass ball lowered from the tower flagpole precisely at midnight to signal the end of one year and the beginning of the next.

Legitimate theater impresarios now fell over one another to open new playhouses in a neighborhood that just a few years earlier none would go near, believing then that Long Acre would never be good for anything but crime, drugs, and prostitution. Before the arrival of the *New York Times,* the square had developed more of a carnival atmosphere than one conducive to a corporate alley. Not long after, dozens of prostitutes worked both sides of the Times Tower, resulting in relatively few new nonentertainment big-dollar investors relocating directly on 42nd Street.

Indeed, the business of sex dramatically increased its visibility on the city's newest and most popular main drag as its purveyors moved to compete for the newly available entertainment dollars by dressing up their street women and fashionably upscaling the houses they occupied. Onetime two-dollar streetwalkers now dressed in high style and proudly walked with umbrellas twirling on their shoulders in the midday sun. They could afford to spend money on clothes and accessories, as most worked two jobs, one as a prostitute and one as a showgirl at the many new dance halls built along the west side of the street—often referred to now as "Soubrette Row"—to accommodate the neighborhood's growing everyday populace. Five years into the new century 42nd Street became the showcase boulevard where merchants of the sunny side competed with hawkers of the shady to sell the workingman his ticket to get into, if not in on, the great American dream.

As for Abram Hewitt, whose original vision of a subway had led to the first great wave of commercial development on 42nd Street, historical anonymity was to be his fate.[*] Hewitt never again enjoyed any widespread measure of public acceptance. Economic decline, meanwhile, eventually befell the New York publishing empire of William Hearst, whose sensationalist moral outrage he continued to vent in his papers. No longer just Jews but Democrats, union organizers, Wall Street speculators, bootleggers, and show business entrepreneurs all came before the loaded barrel of his editorial gun. Nevertheless, none of his publications was able to displace the stalwart *New York Times* as it became the city's, and the nation's, newspaper of record.

N O ONE BETTER EXEMPLIFIED the twentieth century's moral, cultural, and physical shift in the city's body politic than legendary mayor James J. "Jimmy" Walker, who first came to political light as a Tammany supporter of Governor Al Smith. A Democratic state senator in the early twenties, Walker was elected mayor

---

[*]Populist heroes in New York City's history most often are rewarded by having streets or schools, hotels, even airports named after them. Belmont Avenue, a subway stop in the Bronx, bears the name of the founder of the IRT. There is a city street named after McClellan. Hearst and Hewitt have none.

Mayor James J. "Gentleman Jimmy" Walker. The fortunes of the good-time mayor rose and fell with the Street's and the city's cash economy. (Corbis-Bettman)

in the fall of 1925, a halcyon time in America of easy money, easy virtue, and even easier vice. Walker personified the city's rebellious attitude against social restriction in an era that began with the passage in 1919 of the Volstead Act, which enforced the national ban on the sale (but not the private consumption) of alcohol. The purpose of the federal government at first seemed clear enough: to discourage the growing immortality that the nation's newest craze, nightclubbing, had produced, nowhere at the time more concentrated in New York City than on West 42nd Street, which by that year boasted dozens of thriving nightclubs. The day after Volstead, these became "speakeasies," establishments that no longer bothered with quality control, cleanliness, overcrowding, or curfews. By the time Walker was elected mayor, 32,000 speakeasies were operating throughout the city. Entirely in keeping with his political style of governing, he happily looked the other way at the city's booming, if illegal, bootlegging industry. While still a state senator he had helped pass legislation that legalized Sunday post-church entertainment, including baseball, boxing, and moviegoing, which forever endeared him to a working class grateful for anything that helped bring relief to their six-day, sixty-hour workweek, who in turn elected him mayor.

A party loyalist, "people's" mayor, and Broadway celebrity with as much charisma as any of its stars, for the longest time, no matter what he did—and he did a lot—in the eyes of his constituency Walker could do no wrong. Not when a then relatively unknown Congressman Fiorello La Guardia criticized the mayor's giving himself a raise in pay from $25,000 to $40,000. Walker's laughing and effectively neutralizing response was simply to raise his hands in mock astonishment and declare, "Why, that's cheap! Think what it would cost if I worked full time!"

Not even when the very married Walker's well-known penchant for Broadway's feather-clad chorus girls resulted in his leaving his wife for showgirl Betty Compton, a move actually celebrated equally among the me-too fantasists of the decade's high-society swingers and the daydreaming minimum-wagers. This was, after all, the height of the "anything goes" decade. Who was going to complain about what this mayor did on his own time when tax revenues from the seemingly never-ending private real estate deals brought an annual half billion dollars to the city, much of which Walker earmarked for better wages for city employees? "The people" loved him for that. They applauded when he announced that a gambling casino was to be opened in Central Park. They cheered when he dismissed critics who accused him of looking the other way while the sale of girlie magazines proliferated on 42nd Street. When asked about it, he simply shrugged his shoulders, hundred-watt-smiled, and said, "I never knew a woman who was hurt by a magazine." In his spare time—and he had a lot of it—he wrote pop ditties, one of which, the prophetic "Will You

Love Me in December (as You Do in May)?.," became a huge nation-wide hit.

No question, he had the touch. Despite a sizable share of political corruption—the going rate during his administration for mayoral appointees was a Tammany-tradition standard first year's salary—and blatant womanizing, for most of his administration Walker proved a surprisingly effective politician. In 1928, for instance, when a subway strike threatened to cripple the city, Walker used his Irish charm and strong backroom influence to help effect a key settlement that allowed him to keep his spirited vow to maintain the traditional five-cent subway fare, New York's primal symbol of working-class freedom and democracy. It was this tough political victory as much as his freewheeling lifestyle that confirmed his place in the city's populist pantheon.

As 1928 came to a close, "Our Jimmy," as he was known to his constituency, was on top of the world, until his high-life popularity finally proved too top-hat heavy. Walker's fall began, perhaps not so coincidentally, in the days following the 1929 stock market crash. In the morally thick morning aftermath, subway-strike victories were no longer able to balance Walker's flamboyant lifestyle, which to many now contrasted a bit too vividly with the newly depressed economic reality. Almost immediately after the crash, the city's Patrick Cardinal Hayes publicly denounced Walker's personal ways, going so far as to suggest New York's economic downturn and the country's as just retribution for Walker's and other "wayward" leaders' immoral ways.

Things got worse quickly after that for him and the city. On the heels of the prelate's denunciation, worker riots broke out in Union Square, which brought federal troops into the fray. U.S. Attorney Charles Tuttle, who, like the cardinal, placed at least part of the blame for the city's growing social unrest on Walker for what he described as a borough slipping into moral anarchy, demanded an investigation of City Hall. Tuttle soon discovered what even the most casual observer would have: that there was, indeed, an alarming amount of corruption at all levels of the Walker administration, nowhere more prevalent than in the city's court system, most tellingly the women's court, and the police vice squad.

Early in 1930 Tuttle appointed a separate investigative committee, headed by Judge Samuel Seabury. Walker refused to testify, an action that was widely regarded as being tantamount to a confession of guilt. The situation was made worse when eight Democratic district leaders refused to waive immunity and testify. Early in 1931 a prospective witness was murdered, prompting Governor Roosevelt to expand Seabury's investigation to include the District Attorney's Office. By April, Walker's entire city government was under a cloud of deep suspicion.

A year later, in May 1932, after a series of delaying tactics, Walker was ordered by Roosevelt to testify before Seabury and answer all his questions. Walker and Seabury locked horns in court, a series of sensational sessions which saw the mayor effectively elude the judge's more pointed accusations. Ordered by Roosevelt to be more forthcoming, Walker managed to avoid being recalled until after the Democratic convention, held that summer in Chicago, where he openly supported Al Smith against the governor, who got the presidential nomination anyway (and would, of course, go on to win the first of his four national campaigns). That fall, Walker once again went before Seabury, but this time the judge was better prepared, and the mayor was finished. Roosevelt decided Walker had to go, but allowed him to resign. In September 1932 Walker left for an "extended vacation" in Europe, what amounted to self-imposed political exile. As he sailed out of New York Harbor that fall, he took along with him the last fading echoes of the once-roaring decade that had so dominated the city he'd ruled and loved.

Despite the grimmest morning-after of the first three decades of the twentieth century, despite the massive corruption and the worst economic collapse in the city's history, Walker's impact would not soon be forgotten. His visceral, if vicarious, working-man's link to New York's social glitterati lasted until he died in 1946 at the age of sixty-five; by then the fanciful accounts of his glory days having elevated him to folk-hero status. Twenty-five years after he resigned, eleven years after his death, Walker's life was made into a Hollywood romantic comedy starring Bob Hope in the title role as Beau James, the mayor of New York who happily sang and danced his way into the city's revisionist storybook history.

Times Square, looking north in 1935, taken from the New York Times Building. Note the impos-
ing beauty of the legendary Astor Hotel, built by what was then Manhattan's dominant real
estate family in 1904—the same year as the renaming of Times Square, the construction of the
newspaper's namesake headquarters, and the opening of the subway. (Corbis-Bettman)

I N 1930, AS WALKER'S STAR was fading and the grim reality of
the nation's economic collapse began to set in, one of America's
premier industrialists, Detroit's Walter P. Chrysler, aware of the
falling price of 42nd Street's already commercially cheap and available space, decided to build to the east, believing he could transform
that part of the street the way Adolph Ochs and his tower had Times
Square. Chrysler was not alone in recognizing the potential of the
East Side. A generation had already passed since the 1916 opening
of the glamorous Grand Central Terminal on 42nd Street at Park
Avenue, after which the glory of the city's economic upswing followed Walker back over to the razzle-dazzle of the anything-goes
West Side. Walter P. meant to take advantage of this stalled decade
of East Side development by putting his money into a new, eponymous building that would dominate that side of 42nd Street.

The Chrysler Building was completed in 1930, on the site of
one of the city's once most recognizable structures, the all-but-

forgotten turn-of-the-century Bloomingdale Brewery, at the time the city's largest beer-maker. The skyscraper that replaced it remains to this day one of the magnificent monuments of the style introduced at the 1925 Paris Exposition Internationale des Arts Décoratifs, popularly known as Art Deco. Its geometrical roots came from Vienna—an acute German expressionist angularity, set-back collisions from cubism, a lobby of red Moroccan marble, elevator doors inlaid with Japanese ash and American walnut, a ceiling mural 110 feet long and 76 feet wide by Edward Trumball depicting the building, airplanes in flight surrounding it, and scenes from the automaker's factory assembly line, an exterior skin of aluminum applied with the mind-brush of Frank Lloyd Wright, thirty elevators, doors of wood veneer on steel, and a line of idealized automobiles in white and gray brick with mudguards, hubcaps, and winged radiator caps of polished steel in the wall frieze above the twenty-sixth floor of the facade.

Originally planned as an office project and designed by architect William Van Alen for former New York State senator turned real estate developer William H. Reynolds, the seventy-seven-story (1,046 feet) structure was to be topped by a glass dome, lighted from within, to give the effect of a giant glowing diamond in the New York evening sky. Unable to complete it because of the financial downturn, Reynolds sold the unfinished building to Chrysler, who financed it out of his own pocket, boasting that no corporate funds would be used, thus ensuring that his sons would one day inherit his personal monument to his own greatness. Fearing that the Empire State Building, then in its final planning stages, might be redesigned to stand higher than theirs, Van Alen and Chrysler kept secret for as long as possible the addition of the fifty-foot flagpole that would sit atop a 185-foot, seven-story spire, itself clandestinely assembled from the sixty-fifth floor, its five parts lifted by derrick to the top from within a fire tower built in the center of the building.

The completed Chrysler Building immediately became the stuff of 42nd Street legend. The pioneering photographer Margaret Bourke-White occupied an office on the sixty-first floor and made Chrysler's gargoyle ornaments world-famous when she crept out on one to take a picture of the city from that vantage point, even as she was having another taken of the event. A young James Agee, after

*42nd Street's legendary Chrysler Build-
ing had been the tallest building in the
world when the Empire State Building
surpassed it in 1931.* (Corbis-Bettman)

having had a few, was said to have dangled by his hands from the
fiftieth-floor office of *Fortune* magazine, another of the building's
tenants, "for the fun of it." And Chrysler himself kept private quarters at the top, an office suite and an apartment that had a lavish dining room ringed with a frieze of autoworkers in polished black glass
on a field of frosted blue. He had instructed his builders to make
sure his was the highest toilet in Manhattan, so that he could look
down upon the city from his porcelain throne and, as one observer
wryly put it, "shit on Henry Ford and the rest of the world."

In the end, Chrysler never actually moved his corporate head-quarters from Detroit to 42nd Street. Choosing instead to keep his auto company in Michigan and, except for a private apartment, rented the Chrysler Building's office space out to others. Neverthe-less, he saw the building as a self-righteous glorification of his own achievements. No longer simply a building, it was, as architect Philip Johnson once suggested, built to bring its owner close enough to touch the face of God.

A year later the Empire State Building officially replaced it as the tallest building in the world.

ON THE TAP HEELS of Walker's resignation former congress-man Fiorello Henry La Guardia marched to power. La Guardia had run for mayor against, and was crushed by, Walker in the 1925 election, having unsuccessfully campaigned on a plat-form of anticorruption by pointing a morally accusing finger at the flamboyant administration during the good times, when nobody cared. Four years later, with the Depression's tight grip on the nation and the city, the former congressman used 42nd Street as his moral stomping ground to eventually thrust himself to the top of the city's political power heap.

At five feet two inches, the plainly dressed, stocky, pugnacious La Guardia, once described by *Time* magazine as "henshaped," was a puritanical workhorse fusion candidate who took his Depression-age election as a personal mandate to clean up the city's epidemic of crime, corruption, sex, drugs, and bootlegging, by focusing on the evil incarnate embodied on West 42nd Street.* With the zeal of a backwoods preacher, La Guardia denounced as immoral every-

*La Guardia, a former Republican congressman, was the personal choice of Judge Seabury, who was able to convince Roosevelt to support La Guardia in the guise of political neutral-ity against sitting mayor "Holy Joe" McKee, the Tammany candidate FDR considered a cor-rupt anti-Semite. Previously La Guardia had lost his bid for reelection to congress, a victim of the 1932 Roosevelt-led Democratic Party national election landslide. Two years later, in 1934, he was elected mayor of New York City. La Guardia has a street, high school, and Pulitzer Prize musical named in his honor. Upon his resignation, Walker had been replaced by McKee, who served as mayor for two months, until a special election could be held to determine who would serve out the final two years of Walker's second term. John O'Brien was elected, and is remembered, if at all, for his answer to a reporter's question regarding the identity of the next police commissioner: "I don't know, they haven't told me yet."

Mayor Fiorello La Guardia. (Corbis-Bettman)

thing about life on the boulevard of sin that Our Jimmy had once so glorified.

Even as the country's newly elected president, Franklin Delano Roosevelt, was taking historic economic measures to reverse the free fall into chaos and self-destruction, La Guardia determined that the way to political and social salvation lay in moral redemption. After cleaning up what had become the most corrupt police department of any city in America, La Guardia set about to destroy the gambling sites and dens of sexual and alcoholic corruption that had flourished during the previous administration.

The third mayor the teetering city had had in the three years since Walker's resignation, the Little Flower, as he became known (the literal translation of his given name), was a native New Yorker from lower Manhattan's Little Italy, the son of a Jewish mother and an Italian father (La Guardia became Episcopalian by choice). His "no free lunches" style of politics held enormous appeal for the hearts of the increasingly influential, if still largely disenfranchised, New York immigrant voting bloc. La Guardia was determined to destroy the pinball "scourge of the city's children" by declaring war on what had become a national obsession, and to him the symbol of all that had gone wrong in America. With ax in hand, and newsreel cameras always close by, he went on a personal rampage against the city's amusement halls.

The legendary La Guardia crackdown on 42nd Street was intended to make an example of those whose moral breakdown had helped to depress the city economically. One by one he personally padlocked the street's notorious burlesque houses, strip joints, game parlors, and houses of prostitution, among them the China Doll, Billy Rose's Diamond Horseshoe, the Latin Quarter, the Versailles, and the Paradise. Such was La Guardia's at times juvenile manner that often, when speeding down the street holding on to the side of a racing fire engine, he'd stick his tongue out at whatever club owners happened to be standing outside, or raise his thumb to his nose and wiggle his fingers. He also removed 42nd Street's traditional trolley cars, because, he angrily declared, they were too provocative, allowing women's dresses to blow above their knees, and besides they slowed down his beloved fire trucks.

He made fingerprinting of all employees mandatory, outlawed such indigenous rituals as penny gin-rummy card games in the back rooms of restaurants, and threw audits on virtually every nightclub on the street, causing many to go out of business when they couldn't pay their exorbitant tax bills.

La Guardia's grandstand destruction of the shady side of 42nd Street resulted in his accomplishing little more than driving the strip shows, the gambling, the bootlegging, and the prostitution literally and figuratively ever further underground. With burlesque, for example, nothing much changed at first beyond the proximity of naked women's tassels to the street; whereas before they did their thing on little stages above the entrance of the nightclubs they worked, now they did it in basements where the entrance was at the bottom of metal double cellar street doors originally installed to roll down beer barrels. As for the jazz and combo clubs that had once been among the most identifiable signatures of 42nd Street nightlife, they found a new and relatively undisturbed home along West 52nd Street, while the floating gambling dens scattered throughout the Upper East Side before settling into the shaded-window walk-ups of East Harlem. La Guardia fought back, broadening his fingerprint policy so that only those musicians who had secured a city-issued cabaret license could play in any of the boroughs—which was said to be only slightly less difficult to acquire than a gun permit for any performer who'd ever gotten so much as a speeding ticket.

The last "legal" burlesque house on 42nd Street, the Orpheum Dance Palace, where the women were now called taxi dancers (the approximate equivalent of today's strip-club table dancers), was shuttered by La Guardia in 1942. By then it was the only form of live if not exactly "legitimate" theater left on the boulevard. At the height of the turn-of-the-century theatrical boom, seventy-six theaters of one type or another had thrived on or near the fabled street. By 1932, for a number of reasons, among them the Depression, the restrictive policies of the mayor, and the arrival of movies that "talked," the number had fallen to thirty-three. Ten years later, in 1942, with the closing of the Orpheum, it fell to zero. Fiorello's ferocious morality campaign left a cultural blight on West 42nd Street that, except for a brief upturn after World War II, would last a lifetime.

The end of World War II also saw the end of the La Guardia era. The same day that more than a million New Yorkers filled Times Square to celebrate the Allied victory in Japan, the Little Flower announced he would not be running for a fourth term.*

I N 1945 WILLIAM O'DWYER was elected the next mayor of New York City. An Irish immigrant who'd arrived in America in 1910 with twenty-five dollars to his name, O'Dwyer had worked his way through Fordham Law School, become the district attorney of Brooklyn, and gained a flash of fame as the man who prosecuted the legendary mobsters of Murder Incorporated. Defeated by La Guardia in the 1941 mayoral race, O'Dwyer served overseas during the war and upon his return won the city's top office. He was easily reelected in 1949, but the next year found himself ensnared in a nasty series of City Hall scandals centered on police corruption, judges on the take, and a million dollars in illegal bookie-generated payoffs. In 1951 O'Dwyer resigned "for health reasons" and permanently relocated to Mexico City.

He was replaced by Vincent "Impy" Impellitteri, appointed interim mayor by the City Council. Impellitteri, a stylish bon

---

*The figure was 1.2 million, according to newspaper reports for August 14, 1945, the first evening the lights of Times Square, darkened at night during the war, were officially turned back on.

vivant with a touch of the flash and glitter of James Walker, proved to be less than met the public's eye and lost the 1953 election to Manhattan Borough President Robert F. Wagner, Jr., son of one of the most respected politicians in the city.

Wagner was the city's low-profile mayor for three terms (twelve years) and helped to stabilize the city's progressive, if turbulent, economic lurch into the second half of the fifties. At the time of his inauguration a new wave of immigrants, mostly from Europe and South America, had once more radically shifted the city's general census. By then, 56 percent of New Yorkers were either immigrants or sons and daughters of foreign-born parents, and it would be on the shoulders of this new crop of willing minimum-wage day workers that New York would continue its thriving rebound.

By the end of Wagner's first year in office, 40,000 active factories and 100,000 new retail outlets contributed to a citywide gross product of more than $10 billion. After World War II, more than 40 percent of the nation's shipping passed in and out of the harbors of New York City. Postwar prosperity brought a new serenity to the city and allowed its mayor to put a low-profile functionary focus on his role as chief executive officer.

Under Wagner's watch, seventeen acres that stretched from 46th Street down to the eastern tip of 42nd Street, all of which had been donated by the Rockefeller family, developed by William Zeckendorf, and designed by Wallace Harrison (who had worked on Rockefeller Center), began full-time operation as the permanent international headquarters of the United Nations.

The site was separated from 42nd Street by a high brick cliff with inset stone steps originally intended to protect the residents (and buildings) of Tudor City from tidal waves. This stretch of land had been purchased by Zeckendorf, to develop into a futuristic combination housing and retail complex that he planned to call X-City. Unable to raise sufficient funds for the project, Zeckendorf decided to sell it instead and put a price of $8.5 million on the land.

In 1945, Trygve Lie, the first secretary-general of the United Nations, agreed to move the organization from San Francisco to either New York or Philadelphia, depending on which city could offer the best accommodations. By the end of 1946 it appeared that Philadelphia was going to get the United Nations, a situation that outraged Nelson A. Rockefeller, son of John D. Rockefeller, Jr. Knowing Zeckendorf's property was for sale, Rockefeller placed a call to his father, who immediately arranged to contribute the full purchase price of the land to the United Nations. When the deal was completed, Lie announced that Manhattan was to be his organization's new home.

Its highlight was modernist master Le Corbusier's Secretariat Building, which broke ground in 1947. The cornerstone for the Plaza was laid in 1949, and construction was completed in 1954.

A T THE SAME TIME, on West 42nd, a far different kind of development was taking shape. In the years immediately following World War II, a far more explicit, rough-trade pornographic sexual subculture had surfaced west of Seventh Avenue. Much of it had sprung from two sources. The first was the American enlisted man's wartime experiences abroad. Having been exposed to a less puritanical, more aggressive sexuality in Europe and a highly ritualistic eroticism in Asia, the hundreds of thousands of soldiers who left as callow boys returned as sexually experienced men, accustomed to the easily available pleasures they found in the young girls overseas eager to give their American saviors something to savor in return.

The second was the limited options available anywhere outside of the city for its still dead-bolt-closeted gays. The two groups gradually coalesced in the early fifties in a street-savvy proliferation of straight and gay bars and male prostitution rings on West 42nd Street.

Wagner treated that situation and the entire street as the outbreak of a morally perverse epidemic and, to save the rest of the city, in effect quarantined it. His initial counterattack was to have the City Planning Commission rezone the neighborhood so he could legally shut down what would then be the illegal bars that were fronting homosexual prostitution. This move backfired when the bars were quickly replaced by storefront operations that offered a more explicit, if under-the-counter, pornography reminiscent of the "dirty magazines" (gay and straight) that soldiers had found to be so easily attainable overseas and wanted more of back home. A

Mayor Robert F. Wagner, shown here in a publicity shot to raise money for the March of Dimes during the 1950s polio epidemic. Wagner believed 42nd Street west of Seventh Avenue was a moral leper colony and should be avoided by the general public at all costs. (Corbis-Bettman)

weary and frustrated Wagner finally wrote off West 42nd Street as a total loss, a moral leper colony for which containment within its own boundaries seemed the best solution.

It was a decision that, while the complete opposite of La Guardia's hands-on one-man war, was just as damaging to the street. By 1960 the Wagner administration's policy of isolated toleration was seen as an opportunity by the organized crime families of New York to plant their beachhead flags on West 42nd. The Gambinos, especially, would develop a hugely profitable market for the production and sale of totally explicit, industrial-strength pornography, the ultimate come-on that helped turn the street into the sleaze capital of the world. Left alone by a timid mayor, the mob expanded into all of porn's peripherals, including male and female prostitution rings, the deliverance of child runaways to middle-aged male pedophiles, and the distribution of yet one more favorite of World War II veterans: heroin (derived during the war from battlefield morphine), which induced extreme—and extremely addictive—euphoria. Pure white heroin quickly became the drug of choice among the hard-core set that congregated on 42nd Street at Eighth Avenue, where it was always cheap and plentiful.

I N THE EARLY SIXTIES, Wagner's quietly efficient administration began to break down, weakened by a series of internal scandals that smacked of old nineteenth-century Tammany-style bossism. In early 1964 construction of the mayor's and Robert Moses' world's fair in Flushing Meadows was hampered by the revelation of widespread payoffs and accusations of racial discrimination against union leaders. Months later, during one of those hot New York July days when it seems the heat escapes from a hole directly connected to hell, the city degenerated into a four-day race riot that signaled the onset of "white flight" and coalesced the city's minority leaders into a powerful political force.

In one final attempt to contain the festering race issue, Wagner sought to buy a quick-fix social cure by increasing his annual operating budget and earmarking the majority of the new money for construction that included a large number of previously unavailable jobs for minority workers. His plan received a boost when Nelson Rockefeller, who had by then become the governor of New York State, endorsed legislation allowing the mayor to personally reapportion the city's finances. The mayor spent as much as he had and more, running up a massive debt to fortify the impression that the city's minorities were doing as well as he wanted them and everyone to believe.

This round of buy now, pay later economics set the stage for the emergence of an obscure Manhattan Republican congressman, Charlton Heston–look-alike John Lindsay, whose chief asset was the essential one Wagner lacked: youthful charisma in a manner and style reminiscent of John F. Kennedy. Lindsay became the minority party's New Frontier alternative to the city's reigning and increasingly tedious Eisenhower-like mayor. He won the November 1965 election by promising to "turn things around" in a city that, despite Wagner's checkbook politics, was torn by racial strife and an increasingly unstable economy.

Unfortunately for the new mayor, his progressive spin didn't last very long.

Within days of his election, the city, along with much of the Northeast, suffered a massive blackout. New York remained in the dark for fifteen hours (except for the 1963 Kennedy assassination and periods during World War II, the only time the lights had gone out on Broadway and Times Square for that much time), and even before Lindsay's inauguration, the press seized on the notion of a city groping in the dark.

Less than two months later, Lindsay was struck by yet another major blow when he failed to prevent a subway strike by the Transport Workers Union. The strike, led by the union's colorful, long-time leader Mike Quill, lasted twelve days and cost the city $800 million in business revenues and $25 million in wage earnings. The walkout was caused by budget problems, as the subway system, after a series of horrendous accidents and decades of financial losses, was taken over by the city in the fifties and put under the control of the newly created New York City Transit Authority, with a mandate to operate without a deficit.

However, to the citizens of New York, the absurd reality of the eventual settlement was that the average pay of the subway rider was now less than that of the subway worker, whose union had won its members a substantial pay raise based on a new twenty-cent fare. After being held at a nickel from 1904 until 1948, in eighteen years it had now quadrupled.* The blame was put at the new mayor's door, the buck-stop for the city's failure to withstand the

---

*The nickel fare had held for an incredible forty-four years, during which it became one of the few tangible symbols of freedom for the workingman and as such an untouchable totem for any mayor. It finally fell under William O'Dwyer in 1948, a mayor whose misfortunes seemed to begin there and continued until his early resignation less than two years later under a cloud of municipal scandal. In the mid-nineties, when the fare, regulated by the New York City Transit Authority, reached $1.50, tokens were augmented with "Metrocards," which offered discounts on the bulk purchase of rides and replaced the uniquely designed tokens that had to be reformatted with every increase, with highly popular, easily portable magnetic-strip cards.

Mayor John Lindsay. His elitist image help create the term "limousine liberal." (Corbis-Bettman)

force of Quill's bullying. And Lindsay felt the weight on his broad, if sagging, shoulders, a bold example, as one observer put it, of how to run a city so that "the rich get richer and the poor get dumber." By 1969 the city's operating budget had tripled to an unprecedented $7 *billion.*

That same year, the city's spirit temporarily up-ticked when, in January, Joe Namath's Jets pulled off a major upset in the Super Bowl. Unfortunately for Lindsay, the city then made that magic leap from the miraculously sublime to the blindingly ridiculous when a snowstorm a month later paralyzed the outer boroughs. Although the streets of Manhattan were immediately plowed, the blanket of ice and snow was left untouched in the outer boroughs in some neighborhoods for as long as a week. The fallout was the lasting impression that the Mayor only cared about Manhattan—one city tabloid said it took Lindsay so long to do something about the storm because he couldn't *find* Queens, another New York daily wrote that the mayor had "more trouble with Queens than Henry VIII"—and had sold out the real estate interests of the outer-borough residents by granting sizable cooperative residential tax breaks for Manhattan's elite while shoving public housing down the throats of the other boroughs' middle classes.

New Yorkers, citizens of the so-called Fun City, a term first used by sportswriter Dick Schaap, which became the calling card of the Lindsay administration, had their spirits lifted once more when another "miracle" took place that fall: The quixotic Queens-based Mets, New York's "other" baseball team and longest-running joke, somehow defeated the windmill and beat the Baltimore Orioles in the World Series.

However, for all the glory of New York's 1969 Cinderella sports victories, the euphoria in so-called "Fun City" as the Lindsay Administration optimistically dubbed it, lasted less than a year. The glass slipper once more shattered in the spring of 1970 when Detective Frank Serpico accused his fellow police officers of looking the other way when it came to the public's safety on 42nd Street and elsewhere and was among the first to suggest that there was a mob connection between pornography and drugs, the former being the lure for the latter, and that the police knew it and looked the other way while taking a piece of the action for themselves. Serpico's revelations pushed the mayor to create an independent investigative committee. The controversial findings of the Knapp Commission resulted in Lindsay's being labeled soft on crime, and plunged the city's residents still further into an urban landscape of fear and despair.

Nevertheless, for all his problems governing, Lindsay loved the glamour and sizzle of Broadway as no mayor had since the heyday of Jimmy Walker. Unlike so many before him, he never gave up on Times Square. He hoped to save the theater district by tweaking the city's Planning Commission's longstanding zoning restrictions on new construction in Midtown West. Unfortunately, his vision of a revitalized Great White Way was decades ahead of its time, and his courtship of out-of-town developers caused many to wonder if he was selling out New York to a bunch of fat-cat rubes and ultimately cost him more votes than it won. Still, Lindsay might have been able to pull this audacious plan off had it not been for the early seventies national recession that devalued real estate, plunged the city ever closer to bankruptcy, and killed any chance he might have had to star in the real-life saga of his own political salvation.

B Y THE END OF LINDSAY'S administration, New York had had enough of so-called Republican-Liberalism and elected a mayor whose style of Democratic politics was firmly rooted in the legacy, if not the halls, of Tammany.

Former comptroller Abraham Beame took office in January 1974 and inherited a city that seemed once again on the brink of disaster. As if to underscore the dire situation, one month before the new mayor took office a major span of the West Side Highway, one of New York's two major surface arteries, this one connecting Manhattan to the Holland Tunnel, the Lincoln Tunnel, the George Washington Bridge, upstate New York, and Connecticut, collapsed in a dusty, lifeless heap.

Unlike his suave, Wasp predecessor, Beame, a first-generation Jewish American whose parents had emigrated from Poland to New York City at the end of the nineteenth century, was a short, stocky man with a shock of neatly trimmed white hair, the face of a bulldog, and the heart of one too. His political consciousness came from a youth spent in the 1930s socialist whirl of New York's Lower East Side. After flirting with that decade's lurch toward radicalism, Beame shifted his political aim toward the center and began working for the Brooklyn Democratic machine. By the early sixties he was the city's comptroller, a springboard from which, in 1965, he ran unsuccessfully for mayor, losing to Lindsay in the general election.

Eight years and two Lindsay administrations later, Beame cannily took his cue from the pages of the La Guardia handbook, and when his administration ran into fiscal problems, he determined to salvage it by rescuing 42nd Street from the sinkhole of filth, prostitution, and drugs into which it had fallen. However, despite his efforts, West 42nd Street continued to flourish in filth, with no fewer than twenty-five XXX movie theaters, a dozen topless dance stables, unchecked street prostitution and corner drug dealing, and a seemingly endless supply of anything-goes, readily available hard-core storefront porn shops openly operating twenty-four hours a day, seven days a week, fifty-two weeks a year.

In 1977 Beame failed to win his bid for a second term. Instead, the voters turned to the city's newest political hero, the dark horse defender of Forest Hills and one of the frontline warriors in the successful mid-seventies battle to save 42nd Street's Grand Central Terminal from demolition. As it had with so many of his predecessors, midtown's moral redemption became the foundation plank of Koch's successful campaign for mayor. Like Elmer Gantry in pinstripes, Koch vowed to cure all the city's economic and social ills, via the salvation of 42nd Street.

And as the city was about to discover, in the great tradition of politics, New York style, Ed Koch could politically holy-roll with the best of them.

PART TWO

THE CITY
PRIMEVAL

SOME LEGENDS build monuments to themselves; others have monuments built for them. Some provide great terminals; some have boulevards, bridges, and tunnels named in their honor. And some if they live long enough even become cultural icons, perpetuators of the American way, reminders of how every child in America may grow up to be the next father of his country. They have books written about them, movies made of their lives. They become symbols of the nation's spirit, the high priests of morality eternalized in the temples of entertainment. If they were heroic in life, they become saints in death. If they were villainous, they become reconfigured for redemption.

On a clear September evening in 1776, from a hilly vantage point in the middle of a stretch of Manhattan that would one day be known as 42nd Street, the rebel Continental Army led by General George Washington dug themselves in for one more heroic stand against the advancing British. Already in bloody retreat, having fled Brooklyn Heights two weeks earlier in the dead of night by ferry across the East River, Washington's badly outnumbered band of soldiers had faced yet another crushing defeat in the Battle of Kip's Bay (one of a series of skirmishes in the Revolution's six-week Battle for New York). War-weary, dispirited, and on the verge of losing a confrontation in which defeat and surrender would put an end to the upstart American Revolution and a noose around the neck of its leader, Washington's men braced themselves on 42nd Street to fight a redcoat force bent on taking back the country for the pleasure and profit of the king.

The original Croton Reservoir at 42nd Street and Fifth Avenue, which began operations in 1842. (Corbis-Bettman)

49

The rebels desperately needed to hold off the British long enough to regroup and allow the uprising to continue for at least another day. A few miles to the north lay Westchester. If they could get that far, they were assured safe passage to and through New Jersey and into the protective mountains of Pennsylvania, from where the soldiers of the Continental Army could come together and commence their leader's long-range plan of guerrilla counterattack.

At this point, the general's best and perhaps only reliable defense was his faith. He resolutely believed he had God on his side, and this spiritual righteousness would ultimately prove the superior weapon against the single-shot muskets that were even now being aimed toward his men. With time running out and the redcoats advancing ever closer, Washington made one last desperate attempt to inspire his soldiers. Leaping to the top of the dirt hill and drawing his saber high as the enemy opened fire and live rounds flew past, he shouted a defiant warning to the redcoats, then fled with his men into the protective cloak of night.

B Y THE TIME OF Washington's death in 1799, the very hill on 42nd Street where the brave general had fought so valiantly a quarter of a century earlier was unceremoniously transformed into an isolated communal graveyard for a city whose latest invader was a deadly infectious disease spiraling madly out of control.

At the dawn of the nineteenth century Manhattan's population had swelled to an unprecedented 100,000, the majority of which were crowded into unsanitary, unheated, and unplumbed housing on or near the southern docks, close to where much of the city's steadiest work was. That fall another epidemic of the yellow fever that had already devastated Philadelphia and traveled up the coast threatened to do the same to the residents of lower Manhattan. For ten years the disease had systematically ravaged the city's population as it came and went without warning, claiming the lives of more than fifteen thousand New Yorkers. It was a decade of insidious disaster that caused one health official of the day to note, "Death and we shook hands so often in those times, his bony fingers appeared as soft as a lady's glove."

Clean water, or, more accurately, the lack of it, was the major hindrance to an effective counterattack against the viral plague. The shortage caused, among other problems, the pileup of human waste routinely dumped from windows into back alleys. With horse-drawn carriages the only source of land transportation, the unbearable, pervasive stench of human and animal waste permeated the city's air. To avoid constant retching, people anywhere south of Canal Street were forced to hold their noses to prevent the smell of rotting fish, another acrid layer of the already stomach-turning stink that engulfed them.

After a few years of remission the yellow fever returned, now more deadly than ever. Those who could afford to fled for the relative safety of the northern suburb of Greenwich Village, where they hoped to avoid direct contact with what they believed to be the docks' pestilent breeding grounds. Fearing another round of widespread death, Mayor De Witt Clinton desperately sought municipal funding for the provision of an adequate supply of fresh, unpolluted water for the citizens of New York City, and soon found himself in cutthroat negotiation for it with Aaron Burr, whose Manhattan Company held exclusive rights to the upstate Croton Dam, the city's primary source of clean water. Burr, finding himself with the advantage, gleefully demanded an exorbitant amount of money for those rights. Clinton was unable to negotiate a settlement, and as the epidemic came and went with a fresh batch of souls in its ghastly sack, any hope for a citywide municipal water system went with it.

The situation remained unresolved until 1835, when a massive fire swept through and destroyed much of lower Manhattan because volunteer firefighters did not have access to enough water to contain it. This disaster finally moved Mayor Cornelius W. Lawrence to meet Burr's price and led to the creation of the Croton aqueduct system.

The City Council then directed that a new reservoir be built in the city fed by water piped down from upstate Croton to a site far enough north of the existing city settlements so as not to interfere with the chronic shortage of living space, and sufficiently landlocked to avoid contamination from either the Hudson or the East River, which bookended the island of Manhattan. This site was the same 42nd Street hilly countryside turned graveyard upon which

The Crystal Palace and observation deck, which was immediately to the east of the reservoir. (Corbis-Bettman)

Washington had taken his heroic stand during the Revolutionary War. Building the reservoir, construction workers were shocked to discover more than 100,000 skeletons, mostly victims of the epidemics, buried one atop the other. These remains were dumped into Manhattan's surrounding harbors.

The Croton Reservoir, at Reservoir Square at 42nd Street between Fifth and Sixth Avenues, officially opened in 1842. Its capacity was 660 million gallons of water, more than 35 million of which flowed through the city every day.

Atop the huge basin's fifty-foot walls was a circular promenade, accessible by several stone stairways and wide enough to accommodate the large crowds that flocked to marvel at it. The promenade brought a new focus to 42nd Street, and soon became the city's most fashionable place both to see and be seen. Every Sunday, well-dressed families eagerly climbed the two hundred steps to the top of the elevated loop for a very public midday stroll.

Not long after, the adjacent embankment immediately to the east was flattened and made into a paved extension of the square. At its center stood an iron and glass pavilion, the Exhibition of the Industry of All Nations. Modeled after the famous London structure, it came to be known as New York's Crystal Palace. At its completion it became the city's tallest structure, with an adjoining observation post that resembled a giant cannon pointed toward the sky.

The Crystal Palace quickly displaced the reservoir promenade as New York's premiere social gathering place, until one day in 1858 it caught fire and burned to the ground in less than fifteen minutes, even as frantic firefighters tried to figure out how to get any ground-level water out of the high-walled reservoir to extinguish the flames. The once-glamorous grounds were reduced to ruins, and would remain that way for the next twenty years, its wasted land used only as a training ground for Union soldiers during the Civil War, until 1884, when its surface was restored and renamed Bryant Park, in honor of the New York City poet and newspaper editor William Cullen Bryant, who in the 1840s had used his position as editor of the *Evening Post* to lead the movement to create Central Park.

T HE CRYSTAL PALACE FIRE put an end to a brief and genteel era of public socializing on 42nd Street, even as a blaze of another sort continued to burn less than a mile to the east, in the blackened heart of a young thug by the name of Paddy Corcoran.

Corcoran was the leader of the so-called Irish Rat Gang that controlled the quarter-mile riverside turf of nearly uninhabitable tenements known at the time as Corcoran's Roost.* The dockside was as late as the 1860s still overrun by smelly wild goats attracted to the garbage dumps just off the East River that serviced the glue

*Members of the Rat Gang were sometimes known as Corcoran's Roosters. Nicknames such as Paddy were both descriptive and a form of identification supposedly untraceable by police records, especially from one neighborhood precinct to another. Jimmy Curley was Jimmy Carrigio. There was also "Dopey" Benny Fein, Joe the Greaser (Joseph Rosensweig), Pinchey Paul, Little Rhody, Punk Madden, Owney the Killer, Pickles Laydon, Ralph the Barber (Ralph Daniello), Yoske Nigger (Joseph Toplinsky), and Carley the Cripple (Charles Vitoffsky), to name a few of the more descriptive sobriquets to be found throughout the late nineteenth century on Manhattan crime blotters.

factories, slaughterhouses, breweries, coal barges, and gas works alongside the mostly Irish immigrant tenants who lived there. It was not uncommon for goat carcasses to lie in the street for weeks, its bones picked clean by river rats the size of dogs.

These East Side rookeries, or sloping outcrop embankments, were the final destination for New Jersey cattle brought across the Hudson via the Weehawken ferry and driven in herds to the East Side across 42nd Street known as "Blood Alley." The crossing, flattened and widened by the animals' daily journey to the slaughterhouse, was the reason the city had designated it as early as 1837 one of thirteen river-to-river thoroughfares that bisected Manhattan.

Corcoran's Roosters earned whatever honest living they could selling goat's milk and cheese, and meat from stolen cattle that strayed from the herd near the treacherous, hilly, last quarter mile of their final journey. The Roosters' best cash customers were the wealthy neighbors to the north, residents of the new suburbia that reached into the 50s. In 1827 the Winthrops, one of New York's wealthiest Greenwich Village families, had built a country mansion there, an area at the time still considered to be "upstate" New York. Other prominent families followed, including the Kips, the De Voors, the Beekmans, and the Brevoorts (all of whom would eventually have buildings, streets, or neighborhoods in this part of the city named after them).

By 1850 the area's moneyed inhabitants were the perfect targets for Paddy and his gang. When they didn't have enough merchandise to sell them, the young street hoodlums made up the difference at night by robbing, mugging, or murdering the clientele they serviced so politely during the day.

In 1855 the Winthrops, fed up with the ever-present danger from the gangs and the constant and unavoidable noise, stink, and filth from the crosstown cattle drives, sold their mansion and moved farther north, as did most of the other prominent families. This flight of the wealthy caused the East 50s to slip into poverty. The new owners turned the mansion into a hotel and tavern, but soon gave up for lack of paying customers and abandoned it to the animals and the Irish (seeing little difference between the two).

Corcoran's Roosters, whose lawlessness was matched only by their fearlessness, rebuffed any attempts to control them, causing

Artist's rendering of the rookeries that dotted the eastern shore of 42nd Street. Tommy "Paddy" Corcoran, leader of a New York City street gang, ruled this turf and became a legend trying to keep his people from being ousted by the late-nineteenth-century encroachment of corporate interests as Manhattan developed northward. (Museum of the City of New York)

one city official to describe them as "a cancer eating away at the vitals of the city." Even the police feared them, and uniformed patrolmen were relieved when they were instructed not to go after Corcoran, an order that came from the very top of the city's corrupt base of political power. This was the time of "Boss" Tweed's stranglehold on Tammany, and to maintain the voting loyalty of the city's many enclaves of poverty (and help with the collection of tribute money), he enlisted the services of neighborhood ringleaders like Corcoran. Every election, Tweed temporarily "hired" Paddy's boys to make sure their neighborhood voted the way it was told.

The progress of urban development finally accomplished what the might of the city's police force could not. By the late 1870s, horse-drawn wooden trolleys had for the most part replaced covered wagons as the preferred means of Manhattan's street-level transportation. Steel tracks were laid along the streets of every north/south avenue, starting at Fifth and eventually moving west to Eleventh, bringing new pockets of growth and development to the streets known as Hell's Kitchen, yet another shantytown turf, this one controlled by the Irish gang known as the Westies. On the East Side, the laying of trolley tracks succeeded in pushing Paddy and his gang's turf ever closer to the river.

Corcoran's Roost was still further encroached upon when 42nd Street was cross-railed, river-to-river, to allow horsecars to pick up the Jersey steer directly off the ferries. This put an effective end to the daily, messy, thunderous, and, to the gang, highly profitable noontime cattle runs. Paddy took this development as a personal affront to his freedom and in response initiated a murderous reign of terror, whereby he ordered that any face his gang didn't recognize east of First Avenue would leave it on a slab, throat slit by a rusty razor, a signature rat stuffed into the open wound.

By the late 1890s, however, with Tweed long gone, Paddy's gang gradually lost its unofficial police protection, and along with it what little was left of its sanctioned turf. No one was even sure if Paddy was still alive, he would have been in his late sixties by now, and although members of the Roost pledged loyalty to their gang for life, old age was not a common occurrence on these mean streets. The Irish street gangs operated in the tradition of the downtown Chinese triads, dynastic continuums whose founding leaders' spiritual presence was often as powerful, if not more so, as their physical being. Corcoran's name became a rallying cry for the downtrodden of the midtown East Side.

A S THE NINETEENTH CENTURY dissolved into the twentieth, the perimeter of the city's commerce inexorably expanded north, from Wall Street to 42nd Street. By the early 1900s the arrival of new businesses, theaters, the Times Tower, and an interconnected subway made it the most popular boulevard in the city. At the same time, the subterranean contours of the island forced a change in the direction of expansion, pushing major construction east and west, river to river.

The discovery of a major fault line beneath Manhattan's solid bedrock just above 42nd made that street the natural northern boundary for commercial development, and therefore the logical site for a train depot.

The end of the Civil War had marked a new era of expansion by rail across America. As early as 1863, even before the soldiers of the North and South put down their weapons, millionaire steamboat baron Cornelius "Commodore" Vanderbilt began acquiring controlling interest in the Hudson River and Harlem Railroad, which ran through the center of Manhattan to 42nd Street, a crucial link in his vision of a single, grand, continuous railroad line running from one end of the country to the other.

His next move was to build an extension that would run to the Battery, the southernmost seaport in Manhattan. Unfortunately for Vanderbilt, Boss Tweed, fearful of losing a significant amount of street graft from the midtown horse and buggy trade, saw to it the Commodore was denied permission by the city to lay any new track. Not one to take no for an answer, Vanderbilt called in a marker he held with the federal government, which was indebted to him for transporting thousands of Union soldiers by sea during the Civil War, and was soon allowed to run track straight to the bottom of the island. This brought Vanderbilt one step closer to his lifelong dream, one that had begun for him with a single sailboat.

IN 1810 SIXTEEN-YEAR-OLD Staten Island native Cornelius Vanderbilt purchased a small secondhand wind catcher for a hundred dollars borrowed from his mother and began a Manhattan ferry service to and from what was then referred to by the outlying boroughs as the mainland. The Commodore, a nickname given to Vanderbilt by the other ferry operators who made fun of his ramshackle boat, spent the next fifty-seven years building this small, self-operated maritime service into one of the great financial empires of the nineteenth century.

In 1867, Vanderbilt, a millionaire several times over, at the age of seventy-three, sold off the last of his at-sea shipping interests to consolidate and expand his surface holdings.

The New York Central gave Vanderbilt control of all rail lines in and out of New York City as far north as Buffalo, from where the rest of the country could be reached via the Erie Canal. During the particularly cold winter of 1868, Vanderbilt refused to ship any goods in or out of New York City, blaming the weather, which caused the Central's stock to plummet. He then purchased the remaining and now severely undervalued shares from panicky holders, took a seat on the board of directors, and declared himself the new president of the entire line.

By the end of the 1860s, Vanderbilt single-handedly controled an amalgamated rail system of 408 locomotives, 445 passenger cars, 132 baggage cars, 9,026 freight cars, and 740 miles of track. What he needed was a single terminal from which to operate his burgeoning empire. The logical site he chose was the existing Harlem Railroad Depot on the northern end of Fourth Avenue, which stretched over three city blocks, from 42nd Street to 45th.

In 1869 construction began on a major overhauling of the depot. It would take more than two years at a cost of what was then the astronomical sum of $3 million because Vanderbilt insisted his depot rank among the most beautiful structures in the country. He was willing to pay top dollar to import materials from all over the world. To help offset huge budget overruns, the ever-thrifty Vanderbilt sold off his interests in an unused storage building he owned on 26th Street to an investment group led by Stanford White, which converted the site into what became the city's second, and much grander, Madison Square Garden (the first having been built by Vanderbilt's son, William).*

Before work on the depot was completed a series of fatal accidents involving mostly teenagers on the losing end of playing "chicken" with the trains that ran on the new, exposed track below 42nd Street, the city, urged on by Tweed, ordered the Commodore to stop active use of that portion of his route.

An outraged Vanderbilt saw this as nothing more than political maneuvering, and remained convinced Tweed's motivation had less to do with the public's safety than his own profits. The folly of the ban was apparent, as most of the major thoroughfares of the city had by now been covered with one type of surface rail or another.

---

*This Garden was built by White's architectural firm, McKim, Mead and White, at a cost of $3 million, and took up the entire block. It held a 5,000-seat amphitheater, an opera house, a ballroom, a restaurant, and a rooftop cabaret. Atop the structure sat Augustus St. Gaudens's nude statue of the goddess Diana. The Garden was the setting for a major scandal in 1906 when White was shot to death in the rooftop cabaret by Harry Thaw, the husband of chorus girl Evelyn Nesbit, with whom White was having an affair.

Vanderbilt's original Grand Central Depot on East 42nd Street. (Museum of the City of New York)

All along the north/south avenues, for example, thunderous els, whose two-flights-up tracks youngsters enjoyed racing across as much as they did the ones Vanderbilt had laid below 42nd, stood like varicose veins above the skin of the city. And the surface lines Vanderbilt had purchased (which had not been buried at the time of their original construction due to the danger of digging into the uncertain turf) ran unprotected at street level from 57th Street to the depot.

Vanderbilt vigorously fought the downtown ban, until finally, in 1875, after Tweed's conviction and imprisonment, the city granted Vanderbilt the right to resume operations below 42nd Street, but only if he buried the tracks from 59th Street down to the tip of Manhattan, no matter what the personal cost to him might be.

When the first estimates to do the job came in at $6 million, the Commodore vehemently objected, having just spent that much to build his new depot. And there were other problems as well. For one thing, he still had to deal with whatever was left of Paddy Corcoran's Roosters, who took the opportunity of the long impasse between Vanderbilt and the city to make one final attempt at reestablishing their place on the street by preying on the increasing pedestrian traffic in and around Grand Central Depot. At this point, an angry Cornelius, fed up with the city's inability to deal with the situation, organized his own police force. Vanderbilt's goon squads were composed of several teams of tough-guys whose job it was to get rid of the last of Corcoran's gang, using whatever brute force they deemed necessary.

They roamed 42nd Street every night as Paddy's boys once had, armed with guns, clubs, knives, and chains. Vanderbilt's men attacked suspected gang members on sight and put everyone they caught either into the hospital or under the ground. These police-sanctioned vigilantes managed to once and for all put an end to the remaining street toughs who claimed membership in Corcoran's Roosters. The few who survived the Central's street force either wound up joining it, or the already heavily Irish NYPD, or were simply scattered into the dark shadows of the city's underworld, eventually reemerging as low-level runners and enforcers for the new century's local crime bosses.

After a series of at times tense and often acrimonious negotiations, the city finally agreed to Vanderbilt's demand that it pay half the cost of covering the tracks. To try to recoup some of its investment, the City Council voted to put the newly covered land on the open market. As a result of this partnership between the city and Vanderbilt's company, one of the few public-private partnerships in the city's history (the water for the Croton Reservoir deal with Burr was another), the stretch of land north of Grand Central Depot went from a noisy, dirty open-air train route once known simply as Fourth Avenue into the beautifully sculpted, descriptively renamed Park Avenue.

The new boulevards that extended north and south from Vanderbilt's Grand Central Depot added to its exquisite beauty, causing architectural historian Carroll L. V. Meeks to marvel at what was now "one of the first American stations capable of standing comparison with the finest European ones." With its face of red brick masonry, classical fenestration, and ornamental ironwork painted white to appear marble, and highlighted by a great iron and glass shed, the depot was, indeed, one of the most colorful and imposing structures in the city. Standing at the northern tip of commercial Manhattan, its grand entrance rose above the horizon, visible on a clear day nearly to the South Seaport, inviting the city that sat below it and the rest of the world to pass through it to the future.

M ONEY MADE MONEY, and Vanderbilt's rail system thrived, even as the rest of the country suffered through a major economic depression caused in large part by the great Chicago fire of 1871, which devastated that city's terminal and caused an interruption in shipping and a resulting fall in the stock price of several midwestern railroads. Vanderbilt seized this opportunity to expand his empire, and with his eldest son, William, acquired controlling stock in the Ohio, Indiana, and Illinois Railroads, continuing on his quest to control every last foot of rail from the East Coast to the West.

He would not live long enough to see it happen. In 1877, at the age of eighty-two, Cornelius Vanderbilt passed into history, leaving behind thirteen children and numerous grandchildren. William, knowing full well he did not have the ability to run the empire as his father had, smartly aligned himself with banking mogul J. P. Morgan, who subsequently negotiated the sale of 250,000 shares of New York Central stock to Great Britain, to ensure that no other American company would ever be able to buy enough of the Vanderbilt empire to wrest control from the family.

In return for his services, Morgan took a seat on the railroad's board of directors, and a fair share of stock as well. In 1885, during a heated business argument, William suddenly keeled over, instantly dead from a stroke. His share of the family fortune and business passed to his son Cornelius Vanderbilt II. Morgan convinced him the railroad had outgrown his grandfather's original depot.

As a result, less than thirty years after the Commodore had built his $6-million monument to himself meant to stand for ages, Grand Central Depot was dramatically reconceived, torn down, and massively reconstructed as the fifty-seven-track Grand Central Terminal.

Completed in 1899, the new terminal emerged as the defining symbol of the recently incorporated city's entrée into the twentieth century, marking 42nd Street as the city's new capital of commerce.

To the west lay the future site of the *New York Times,* a section of the street already alive with nightclubs, hotels, and brothels. To the north lay Park Avenue, which, due to technological advances in construction developed during the covering of the tracks, allowed developers to build luxury housing on either side of the now-flowery boulevard all the way north to Central Park. To the south, new housing and corporate offices brought radical change to what remained of the old Fourth Avenue, rechristened Park Avenue South. And to the east, businesses large and small flourished by taking advantage of the pedestrian traffic generated by the grand new terminal. There were numerous cigar stores, wholesale liquor outlets, taverns such as Charley Conners and the Sherman House, the Ruptured and Crippled Hospital, the Manhattan Storage Warehouse, and everyone's new favorite hangout, the immensely popular and endlessly social saloon in the splendidly wood-paneled lobby of the fabulous Grand Union Hotel, where every night its colorful proprietor, the eminent humorist Simon Ford, could be found holding court for locals and overnight travelers alike.

In the back room, "burny," the common name for the city's newest fad, the smoking of crystallized cocaine, became the recreation of choice for young men in preparation for a visit to the West Side's brothels. With the Irish street toughs on the run, midtown distribution of coke, which they had once controlled, was taken over by gangs of immigrant Jews, led by the notorious Monk Eastman, and by their chief rivals, the Italians, led by Johnny Torrio, Frankie Yale, Lucky Luciano, and one member of the notorious South Brooklyn Rippers and later the Five Points Juniors, a scarfaced self-styled ladies' man with an insatiable thirst for sex and violence by the name of Al Capone.

Just three years later, in 1903, plans were made for yet another renovation of the terminal because of the need for complete electrification to accommodate the next generation of motor-driven trains. Its design evoked the triumphal gateways of ancient Rome. Above the central arch and the fifteen-foot-wide clock stood Jules Coutan's forty-foot-tall statue of Mercury, the god of speed, supported on either side by Hercules (moral energy) and Minerva (mental energy). The main concourse, designed by Reed and Stern of Minneapolis, was 275 feet long, 120 feet wide, and 125 feet

The expanded, electrified Grand Central Terminal. (Museum of the City of New York)

high, styled in Ecole de Beaux-Arts Eclectic, set apart by and dominated by three enormous arched windows facing south on 42nd Street.

The new Grand Central Terminal became an even greater tourist attraction than its predecessor and spurred another round of commercial development, particularly to the east. Everything that had stood before, including the popular Grand Union Hotel, was slated for demolition, replaced by three new hotels all within walking distance of the new terminal. The majestic Biltmore went up on the aptly named Vanderbilt Row. The Commodore, also named for Vanderbilt, went up on 42nd Street between Lexington and the terminal. The Ambassador laid claim to Park Avenue at 51st, land still owned and controlled by the Vanderbilt-Morgan confluence.

I N 1848, THE LAST YEAR of his life, John Jacob Astor, looking to leave his initials on the soul of the city, committed himself to building a public library for the city supposedly in memory of a favorite childhood schoolteacher who urged the multimillionaire to leave "fitting testimony to his adopted country by its richest citizen." Astor's will left $400,000 and a plot at Lafayette Place for a library (on the Lower East Side, where the Joseph Papp Public Theater stands today). Although it was completed in 1854 and opened with great fanfare, its availability to the public remained limited, a monument more to be admired than used.

Robert Lenox, a Scottish immigrant, had made his fortune, like Astor, in New York City real estate. When he died, his son, James, donated a portion of family-owned land on Fifth Avenue between 70th and 71st Streets as the future site of a library, intended for use without charge, but only by scholars. Founded in 1870, it proved more costly than anticipated and its use was necessarily severely limited.

When former governor Samuel Tilden died in 1886, he bequeathed $4 million to be used to support a free library and reading room, an amount that was significantly reduced after a series of successful legal challenges by his surviving children. As a result, the library ran into early financial difficulty. Thus, in a relatively short period of time, New York City had three fancily built but largely impractical libraries, none of them especially usable by the public.

In 1885, meanwhile, a small group of women associated with the Grace Episcopal Church managed to collect a few hundred donated books to use as the basic inventory for a free public reading room. This small, unadorned library proved so successful that for the two hours each week the women could afford to keep it open, people lined up around the block for a chance to get inside. When word of the reading room's popularity reached City Council President Adolph Sanger, he allocated additional public funds to ensure the library's ongoing availability. In 1901 Pittsburgh steel magnate Andrew Carnegie donated $5 million to the project, which became the New York Public Library.

The search began for a central locale to serve as its official site. Columbia University's Madison Avenue campus, between 49th and 50th Streets, was considered, but estimates of the needed renovations proved too expensive. The Tilden mansion on Gramercy Park was rejected for being too small, the Astor Library for being too far south, the Lenox too far north.

The New York Public Library under construction at Fifth Avenue and 42nd Street, on the site of the old Croton Reservoir. The famous lions have not yet been set in place. (Corbis-Bettman)

There was one place, however, that everyone agreed was perfect: the empty shell of the old Croton Reservoir, which fifty years earlier had provided a vital water link for the city. Once the site was chosen, a great rush of excitement accompanied the city's request for independent bids for the design of the new library. A carnival-like competition took place, daily details of which were breathlessly reported in slanted letters on the front page of the city's dozen daily newspapers, climaxing when a relatively unknown company, the French and American partnership of John M. Carrère and Thomas Hastings, was granted the contract. The city purposefully chose them to avoid a "sameness" about the architecture that had begun to dominate the corporate side of 42nd Street. Carrère and Hastings were asked to design a building that would maintain the atmospheric intimacy of an academic alcove while utilizing what was, admittedly, a monumental amount of space.

Several times the project was nearly abandoned as construction costs kept ballooning until the original estimate had nearly doubled, passing the $9-million mark. At its completion, Carrère and Hastings had proved their worth, having erected a unique Beaux Arts structure modeled in part after the Parisian Louis XIV Louvre and the Place de la Concorde, complete with a matching terrace overlooking the adjacent Bryant Park.

The library's magnificent design was offset with a light touch when two Tennessee-marble lions were placed at the steps of the Fifth Avenue entrance. Intended at first to be used only for the opening ceremonies, they had been commissioned from and carved by Edward C. Potter at what was considered the bargain price of $13,000. However, they proved so popular they remained in place, a permanent symbol of not just the library but the leonine prowess of New York intellectualism. Later nicknamed Patience and Fortitude by Mayor La Guardia, they became a favorite of New Yorkers, offering visitors a chance to "read between the lions."

 AND SO THE twentieth century began with New York City politically incorporated and physically reconfigured. Forty-second Street was now New York's grandest showcase boulevard, much of it having been developed by such native giants as Vanderbilt and Astor, whose imprint in turn lured other great names of American industry to it, national figures that included Rockefeller, Ford, Chrysler, Carnegie, and Morgan.

Residential housing flourished as well at both ends of the crossroads, the most lavish of projects being "Tudor City—A little piece of Heaven on East 42nd Street," as described by real estate developer Fred French who built it to his own sixteenth century–style specification. Erected in 1928 on the very land that once served as the home of Corcoran's Roosters, Tudor City offered twelve apartment houses, three thousand apartments, a post office, a hotel, two private parks, and that gigantic wall that separated it from the banks of the river.

However, less than a year later, after thirty years of unparalleled growth and development, the economic ax fell hard, sharp, and fast across the country, cutting deep into its financial capital, New York City. With the 1929 collapse of the stock market, much of midtown's finest locales turned into shantytowns. Bryant Park, already physically ripped apart by the construction of the new Sixth Avenue subway line, became the newest homeless encampment. Grand Central Terminal became the last stop for those with

Designed by a ten-man international team under the leadership of architect Wallace Harrison, who'd conceived the Trylon and Perisphere for the 1939 World's Fair, the acknowledged influence on the United Nations was Swiss-born modernist Le Corbusier; the two later fought over accreditation. Here in the mid-1950s is the view looking east, onto "Blood Alley," the once slum-infested waterside of slaughterhouses and rookeries. The U.N.'s Secretariat Building, the first glass-walled skyscraper in the world, looms above the neo-Classic residential housing complex Tudor City. (Note its French-style rooftop name-in-lights.) The design of the General Assembly Building was amended to appease Congress, which was reluctant to release federal funds for U.N. construction unless an American-style dome was included. (Corbis-Bettman)

nowhere to go but down, into its cavernous main concourse, where the once ornate waiting rooms became bedrooms for those lucky enough to snag a spot of bench. The steps of the library were filled with bodies every night, lying end-to-end, covered with blankets in winter, seeking rest and shelter from the economic storm.

The stages of 42nd Street's great theaters, once the center of the city's gaiety, laughter, prosperity, and performance culture, were

"Mugsy," the character portrayed by Leo Gorcey (second from left) *in a series of feature and short films, was the leader of a New York City street gang (loosely based on characters created by Sidney Kingsley for his Depression-era stage play* Dead End, *which was later made into a movie) that many believed was based on the legend of Tommy "Paddy" Corcoran and his "roosters."*

(Corbis-Bettman)

either empty or abandoned or had been converted to movie houses, showcases for Hollywood's endless supply of cheap entertainment designed to take the nation's mind off its problems for an hour or two.

Occasionally a film did manage to come along that attempted a more realistic view of life. Some were originals, others based on Broadway shows. One such movie was an adaptation of Sidney Kingsley's play *Dead End,* turned into a 1937 Depression slice-of-lifer that starred Humphrey Bogart as an aging, dying gangster, a personification of the so-called Roaring Twenties. The story was set on the East Side of Manhattan, along the midtown embankment, and featured as one of its supporting characters a tough teenage gang member by the name of Spit with a bold sneer and a quick punch. As portrayed by Leo Gorcey, a Jewish actor out of New York's Yiddish theater who created the role on Broadway, the character proved so successful that both he and his Dead End Kids, renamed the East Side gang, were featured in a sequel the following year, *Angels with Dirty Faces.* Spit's character was softened and renamed the less graphic Bim. A series of low-budget "New York" teenage gang films followed that were shot on the soundstages of Hollywood.

Over the course of time, the popular image of Gorcey and his gang of street thugs was softened and relocated to the Lower East Side, where they became the Bowery Boys. Mugsy, as he was now called, took on a comic, goofball-with-a-heart-of-gold nonethnic persona who loved his mother, God, and country. He became a model citizen of sorts, a symbol of the irrepressible good nature of American nonethnic urban youth, a boy who'd grown up poor but through humor and an inherent morality managed to discover the true meaning of self-worth, as characterized by his enduring heart of gold. The Depression, according to these movies, was merely a test of character that perseverance would inevitably conquer.

As a harmless comic figure, Mugsy became a Saturday matinee favorite of kids for twenty years, and may still be seen every weekend in syndication on early-morning TV all over the country and around the world.

Years before the turn of the century, a ghostly figure was said to haunt the Irish bars along the East and West Sides. On any given night, for the price of a beer, the old coot was good for a wild tale or two filled with blood and violence, about his days as the leader of a gang of young dock toughs dedicated to protecting the neighborhood from wealthy real estate developers. His stories became the stuff of New York City legend, told and retold forever, long after he finally died, in every Irish haunt. Eventually these tales found new life in Sidney Kingsley's *Dead End* in the modernized fury of Leo Gorcey's East Side tough kid they called Spit.

There are legends, and there are legends. The old man's name was Paddy Corcoran.

3

E VEN BEFORE LONG ACRE was renamed Times Square, the business of sex had become an integral part of what smiling New York City gentlemen in the last half of the nineteenth century referred to behind their wrists as the Crossroads of the Girls.

Wherever new residential or business areas developed, the operators of brothels quickly moved in. By the time John Jacob Astor died in 1848, his $500,000 worth of Manhattan farmland that stretched from 42nd to 46th Streets and from Broadway to the Hudson River had increased in value to nearly 20 million mid-nineteenth-century dollars. A year after his death, the executors of his estate divided the raw land into separate parcels roughly the size of city blocks and built residential dwellings on them. Once a parcel was sufficiently developed, the operators of chains of brothels would buy out the renters' leases, offering handsome bonuses and moving expenses to get them to leave, a gesture that hastened the development of new residential areas to the north and west of 42nd Street.

By the last decade of the nineteenth century, brothels had become a familiar, if not welcome, fixture in every neighborhood in Manhattan, but nowhere were they more popular than in the streets

The northwest corner of Seventh Avenue and 42nd Street at the turn of the century, when the Rialto stretched northward to the west of Long Acre Square and into the heart of the Tenderloin district. In one form or another, the cigar store would remain in existence for nearly one hundred years, before finally being torn down in the mid-1990s to make room for a corporate high-rise.
(Corbis-Bettman)

that surrounded Long Acre Square. This was where Broadway's celebrated mile and a half Rialto of social recreation and entertainment officially came to an end, although by the mid-1890s it was increasingly difficult to tell one from the other.

The Rialto's grand promenade began at 23rd Street and Madison Square. From there to 41st Street, dozens of theaters, nightclubs, gourmet restaurants, hotels, shops, and sawdust bars lined the streets. Every night, visitors loudly and loosely stood all along the sidewalks of Broadway, drinks in hand, arms around each other, sharing in the party atmosphere of this urban midway.

Each street of this boulevard offered a different theatrical "specialty." Just above 24th Street stood the Fifth Avenue Theater, which presented the biggest stars of the day in tailor-made extravagances. The Lyceum, also on 24th, was the best place to see the latest drawing room melodrama, which at the time was one of the most popular forms of live theater. On 30th Street both the strip's namesake theater, the Rialto, and Wallicks offered "realistic" melodramas that dealt with social issues such as marriage, economics, politics, and crime. Next came Daly's, which presented Shakespeare's plays in permanent rotation, and its neighbor, the Standard, American home of the works of Gilbert and Sullivan. On 39th Street stood the magnificent Metropolitan Opera House, where Arturo Toscanini and Enrico Caruso regularly performed to sold-out crowds. At 41st, the Broadway Theater marked the northernmost boundary of the Rialto, above which the Tenderloin took over.

Strolling the Rialto before dinner, taking in a show, and going out after for a nightcap and a little dancing became an essential part of Manhattan's turn-of-the-century social life. The streets along this colorful strip of Broadway provided a theatricality often as entertaining as what went on inside its many playhouses, with wanna-be performers on every corner singing, dancing, reciting, or merely posing in the hopes a casting director might spot them and bring them "inside." Close to the northern end, hookers openly languished outside their fancy brothels, ready as well to be taken in at a moment's notice. As historian Lloyd Morris described the scene,

The {Rialto} was a city in itself, the domain of a society that flourished through the night . . . a city of beautiful nonsense. Here they all

met on common ground—Wall Street financiers, industrial magnates,
gilded factions of the Four Hundred, gaudy playboys, journalists,
celebrities from Bohemia or the arts, the greatest stars of the theater,
gamblers, jockeys, pugilists, professional beauties, chorus girls, kept
women—notorious votaries of pleasures, the cynosures of a vast,
prosperous public. Mingling with the crowds that surged up and
down Broadway under the garish lights you saw streetwalkers
and confidence men . . . panhandlers, dope-fiends, male prostitutes,
and detectives.

In 1893 the Rialto's northern border for the first time extended
into the heart of the Tenderloin when T. Henry French, the son of
Samuel French, head of the play-publishing empire and former
manager of Stanford White's Grand Opera House at 23rd and
Eighth, decided to branch out on his own. He raised enough independent money to build the American, the first legitimate theater
to be erected on 42nd Street, on the north side and closer to Eighth
Avenue than Seventh, where a few land parcels were cheap and still
available. Surrounding his theater were two of the boulevard's more
opulent brothels. Despite threats from their owners that his new
theater would surely be burned down, and the constant appearance
of menacing characters lurking outside its entrance, not only did
French's American manage to survive, its opening production, *The
Prodigal Daughter,* was a smash. It played to sold-out audiences,
with customers lining up to buy tickets as early as ten o'clock in the
morning each day. The big draw was the extravaganza's "3-D" cli-
max, complete with ten steeplechase horses racing diagonally
across the stage on treadmills to create the illusion they were running straight into the audience. Even with its high-priced tickets—orchestra seats began at $1.50, with boxes going for as much
as $12—the theater was an immediate hit and before long one of
the most popular attractions in Manhattan.

Before the year was over, French added a rooftop garden atop
the American, even as other theatrical entrepreneurs broke ground
on several new theaters on this extension of the Rialto. Overnight,
42nd Street playhouses sprouted alongside the older, illegitimate
houses of play. A competition of sorts for the public's entertainment
dollars developed, as each establishment promised its customers a

little bit of what the other actually offered. The red-flocked, lamp-lit, and heavily perfumed parlors of 42nd Street's upscale brothels became even more dramatically laid out, with costumes and scenario role-playing "ingenues" offered to customers. At the same time, the interior design of the new legitimate show palaces became ever more extravagant, and producers advertised their shows in life-size billboards of elegantly undressed, overly made-up, and suggestively posed leading ladies outside their theaters. Bordello sexuality became more theatrical, while the legitimate theaters' atmosphere turned more overtly sexual. As the Rialto and the Tenderloin continued to blend into each other, so, too, did the content of the products they offered until, in the eyes of the authorities, one legitimate production went too far over the legal borderline of what they considered to be acceptable material for public consumption.

It happened in 1896 when independent producer John Hamilton rented out French's rooftop garden for his presentation of *Ten Minutes in the Latin Quartier {sic} or, A Study in the Nude,* in reality nothing more than a naked woman sitting on a chair. Both Hamilton and his star, Hope Booth, were arrested on opening night for violating public decency, an action that angered the Rialto's other legitimate producers. Everyone in show business knew 42nd Street's biggest open secret: that when it came to what was going on inside the brothels there were no limits. New York was a "wide open" city, with the police well paid not only to look the other way but keep out the legitimate competition as well. To them, the bust was more of a shake-down than a cleanup.

In response, a group of Broadway producers and theater owners formed the Theatrical Syndicate, a protective "trust" of producers to legally defend any one of their productions from being unfairly shut down. Among its charter members were three of the biggest producer/theater owner teams on the street—Hayman and Frohman, Nixon and Zimmerman, and Klaw and Erlanger, the last joining even as they were building a massive and elegant new theater for the south side of 42nd Street just west of Broadway they planned to call the New Amsterdam.

Not long after its formation, the Syndicate announced that it intended to standardize all material presented in any of its houses, a form of self-regulation meant to avoid police interference. Several independent producers who initially resisted affiliation with the Syndicate, fearing it might interfere with the content of their shows, nevertheless offered to cooperate with the organization's stated uniform standards of presentation. Among those who were sympathetically but unofficially affiliated were Sam, Lee, and J. J. Shubert, three young brothers new to the street by way of a single theater, the Lyric, on 42nd west of Broadway, and an independent young millionaire determined to build the greatest theater the city and the world had ever seen.

OSCAR HAMMERSTEIN was a five-foot-six potbellied German-born Orthodox Jew brought by his parents to the New World. As a teenager, the penniless Hammerstein worked a number of odd jobs, including hand cigar rolling, which so bored him he invented a series of machines to do the job more efficiently and therefore more profitably. His patents on these devices made Hammerstein a millionaire before his twenty-fifth birthday.

He then turned to his first love, show business, and, as the new century approached, determined to produce European-style grand opera in English and at affordable prices. Originally looking to acquire one of the existing theaters along the Rialto, after French's successful venture onto 42nd Street Hammerstein decided to build his own from the ground up. He soon discovered what he considered a great bargain—eight adjacent lots of a weedy horse-grazing patch on Broadway and 43rd Street, one block north and just to the east of Long Acre Square. It didn't seem to matter to him that this parcel was part of a larger no-man's-land, a dark and dangerous strip of midtown known and feared by the neighborhood's patrons as Thieves' Lair. Undaunted, even before breaking ground on his first theater, Hammerstein bought an additional 203 feet of adjacent land, stretching his Broadway holdings north to 45th Street. The price of these acquisitions came to more than a million turn-of-the-century dollars, which Hammerstein paid for with cash.

He now imagined building a self-contained show business emporium big enough to rival Stanford White's grand Madison Square Garden at the southern end of the Rialto, except his would be more magnificent and more magical, Manhattan's premier show-

Oscar Hammerstein I, the visionary whose grand theatrical empire helped turn Broadway into a twentieth-century boulevard of electric spectacle. The first to add lighted signage to his establishments, Hammerstein is generally credited with having turned the street into "The Great White Way." The one-time cigar roller is seen here in his ever-present top hat and tails. (Corbis-Bettman)

case for the finest plays, performers, and circus acts in all the world.

In November 1896 Hammerstein officially opened the Olympia, and as he had promised, it quickly became the most sensational show palace on the Rialto. It was an architectural wonder with a glistening exterior of Indiana limestone, two huge external support pillars of polished granite, two hand-carved doorways, a marble foyer, three theaters, billiard rooms, a bowling alley, a Turkish bath, a half dozen cafés and restaurants, and one of the newest and at the time most modern of inventions: an Otis elevator to whisk passengers to the by-now-obligatory, and in this instance utterly breathtaking, roof garden. Riding the Otis became a major audience attraction all its own, bringing as many people to the Olympia as the shows it took them up to see.

Now that he was a successful theater man, Hammerstein decided to refine his appearance to reflect the way he believed a successful turn-of-the-century owner/producer should look. He never again allowed himself to be seen in public wearing anything but the immediately identifiable outfit he chose for himself that contained elements of his Jewish Orthodoxy and his sense of theatricality—namely, a heavy black Prince Albert coat with velvet lapels, silver-and-black-striped pants, and a big black silk top hat. He kept his round and pudgy face hidden behind a beard, and the butt of a cigar forever clamped between his teeth. His sense of humor was as singular as his appearance. One of his favorite practical jokes was to stand backstage and drop cold coins down the backs of actresses' dresses just as they were about to make their entrances.

In 1898 Hammerstein had a huge sign erected entirely of lightbulbs to illuminate the marquee of the Olympia, the first theatrical establishment to take advantage of the power grids that had recently been installed in the neighborhood. Every day at dusk, Hammerstein took great pleasure in personally throwing the switch that lit up his piece of the Rialto, an act that gave Broadway a new calling card. It would soon be known the world over as the Great White Way.

Hammerstein now decided to expand his empire southward by working his way back toward 42nd Street. He opened two new "fully electric" theaters adjacent to the Olympia: the Music Hall, the "finest vaudeville house in the city," and the Concert Hall, the largest anywhere in the world whose massive exterior was completely hand-leafed in red and gold. The auditorium had eleven tiers of boxes, a centerpiece chandelier with six hundred arc lights, and dozens of statues and paintings offset in a cream and gold motif.

That same year, 1898, annual attendance at Hammerstein's theaters passed the 2-million mark, which significantly added to Broadway's booming annual box-office take of more than half a *billion* nineteenth-century dollars. While many credited his theaters with helping to modernize and expand the New York theater scene, within his own professional community Hammerstein was not especially well liked. For one thing, he not only refused to join the Syndicate but in direct violation of their policy of establishing set prices (always the highest on the street) kept his admissions lower than any other on the Rialto. Tickets to one of his all-star entertainment revues usually began at fifty cents for standing room and went up to a modest $1.50 for the best seats in the house, significantly less than what Syndicate theaters usually charged.

Flush with his success, Hammerstein looked to expand his growing empire yet again, but this time ran into an unexpected resistance for which even he had no immediate answer—a post-incorporation, fin de siècle lull that hit the entertainment industry and lingered. A cultural gloom hung over Manhattan like a dark cloud, a pervasive sense among older and well-to-do islanders that while much had been gained, something unique had been lost in the December 31, 1898 incorporaton of the five boroughs into the single metropolis of Greater New York. After an initial burst of celebration, a malaise set in among Manhattan's elite. Even the great Diamond Jim Brady, whose enormous dinners every night at the famed Long Acre Rectory eatery had always drawn crowds of gawkers, appeared to have grown sullen, now eating each meal as if it were his last before watching Manhattan go to the gallows, taking the so-called "Gay Nineties" with it.

Not long after incorporation, the Olympia, which had huge operation costs, for the first time began to lose money. This sudden and steep drop in cash flow forced the financially extended Hammerstein to close his beloved theater, even as he was about to break ground for the Victoria on the "independent," non-Syndicate north side of 42nd Street at Seventh. To avoid some of the Olympia's more persistent creditors, Hammerstein formed a new corporation with his two sons and listed the theater as a joint venture among the three of them.

Looking to save on construction costs, Hammerstein cut too many corners and when the Victoria failed to meet the current commercial building code it was not allowed to open. He suspected the city's action had more to do with the influence of the Syndicate than the building code, and in response declared the Victoria not a "legitimate" theater at all, but an elaborate nightclub and therefore perfectly legal.

He opened the Victoria in the winter of 1899, and, because he knew that the city and the Syndicate were both watching to make sure it wasn't in fact a legitimate theater, Hammerstein produced a nightly rotating roster of acts that showcased sexy showgirls and other, more family-oriented musical and variety acts. This new something-for-everyone hybrid style of entertainment—a string of unrelated acts held together by a series of placards announcing each, as if they were individual rounds of a boxing match—proved an immediate hit. To underscore the difference in the Victoria's fare from the theatrical fare being presented on the rest of the street, Hammerstein called his shows vaudeville, after the French cabaret style of entertainment.

The Victoria reinvigorated Broadway and relined Hammerstein's pockets. He quickly opened yet another emporium, the Paradise Roof Garden, next door to and in association with another of the north-side 42nd Street independents, the innovative T. Henry French and his American Theater. He then built the Republic, which, to recoup some of his start-up costs, he leased to independent producer/impresario David Belasco. The next year, the first of the new century, Hammerstein added two more theaters, the Empire, on 41st and Broadway (bringing the total number of legitimate theaters in Times Square to forty), and farther uptown, the Harlem Opera House, for which he booked the most popular acts that had played his midtown theaters. He also brought the best Harlem acts downtown, which made him the first Broadway producer to hire black performers for integrated midtown venues on a regular and equal-pay basis.

Hammerstein then introduced a popular new novelty into his theaters, moving pictures, which he discovered was a cheap and easy way to keep audiences entertained (and eating and drinking) before the start of his live shows. After hanging a sheet between two poles stuck into his roof, he'd start every evening's program with a film short, given to him for free by the inventor and filmmaker Thomas Edison, eager to have his company's newest product exposed to the public. To Hammerstein's amazement, the movies always brought the audience to a quick and attentive hush, captivating them in a way no live act ever had. He had never seen anything like it.

No one had.

BY 1904, THE YEAR LONG ACRE officially became Times Square, eighty-four theaters were in full operation on or north of 42nd Street, bringing the total in the city to nearly seven hundred. The IRT subway station had brought unprecedented numbers of new theatergoers and huge profits to the theater owners of 42nd Street.

The Theatrical Syndicate had grown as well, a controlling force to be reckoned with in more than five hundred theaters, and had helped divide West 42nd Street into two distinct theatrical camps, one on the north, or independent, side, where Hammerstein ruled, and one on the south, Syndicate-dominated side. That spring, the Syndicate invited independent theater-owner and producer T. Henry French to join them, a move many in the theatrical community believed was nothing more than an attempt to divide and conquer the independents. An outraged French turned the invitation down by announcing his intention to cross the Syndicate's invisible border and build a new theater on the south side of 42nd Street. Less than a year later, unable to book the stars he needed to fill seats, or prove what everyone on the boulevard knew was true—that the Syndicate had threatened any performer who worked for French with permanent banishment from any of their theaters—one of Broadway's pioneers went bankrupt, lost all of his playhouses, and left the street forever.

The Syndicate, meanwhile, continued to expand its realm of influence throughout the country, buying theaters and developing touring circuits to bring Broadway-quality productions of its member producers to the rest of America. By the end of the first decade of the new century, "Broadway" no longer merely defined a Manhattan location but a national industry. Once the final hoped-for destination of a regional theatrical production, New York now became the starting point for star-studded tours that traveled coast-to-coast, making it possible for every city in the country to offer its citizens the opportunity to see a "Broadway" show.

To accommodate its ever-growing New York audiences, new and more glamorous playhouses were built along Broadway, with ever-fancier restaurants and hotels filling out the newly re-named Times Square district. The most luxurious of these, the Astor, opened its doors in 1904, as did the equally fashionable Knicker-bocker Hotel, located on the south side of 42nd Street, to the southeast of the new Times Tower. The Knickerbocker quickly became the essential eating, drinking, and rooming establishment in the giddy atmosphere that now enveloped the neighborhood.

As business in Times Square continued to expand, the Syndi-cate demanded the police do something about what remained the-ater's biggest competitor on 42nd Street: the salacious, increasingly upscale trade of sex for sale. Dozens of brothels still openly operated on West 42nd Street. Nevertheless, as late as 1904, for whatever reason, the city's official position remained one of tolerance, its leaders insisting that visiting a prostitute was an accepted rite of passage for every young man, what turn-of-the-century mayor Robert A. Van Wyck called nothing worse than "what I did when I was a boy."

Left unspoken by Van Wyck was the hard truth that prostitu-tion was more than ever before a vital part of the city's cash-flow economics. Johns who frequented brothels often went for some-thing to eat afterward and patronized the many stores and vendors on the street, buying boots and shoes, dry goods, groceries, and newspapers or magazines. They bought drinks at any one of a num-ber of saloons before and after they took care of business. Those who preferred street prostitutes often rented rooms at one of the street's many smaller and older hotels, which had managed to keep their doors open by catering to customers who preferred the always avail-able twenty-minute "short-stay special."

Not surprisingly, Van Wyck's comment outraged the Syndicate that was no longer able to buy into the corrupt city politic, and pro-vided the excuse it had been waiting for to turn itself into a political force all its own. Aware of the additional money it stood to gain if the brothels could somehow be eliminated, the Syndicate officially came out in support of George B. McClellan in the upcoming may-oral election after he publicly vowed to help eliminate "illegal" sex from 42nd Street. That fall, McClellan won in a landslide.

In 1904, his first year in office, the new mayor invited representatives of the Syndicate to City Hall, to discuss how best to bring "a new morality" to midtown Manhattan. He presented them with his plan for the Society for the Prevention of Crime, an organization he insisted would quickly and effectively wipe out "the vilest haunts frequented by the sons of our best-esteemed citizens."

It didn't. Less than a year later, the number of men in Manhattan who willingly paid for the services of women rose to an all-time high of 150,000 a day.

The next organized attempt to wipe out prostitution in midtown came later that year with the emergence of a group that called itself the Committee of Fourteen, a nontheatrical, civic organization made up largely of local businessmen and the clergy. The Fourteen, enthusiastically welcomed by the Syndicate, aligned itself with the powerful pre-Prohibition Anti-Saloon League to mount the strongest campaign yet to "clean up" 42nd Street. Their combined pressure actually brought about the shuttering of some of the street's more prominent brothels and succeeded in getting short-stay check-ins outlawed by the City Council, a move that for the first time effectively reduced the presence of streetwalkers in front of the theaters.

The Fourteen's and Anti-Saloon League's midtown efforts coincided with those of several related nationwide populist organizations, including the newly emboldened women's rights movement and the first organized attempt to regulate child labor. The Fourteen's popularity soared after it combined the mass-appeal sentiments of these two groups and announced it really considered prostitutes, especially underage ones, not criminals after all, but victims of an economic system that forced women to lie on their backs as the only way they had available to stand on their own two feet.

The organization now took on an even more powerful life all its own. In 1907, Democratic mayor George McClellan, long considered one of the city's more liberal politicians, facing reelection, came down on the Syndicate, announcing a crackdown against what he angrily described as the real moral threat to the city, Broadway's increasingly risqué Syndicate-sanctioned productions. The organization had lost its political base to the more militant, and more powerful Fourteen, which backed the mayor's forced closing of George Bernard Shaw's *Mrs. Warren's Profession,* a play about prostitution, on the grounds that it was blatantly immoral. The result was the elimination of the subject of sex, the appearance of so much as a flash of a woman's bare leg from any legitimate Broadway production.

B Y 1909, HIS LAST YEAR in office, McClellan had become one of the most popular mayors the city had ever had. A populist hero for not only helping to bring the subway to Times Square, but his role in cleaning it up as well. Shortly before his term ended, he met with his Board of Estimate to discuss the latest proposals offered by the Fourteen—the physical widening of Broadway and the introduction of a new subway line to run under Fifth Avenue. McClellan agreed that the elimination of the more risqué elements of Broadway had made 42nd Street a more attractive place for corporations to invest, even if it meant eliminating the show as the price of increasing the business.

M CCLELLAN WELL UNDERSTOOD the political link between real estate and morality was the board's plan to widen the street and increase property values. The competition—the once-tolerated hookers and pimps who had occupied the Tenderloin for at least half a century—were now seen as a roadblock to profit, and since money was the best evaluator of spiritual worth in this Industrial era, anything that interfered with the value of real estate was seen as inherently immoral. This was why McClellan had no problem going after the Syndicate *and* the streetwalkers, as both seemed, to him, the same seamy side of a coin that could be better spent on business than either the Babes of Broadway or the ones in the bordellos. As his own career had proved, a righteous moral stand was good politics as well as good business.

Which was why he was so surprised when his proposal was met with skeptical resistance from Times Square's existing commercial property owners and fierce opposition from those who worked in the neighborhood and understood far better than the mayor and the Fourteen the economic realities of Times Square. Most businesses, including the *New York Times,* to some degree depended upon the theater. The "newspaper of record" not only considered Broadway a legitimate news beat but made a lot of money from producers' advertising dollars. And there were the numerous costume makers, piano tuners, scenery builders, billboard operators, script printers, agents, managers, musical arrangers, choreographers, teachers, makeup artists—all of whom operated on West 42nd Street and feared that the arrival of big businesses would result in the elimination of their tenement-office workplaces.

After much heated debate, a compromise of sorts was reached among the Fourteen, the mayor, and the Times Square business community. One new subway stop would be added on Sixth Avenue and 42nd Street, after which all further corporate construction on the West side would be put on indefinite hold. This pleased the Fourteen, who believed the new subway stop would encourage new business to the east of the theatrical center of 42nd, while those who worked in the industry no longer had to worry about the continued existence of the buildings housing their mom-and-pop businesses.

This delicate three-way balance lasted less than a year when the latest rage hit Times Square: a fifty-foot electric "moving" sign for Heatherbloom petticoats ("Silk's Only Rival") showing a girl caught in a storm, her skirts fluttering back and forth from the force of elaborately constructed driving rains and gusts of wind (its elaborate electrical effects rumored but never proved to have been underwritten by Oscar Hammerstein). Although the Fourteen complained the sign was far too risqué, it was an immediate hit with the public. In 1911 the organization revived its militant tactics and forced the shutdown of the tony Metropolitan Opera's "too racy" production of Richard Strauss's *Salome.*

Undaunted, by 1912 the street fairly shimmered with lighted animated billboards using sex as the basis for their hot commercial come-on. Among the more popular was a nearly nude young girl enthusiastically undulating as she rode bareback on a wild stallion for a skin products company. Another offered a pretty young winking girl chewing gum (the gum was the product). And still another showed a woman drenched under a "fountain" of sparkling water selling skimpy underwear, her all but naked body clearly visible in the "flowing" lights.

A year later, in 1913, William Hammerstein, Oscar's son and partner, was arrested for presenting something publicly condemned by the Fourteen as the "immoral" *Dance of Fortune* at the Victoria, which was performed partly in the nude. The group then petitioned City Hall for the right to take over some midtown law enforcement duties from the local police.

The organization had stepped up its moral campaign believing prostitution could not still be so widespread without protection. It initiated a fierce public campaign that eventually pitted it against the new mayor, former state supreme court judge William Gaynor. Gaynor, a solid Democratic machine politician, had been the retiring McClellan's handpicked choice. He had won the 1909 election despite a relentless print campaign against him led by midtown's aging watchdog and active supporter of the Fourteen, the relentless William Randolph Hearst. His newspapers openly attacked Gaynor, hinting that he was a "lapsed Catholic," and therefore unfit to be mayor. In the wake of Hearst's daily attacks and continued pressure from the Fourteen, Gaynor, fearing he could be driven from office, reluctantly surrendered the police department's "powers of moral regulation" to the organization.

By 1914 the Fourteen had reached the height of its power and influence. It now diligently policed 42nd Street in search of the slightest sexual provocation it could then use to shut down any show it deemed unacceptable and arrest its participants. The result was a serious diluting of whatever role legitimate theater had as a forum of social or political ideas, the voice of the disenfranchised, the playful idealism of erotic fantasy, the realm of creative imagination. Broadway's producing organization, the long suffering Syndicate, finally sided with the Fourteen, willing to do whatever was deemed necessary to pass its censorial eye.

By the dawn of the so-called Roaring Twenties, Broadway's affiliated commercial mainstream had more or less been split into two profitable tributaries. Nonmusical productions became increasingly bland, their female stars ever more clothed. The most popular "straight" Broadway production of the twenties was a comedy about a Jewish–Irish Catholic marriage called *Abie's Irish Rose,* which held about as much sexual allure as an episode of *All in the Family.*

At the same time, several of Broadway's biggest independent

producers continued to present burlesque girlie shows dressed up with just enough shiny underwear to allow them to win a pass as legitimate entertainment from the Fourteen. By now it was common knowledge along the Great White Way that several members of the organization routinely accepted illegal tribute from the producers of burlesque to keep the doors open.

WHILE BROADWAY DRAMATICALLY floundered in the iron grip of the Fourteen, Hollywood, as yet unencumbered by any uniform governmental regulation, flashed its long legs across the silver screen and found a worldwide audience willing to pay to see them. Films primal shift from Hammerstein curtain-raiser to main attraction came in 1915 when D. W. Griffith's unprecedented *The Birth of a Nation* held its world premiere at Klaw and Erlanger's "legitimate" Liberty Theater on 42nd Street, the same house where only eight years earlier Flo Ziegfeld had wowed Broadway with the first edition of what would go on to become his internationally famous *Follies*. The film proved a sensation, and soon, all across the country, legitimate theaters, particularly those not controlled by the national live touring chains, were able to switch to film and show the latest movies to packed houses the same day they opened in New York City.

Hollywood's movies quickly became the dominant and most profitable form of American public entertainment. Stars no longer had to pack their bags and take their shows on the road, and producers no longer had to pay them to do so. A single performance captured on film could earn a thousand times more than a thousand live performances that had to be repeated nightly, which made the silver screen the new career goal of many stars and backers whose faces and productions once lit up Broadway.

Things got noticeably better for film, and worse for theater, when 1927's *The Jazz Singer,* generally considered to be the first "talkie," brought the added element of synchronized sound to the movies. The film starred Al Jolson, a twenty-year Broadway veteran the Warner studio had plucked from the New York stage and repositioned for cinematic superstardom. His phenomenal leap from

Broadway to Hollywood personified the mainstream shift from live theater to movies. The success of *The Jazz Singer*, a standard rags-to-riches "show business" saga with a Jewish immigrant as its hero, spawned numerous imitations of setting (Broadway), story (unknown overcomes great personal obstacles to become a big star), ethnic origins (Italian, Irish), and star (almost always a box-office stage legend cast in the lead).

As movies became the nation's first choice for instant, inexpensive, and endlessly entertaining escapism, for the first time since their turn-of-the-century boom, the theaters of 42nd Street, once according to film historian J. Hoberman, "the best-lit stage in American culture," became increasingly difficult venues of first-rate entertainment. *Variety* in 1938 described their few new presentations as decidedly "cut-rate." Critic Ferdnand Legér took it even further when he wondered if Broadway shows could still "be considered as one of the fine arts."

The grim reality for the Great White Way was that the night Jolson first "sang" on-screen, its only still-profitable theater was Morton Minsky's 42nd Street Burlesque House, which featured Gypsy Rose Lee, by far the most sexually provocative legal act on the boulevard. Although he had been closed down several times by the Fourteen and the police (Minsky steadfastly refused to pay off the Fourteen), he continued to present not-so-innocent (or legal) starry-eyed "ingenues" performing the second and third shows of the night in the nude. Minsky (one of four brothers who were all partners) managed to stay open by moving his later shows to the basement, where the girls got a little bolder, and the sex, both on and off the stage, a lot harder.

Minsky, one of the few adventurers left on Broadway, had learned that the only way to compete with the movies was to offer the public something they couldn't find on-screen—live, hot sex. By the time Jimmy Walker took over as mayor in 1926, despite his enthusiastic support of the street's nightlife, most of Broadway's supposedly more provocative productions had become stale, overpriced imitations of movies.

When the Depression hit, film had become the great nickel escape route for a nation faced with the harsh realities of poverty and unemployment. Its favorite and most popular subject continued to be the glorification of the theatrical high life on 42nd Street it had helped to bury, using idealized nostalgia as a way of holding back the harder reality of the present day. Of all the Hollywood backstage musicals that opened on the street, Busby Berkeley's 1933 *42nd Street,* starring Ruby Keeler and Dick Powell, was the biggest, the best, and by far the most successful. About this landmark musical, Hoberman wrote, "42nd Street is a prime chunk of fantasy real-estate—not just a movie, but a novel, a song, a play, an act, an attitude, a dream, a racket, a rhythm, a way of life . . . it's the tale of how America licked the Depression, how the Warner Brothers elected Franklin Roosevelt, and how Hollywood got to out-sing, out-dance, and out-entertain Broadway."

The film opened in New York City on March 9, an event celebrated by the arrival of the "42nd Street Special," a private, star-studded train that had pulled out of Hollywood, California, three weeks earlier on a publicity junket whose final destination was Grand Central Terminal. Upon disembarking, movie cowboy Tom Mix, like Caesar entering Rome, triumphantly led the cast in a victory ride by horseback up the street to the Strand, where the film had its world premiere.

With live theater all but dead, most of the legitimate theater owners began to convert their venues into movie houses. One year after *42nd Street* opened and continued to run on its namesake boulevard, only four theaters there were still presenting live shows. And two years after that, the Times Square, where only five seasons earlier Laurence Olivier had made his live American debut with Noel Coward and Gertrude Lawrence, and Hammerstein's wondrous Apollo, two of what had once been the most successful theaters on Broadway, were both converted to movie houses. In 1935 the Brandt Organization, a new and aggressive film distribution company, became the latest, most powerful show business entity on 42nd Street when it gained operating control of the Liberty, Hammerstein's Lyric (where the Marx Brothers first gained fame in the live version of *The Cocoanuts*) and Republic (which became the new Victory), and the Eltinge burlesque house.

By 1940 live legitimate theater could no longer be found anywhere on 42nd Street.

O NCE FILM ESTABLISHED itself in the mainstream, it faced the same wave of moral righteousness that had all but killed the creative thrust of the American theater. Ironically Hollywood accepted the close and regulating eye of the Hays Office and agreed to eliminate any content deemed sexually explicit or politically subversive. This helped create a compensating, uniquely elliptical style of suggestion-by-montage that finally elevated film from the novelty of a derivative medium, filmed theater, to a separate, subtextually sophisticated wholly original and extremely popular form of entertainment, if not a totally unique American art form.

Meanwhile, Broadway's commercial free fall continued to spread from 42nd Street throughout Times Square. Hammerstein, before he died in 1919 penniless and nearly forgotten, had sold his beloved Olympia to a group of investors who in 1940 split it into two movie theaters, the New York and the Criterion. The rest of what had been Broadway's glittering strip of real estate above 42nd Street was sold off piecemeal by its various owners, mostly to nontheatrical businesses, among them Regal shoes, Loft's candy shop, Woolworth's, the King of Slims tie shop, and Bond's clothing store. From the roof of the Hotel Claridge, designer Douglas Leigh's legendary Camel billboard blew giant smoke rings nightly over a Broadway that in the forties was reconfigured by movie theaters, retail establishments, and very few live plays.

New York theater's near-death experience would, ironically, provide the perfect atmosphere for a new generation of rebellious talent no longer tied to a tradition that had been destroyed, or destroyed itself, and that, either way, no longer held any meaning for them as a place to create "real" drama. Quietly, in the so-called "Roaring Twenties," amid the aging *Follies,* the facile *Abie's Irish Rose,* and the endless (and mostly imported) revivals of Shakespeare, a new American theatrical voice had slowly begun to emerge.

Names like Saroyan, Wilder, Kingsley, Rice, Anderson, and others, with plays like *My Heart's in the Highlands, Our Town, Dead End,* and *Winterset,* began to deliver a less-formulaic, more dramatically dynamic choice to those who looked to Broadway for the stuff that drama was made of.

The first and greatest of these new voices undoubtedly belonged to Eugene O'Neill, whose darkly poetic plays pulled apart the very essence of what made Hollywood movies so appealing to audiences. As depicted by the studios, most of which had been created by European immigrants who often saw themselves as the heads of one large, happy family of actors who behaved like children (or children who behaved like actors), the family stood as the single unassailable symbol of the American way of life. And it was the American family that O'Neill brilliantly deconstructed on stage as a way of exposing its disturbingly dark dysfunctional side. Accepting as a given the many brilliant exceptions in both film and theater—the challenging, subversive films of independent filmmaker Charlie Chaplin, for instance—Hollywood movies, particularly during the Depression and continuing through the propagandist war years, for the most part played up and off the idea that the spirit of the American family remained the unassailable foundation of the nation's strength, while O'Neill and others dramatized the reasons for, and consequences of, what they saw as its and the country's parallel breakdowns.

Born in a theatrical residence hotel on Broadway and 43rd Street to the legendary actor James O'Neill, Eugene grew into manhood haunted by the memory of his own disturbed family's behavior, a recurring nightmare that formed the dramatic basis and shaped the themes that dominated his work, much of it in his lifetime considered too controversial by Hollywood to be adaptable for film. None of the studio moguls wanted to make movies about irredeemable losers, dead-end alcoholics, and never-coming-back prostitutes, the main characters of O'Neill's ongoing examination of the dysfunctional American family (which, viewed in the context of the playwright's chosen settings—bars, waterfronts, his own family's lifeless living room, and his father's chosen career—served him well as a particularly vivid metaphor for the fall from commercial grace of the American theater).

O'Neill made his professional Broadway debut in 1920 with *Beyond the Horizon.* A bold standout among the bland musicals and repetitive revues, *Horizon* won the Pulitzer Prize, established O'Neill as a leading dramatic voice, and helped begin the long road back to redemption for a form of entertainment whose context had been shattered and whose art was all but lost. Through O'Neill,

Broadway slowly began to regain its hold on the nation's imagination, a long, creative, and not especially profitable rebirth that slowly developed in fits and starts until, of all things, a 1943 musical with nary a bare ankle on display managed to bring audiences back to Broadway in droves and Broadway back to relevance. Written by the new team of Richard Rodgers and Oscar Hammerstein II (Oscar Hammerstein's grandson), *Oklahoma!* was set in the purest of sunny American landscapes, the western plains, and offset by a Freudian-driven center-stage plotline with a psychological subtext performed in italics via Agnes de Mille's dream dances.

After the resounding success of *Oklahoma!* Broadway continued to capture the public's imagination by providing something movies couldn't, or refused to: an ongoing examination of the dark side of the American dream. In the movies of the 1940s, love was free and conquered all. On the stage, love came with an emotional price tag that had little to do with liberation. Tennessee Williams deepened Broadway's cultural perspective by peopling his plays with explicitly homosexual antiheroes, officially off-limits in the studio-dominated era of American movies. In film, men were men, women were women, and gays, if they were allowed to exist at all, were almost always wisecracking "sidekicks" who never expressed any interest in or competed in any way for the girl.

In the movies, winning a woman's love was only part of the bargain, "happily ever after" being the rest of the pact. On the other hand, Tom, the protagonist of *The Glass Menagerie*, Williams's prototypically gay southern existentialist, turns heroic if not hetero when he abandons his "straight" family to wander into the existentialist night. This was Broadway's darkest response to Rhett Butler, Hollywood's straight southern idealist. With *Menagerie*, Williams irrevocably altered the romantic roadmap of modern American theater.

Arthur Miller's postwar titanic *Death of a Salesman*, while no less devastating, further abstracted Broadway's investigation into the increasingly fragile state of the American family. In his play Miller examined the crumbling world of the postwar sacrificial patriarch, driven to madness and finally suicide when he tries and fails to discover what there is about his life, including life itself (and, by extension, the stage upon which that life is presented), that still holds any meaning. *Salesman's* dramatic structure sharpened the focus, and therefore the metaphor, of the theatrical, gauze-draped proscenium of *The Glass Menagerie,* and by doing so allowed audiences to observe Miller's interior view of the modern dysfunctional world (of creativity) through Willy Loman's privileged, if distorted, vantage point.

Finally, Edward Albee's 1963 *Who's Afraid of Virginia Woolf?,* in which Mr. and Mrs. America, a pretentious college professor and his drunken wife (named George and Martha, in case anyone missed the point), are the embittered parents of a reason-they've-stayed-together child that in fact doesn't exist. This explosive evening in the theater once and for all pulled the plug on the characters of the realistic American family, and the character of American theatrical realism. Two years later, Albee offered his *Tiny Alice,* which author Philip Roth famously dismissed, and along with it Broadway theater, as "a homosexual dream."

Albee completed the cycle of Broadway's self-examination and the theater once more retreated into the klieg light of commercialism with a series of highly profitable if hopelessly benign stage comedies (*Any Wednesday, The Odd Couple, Same Time Next Year* typical of the fare) that could just as easily have been made into movies or TV sitcoms (many were) without changing a word of the script. Also returning to popularity to fill the void was the uncomplicated musical, the biggest of which would be a remake of an early Thornton Wilder comedy, *The Matchmaker,* tunefully resuscitated into the financially boffo but intellectually barren *Hello Dolly!*

Toward the end of the sixties, the pseudo-hippie, cultish, non-book musical *Hair* opened on Broadway, and the theater returned to its oldest, most reliable, and least creative draws. The top box-office attraction of the 1969 season, *Hair* was a musical whose highlight was the brief, totally nude onstage appearance of the entire cast. Barely two months later, *Oh! Calcutta!,* a title roughly derived from the French for "What a beautiful ass!," opened and ran for nearly a decade. With a curtain-raiser that also featured a naked cast, and parlor skits built around leering nudity, the familiar, collective cry that had been heard so loudly since the turn of the century echoed like a dissonant Greek chorus. Once more a barrage of critics proclaimed, and the public seemed to agree, "The theater is dead!"

It was and it wasn't. For even as Albee's plays cued the entrance for the next phase of mainstream theater's retreat into meaninglessness, a new, alternative form of theater was already emerging on an all-but-deserted stretch of real estate, an even raunchier version of the old Rialto, on, of all places, 42nd Street, just west of Eighth Avenue. What had long been Manhattan's cultural and commercial Siberia, a bleak stretch of sidewalks native New Yorkers considered one block beyond the last acceptable outpost of civilization, was about to undergo a remarkable transition in what would be a valiant attempt to physically extend the boundaries of New York theater and, along with it, the commercial horizon of mainstream America.

BY THE MID-FIFTIES, life along the once-glorious West 42nd Street had become an urban anachronism, the last dirt road exit to Eisenhowerville before the entrance to the superhighway of JFK's New Frontier.

In January 1954 the stiff-white-collared *Business Week* grimly reported what anybody who'd recently been there already knew, that the strip of 42nd Street between Seventh and Eighth Avenues, once the most glamorous single block of theaters in New York City, had turned into a nightmare of pinball arcades, souvenir shops, "dirty" bookstores, suspicious auction rooms, hot dog and orange drink stands, flea circuses, and soapbox pulpits for Sunday morning Bible-waving corner preachers, political extremists, and end-of-the-worlders. The street's once-grand show palaces, the magazine noted, were reduced to playing tired or titillating movies, newsstands sold girlie magazines that hung by clothespins off the sides of green wooden kiosks, and penny arcades were the new favored hangouts for prostitutes, pedophiles, and pushers. Forty-second Street, the magazine somberly concluded, was "not what it used to be."

What it was, was something else again, a street, like the city itself, and the nation to which it belonged, in transition from the brief postwar burst of youth and energy that had temporarily relit

A stolen kiss in Times Square during the wild street celebrations that greeted the end of World War II. Having experienced a freer sexuality overseas and the effects of powerful pain-killing narcotics, GIs returning to the U.S. via New York City's harbors and ports were point men in the postwar sex and drug revolution. They would find all they wanted of both on 42nd Street.

(Corbis-Bettman)

it. In truth, 42nd Street's post-war fall from grace provided a unique potpourri of bargain-basement entertainment more fascinating and bizarre than anything East Side, West Side, all around the town. Here were twenty-four-hour venues for any and all types of edgy recreation, creative experimentation, sexual exaltation, and antisocial lamentation. What by and large had turned off the general populace was precisely what turned on its fringe—all-night play-offs of sex and so-called B movies, shots-only bars with bare lightbulbs hanging from tin ceilings, and an endless supply of corner character weirdos.

The street's row of once-legitimate theaters offered an endless supply of documentaries featuring pretty young girls playing volleyball in the nude, but also a fair share of westerns, horror films, foreign releases, and other genre-specific second, third, and fourth runs that, in the days before video and cable, were not easily available to the general public. In truth, 42nd Street had, after the war, evolved into something of an unplanned, informal American cinematheque.

Around the corner, on Broadway, the most ornate movie palaces in the country, including the Roxy, Loew's State, and the Paramount, and also at Rockefeller Center's Radio City Music Hall, reserved-ticket first-run films played at four dollars a seat for such wide-screen adventures as *Giant* and *Around the World in Eighty Days*. At the same time, these very same films were quietly squeezed in on double and triple bills along 42nd Street, unadvertised (by contract), playing around the clock for twenty-five cents during the day, thirty cents at night. These became the theaters of choice for the culturally disenfranchised, the hipsters, students, cineasts, minorities, gays, the unemployed, the retired, and anyone else looking for a bargain-basement admission into the world of wide-screen dreams. For most of the fifties and half of the sixties, the movie theaters on 42nd Street were so popular that even at their discounted prices they regularly outgrossed the combined take of the rest of the city's hundreds of movie venues.

Each theater on the street had a specialty that attracted its own loyal following. The Times Square presented westerns. The Hudson offered violence and action-genre films. The Victory offered war movies, the Empire domestic, nonmilitary violence (e.g., Fritz Lang's *The Big Heat*), the Lyric showed nonadvertised first runs. The Selwyn ran second-run box-office flops, and the Liberty less successful, third-run mainstream misses. The Apollo specialized in foreign films, and the Rialto "art," mostly horror and soft-core sex.

These films shared time and space on a street where, in 1960, forty cents bought an hour at John Fursa's Chess and Checker Club, the "flea house," as it was known to regulars, a dimly lit "decrepit walk-up" that stood next to the dusty, darkened exterior of the New Amsterdam, the long-forgotten and sadly neglected onetime jewel of the boulevard.

A street where Huberts' Museum and Flea Circus operated, an oddball emporium housed between the Liberty and the Harris Theaters in the Percival, in another time a residential dwelling among the city's most luxurious. Huberts', for fifty cents, offered a variety of nightly rotating flea acts with fleas that dangled from dental floss or flew in circles on a contraption made of toothpicks. "Performers" included Ajax the Sword Swallower, Libera the "double-bodied individual," Chief Amok, a certified African headhunter, Albert-Alberta, half-man, half-woman, and Waldo, whose specialty was eating live mice onstage ("photo-documented" by the *Daily News*).

A street where tile-walled Nedick's sold a doughnut, fruit drink, and coffee for fifteen cents twenty-four hours a day, a midtown ritual otherwise known as breakfast at "the Orange Room," where a nickel cup of Joe and fifteen cents' worth of mashed sweet potato could be gotten at the Third Avenue Horn and Hardart Automat, and a T-bone steak, baked potato, garlic bread, and tossed salad for $1.09 at Tad's Steaks.

A street where ninety-nine cents bought the single most popular item sold at the Funn Store, the infamous whoopee cushion; where men pulled the brims of their hats over their faces and stood at the rear of the United Cigar Store on the northwest corner of Seventh taking slips for the daily numbers game; where fifty cents bought a workout with the house palooka in a professional boxing gymnasium; where now-empty, out-of-breath, and exhausted storefronts painted their windows the same pale green color as the skin of aging junkie whores who broke into them to shoot up.

A street where winos sold their soul for five dollars a pint at the white-walled blood bank, then killed the afternoon getting high and playing Fantasy or five-cent Pokerino at Playland.

A street where the shifting winds of change had left a cultural vacuum that sucked onto its sidewalks a handful of the city's hippest creative fringe: the poets, kooks, and cavorters squeezed in between the Beats and the folkies, all of whom for however brief a period turned 42nd Street into the personal playland of the blue-jeaned avant-garde.

J OE FRANKLIN, a 42nd Street–based fixture on New York radio and television for more than fifty years, recalled what it was once like going to the movies on 42nd Street. "I used to live on East 84th Street in Manhattan. A few blocks away was my good friend Tony Curtis, whose name then was still Bernie Schwartz. Every Sunday we'd take the subway for a nickel to Broadway and 42nd Street. There we'd buy a hot dog at Grant's Cafeteria for a dime, maybe have a nickel doughnut at Toffenetti on the ground floor of the Times building, then go to a five-cent theater between Broadway and Eighth Avenue called Laff Movie, which previously had been the Republic burlesque house, and where now every day they showed one full-length comedy with W. C. Fields or Laurel and Hardy and about six shorts, always a Three Stooges and a Charlie Chase. The theater was always packed with kids. After the show, the last nickel got us home. Right across the street from the theater was a big sign that read "Child's Bar." It was for a restaurant that was part of a successful chain in New York City, but it always used to make Bernie and me laugh and say the same joke every week. How could kids have a place of their own where they could drink whiskey? These were the good old days on 42nd Street before the big change came in the fifties and everything went downhill."

"There were never any 'good old days' on 42nd Street," according to film critic and historian Andrew Sarris, "at least not to anyone who actually spent some time as an adult down there." In the early sixties, before he became the founding voice of *auteur* film criticism in America, native New Yorker Sarris was the editor of a limited-edition English version of the French film magazine

*Joe Franklin, a legendary 42nd Street broad-
caster and social pop-culture chronicler who spent
more than half a century working the West Side.*
(Photo courtesy of Joe Franklin)

Cahiers du Cinéma. To do so, he rented the cheapest office space he
could find, a second-floor walk-up at 303 West 42nd Street, on the
corner of Eighth Avenue, where he split the costs and shared the
space with another young movieholic, then unknown filmmaker
Martin Scorsese, who was still struggling to complete his first independent feature. Working on the street in the days before video-
cassettes, each quickly discovered the wealth of movies that played
there twenty-four hours a day, films they would not otherwise have
such access to, films that were to enrich Sarris's critical overview
and enhance Scorsese's cinematic output.*

As Sarris later recalled, "I remember when Lincoln Center
began its Film Festival in the early sixties and everyone wanted to
have the first opening night on 42nd Street. These were people who
I was sure had never stepped foot down there and had no idea what
the street was really like. What it wasn't was *Guys and Dolls,* all

---

*The 42nd Street of this period shows up as a locale in several Scorsese films, including *Mean
Streets* and *Taxi Driver.*

Broadway glamour and Technicolor crap games and romance and beautiful women. That was Hollywood's mythic take on Times Square. Yet there was *something* there."

The street's gritty charm made it the favorite haunt of the Beat poets and novelists, and their comic counterpart Lenny Bruce, all of whom loved going to the movies on the Deuce. To them the seediness of the theaters held a special homey comfort, the dank orchestra sections not unlike the apartments they rented: dark, smoky, damp, cavernous, a cool place to hang. The Kerouac crowd made them the "hip" places in town to see a movie. Into the sixties the Village coffeehouse circuit of folksingers, which included Bob Dylan, David Blue, and Phil Ochs, eagerly sat through all-night runs of John Ford westerns starring John Wayne, by far 42nd Street's most popular and enduring movie star. Favorite Wayne films *The Searchers* and *Fort Apache* ran in rotation for years. And when a theater ran a marathon five comedies on a single bill, the singer-songwriters went to practice their sullen onstage poses, training themselves not to smile or laugh at anything they saw, no matter how funny they thought it was.

Others not as attracted to the street's inherent movie charm or hang-out hipness came for the relatively low price of admission to the still forbidden world of sexual fantasy. "It was the very beginning of the soft-core porn scene," Sarris remembered. "In the late 40s and early 50s the movie theaters would show films where people would play volleyball, those nudist colony things, 'health films' as a legitimate excuse to show the audience people on-screen with no clothes, which really opened the gates a little because these were films with no pretext. Those were followed by other soft-core things, titillating little movies where pretty women were 'patients' and doctors gave them fairly explicit examinations."

"I used to rush down there to West 42nd Street at eleven o'clock in the morning," recalled pop culturalist Phillip Lopate of his school days in the late fifties and early sixties. "I didn't know where to start to turn my head around and look. Heaven for a film-lover like me was ten marquees that changed bills every day. I used to cut classes to see *Rules of the Game* with my legs dangling over the Apollo balcony. And it was there I caught up with all the flicks that opened and closed in three days and that nobody else would show: the great westerns of Raoul Walsh and Howard Hawks, all the Otto Preminger melodramas."

"It was, I guess, *some* kind of cinematheque," says Sarris, "although at the time there were always other and better places to see a much wider span of revivals, like up at the New Yorker, or the Thalia, or downtown at the Bleecker Street Cinema in the Village. These were places where there were programmed, thought-out series, while on 42nd Street, besides the bargain-basement block-busters, it was simply a matter of what was available that no one else wanted. Still, I did occasionally go to the movies on 42nd to catch up on certain films it was difficult to see anywhere else. They showed a lot of foreign films, in many instances the only place you could see them in America. They had subtitles, and the theaters that featured them became something of a haven for deaf-mutes. I'd always see them standing in front of the theater talking to each other before the movie using sign language.

"Some of the theaters that weren't showing soft-core or action genre films, which were always very big, either doubled up new releases or showed those that couldn't get major distribution for one reason or another on what was called 'delayed-run' release. Orson Welles's *Touch of Evil* was a genuine 42nd Street phenomenon. I think the John Ford movie *The Man Who Shot Liberty Valance* opened in Brooklyn for its first run, and the only other place you could see it in the city, certainly the only place in Manhattan, was on 42nd Street. Not because the audience was especially esoteric or into John Ford, but because genre movies, action films by anybody, had become very popular there. The audiences loved them, particularly the black audiences.

"This period in the fifties and early sixties happened to coincide with the golden age of westerns that were sexy and rather intelligent, movies by talented directors like Bud Boetticher and Anthony Mann. They had stories that were tough and evocative. In *Man of the West,* Julie London is forced to do a striptease for the villains, which happened to be one of the most erotic things I'd seen in an American movie to that point. Westerns were particularly popular with the 42nd Street crowd. The plots were prearranged, the good guy versus the bad guy, the tough babes, it was all there. Young black men would come into the theaters with toy six-shooters and talk out loud back to the screen, saying things like, 'All right, Hoppy, I'll take care of him for you' and 'shoot' at the screen."

For their diligence, audiences were occasionally rewarded with rare film treats. Even the most elusive of legends played at the Apollo on 42nd Street. Brigitte Bardot was America's officially designated foreign sex siren of the fifties, but very few people in America other than those hearty souls who ventured down to the Seven/Eight, the strip between Seventh and Eighth Avenues on 42nd Street, ever got to see what the panting was all about. For the most part invisible on the nation's mainstream movie circuits and American television, Bardot spoke no English, and almost all of her films were shot in France, where nudity and sensuality were taken as sweet liberties. Her films became favorites of the 42nd Street fringe, an erotic alternative to the much more accessible, all-American Marilyn Monroe, whose neurotic virtues were prepackaged by the studios in regular and ample doses.

Sarris: "The Rialto [around the corner on Broadway between 42nd and 43rd] used to specialize in horror movies and always had a steady patronage. I think they showed a lot of Val Lewton's work, which was dark, violent, and sexual. In other words, perfect for Times Square.

"Still, toward the end of the sixties, the movie theaters shifted more and more to hard-core porn, they became dirty and smelly, and there was a lot of cruising that went on in them. The romance of the street, such as it was, had evaporated. People now liked to throw lit cigarettes into the audience from the balcony. They also had four of the back rows in the auditorium of the Apollo reserved entirely for women, to prevent mashers coming on to them. And there was a lot of homosexual activity. You get a sense of what it was like in *Midnight Cowboy*, which was actually filmed in one of those theaters. I remember one time at the Apollo, I went to the men's room and discovered it really wasn't a men's room at all, just a lot of urinals with no private booths. I stood there trying to figure out why, when I noticed some guy had followed me in there and was about to proposition me."

E ROTICISM, IN PRINT and pictures, became one of the great diversions of American soldiers during World War II. Those who left home as innocent boys returned from overseas grizzled veterans. As they returned to their hometowns (via the European theater port of reentry, New York City), they brought their war wounds, their scars, and their newly awakened sexual heat back with them. A look at any one of the many photographs taken in Times Square of tough, young, victorious returning sailors on V-E Day bending submissive nurses backward in their arms suggests how much more aggressively sexual American GIs had become as a result of being stationed overseas. The message was clear: You *couldn't* keep them down on the farm after they'd seen Paree.

And as they soon discovered, anything even approaching the sexual thrills of their army days could only be found stateside in the for-sale sexuality of 42nd Street's underground strip clubs, one of the few reliable locales where they could fill their noses with the familiar, if approximated, musky scent of anything-goes girls.

Or boys.

The underground "straight" sex clubs on 42nd Street peacefully coexisted with those that catered to the city's anonymous and closeted gays who'd never made it overseas and found their glory in sleek young boys in whose reflection they sought the idealized, liberated image of their own repressed boyhoods. In the fifties one of the most frequented "nightspots" on West 42nd Street wasn't a club at all, a tavern, or even a movie theater. It was the Times Square baths, where gay men frolicked, as it were, alongside otherwise "straight" American veterans who had first experimented with homosexuality on the front, and now sought a place to revisit and perhaps replicate those so-called illicit pleasures, the hot link to the forbidden glory of their war-torn sexual liberation.

On 42nd Street, the sale of hard-core pornography benefited from an ongoing legal battle that had begun 150 years earlier.

The first recorded court decision in America involving obscenity came in 1815 when six Philadelphians were convicted of publicly displaying an indecent work of art. Federal restriction of pornography officially began in 1842, with the passage of a law forbidding the import of obscene pictures. In 1865, using the mail to send pornographic materials was made a felony, a result of the growing fear among the Northern commanders that smut circulating among Union soldiers was corrupting their morals (presumably they'd gotten it by post). After the war, a sizable new generation of young and randy veterans settled permanently in New York City, prompting City Hall clerk Anthony Comstock to launch a national crusade for stiffer laws against "smut," which helped form the basis of what became the nation's legal restriction of pornography. It was a position that remained essentially unchallenged until 1933, the same year that Prohibition was repealed, when District Court Judge John Woolsey declared the James Joyce work *Ulysses* "nonpornographic." This marked the beginning of several key anticensorship victories that included successful defenses of *Mademoiselle de Maupin, Casanova's Homecoming, Frankie and Johnnie,* and *God's Little Acre.*

Things then pretty much wheeled freely during the postwar years on 42nd Street until the Supreme Court once again intervened with its 1957 landmark decision in *Roth v. United States,* which attempted to formulate a more specific definition of "obscene." The case involved New York businessman Samuel Roth, a local retailer who sold what today would be considered soft-core magazines and books. Although Roth was convicted, his case is remembered for establishing a new legal standard for obscenity. The court declared that a work can be judged obscene only if its predominant appeal is to "prurient interest," it goes "substantially beyond customary limits of candor in description or representations of such matters," and it is "so offensive on its face as to affront current community standards."

The liberal Warren Court went still further when, in 1966, it limited the legal definition of "obscenity" to material judged to be *"utterly without redeeming social value."* It was the use of the word "utterly" that finally opened the floodgates. Not long after, virtually every theater on 42nd Street converted to the newly allowable and extremely popular pornographic movies. Later on, Sarris, writing in the *Village Voice,* reflected on the fallout from the new permissiveness: Times Square "languishes in this *quartier Latin,* and the Times still lingers there, along with about two dozen respectable restaurants. The rest is raunch and hustle in this after-hours animal kingdom. To watch [Broadway] theatergoers fleeing for their lives after the final curtain is to experience some of the primitive terror of the last days of Pompeii."

Sarris was, of course, correct in his reaction to the infectious spread of pornography on West 42nd Street. The accompanying sleaze that porn brought to the dance managed to once again bring the neighborhood's legitimate theaters, which had been surviving on bargain-rate genre movie cards, perilously close to insolvency. Every evening, as the last remaining day patrons left the boulevard, 42nd Street came alive with a parade of shadowy drug peddlers and con artists, vagrants drinking beer from cans wrapped in paper bags, men dressed like women, and teenagers from the burbs looking to come down to the "Deuce" to get high.

Ironically the street's commercial devaluation made it the prime target of a growing band of theatrical producers looking to present works that were less commercial and at the same time more profitable than the standard Broadway fare. To do so, they had to find makeshift theaters and converted church basements to stage their presentations. It was a period of theatrical development known as off-Broadway that had until the early sixties flourished mostly in the small nonunion theaters and window fronts of Greenwich Village.

Off Broadway's journey to 42nd Street began with Irving Maidman, an aging small-time real estate developer, who had, by the early 1950s, invested in a string of low-rise, mostly vacant properties between Ninth and Tenth Avenues, a no-man's-land between the vague and sleazy void to the east and a surprisingly booming, if somewhat oddball, tourist boom of sorts to the west. The only action to be found within shooting-up distance of his buildings was a row of cheap, gaudy motels that had opened up on 42nd and Twelfth, fifties-style pillbox structures with mattresses and pools perfectly suited to the new generation of motor tourists who preferred these drive-in pit stops to the city's more traditional midtown stops. With easy access from all points south of the Lincoln Tunnel and a price range perfectly suited to the wife-two-kids-and-a-car budget-minded, the motels of 42nd Street, highlighted by the Sheraton Motor Inn, which the *New Yorker* described as "a startlingly classy pioneer in a somewhat declasse neighborhood," had become by the late fifties something of a travel sensation. These rest stops for the new Interstate 80/Jersey Turnpike interchange on the other side of the Lincoln Tunnel even caught the imperious gaze of the *New York Times* when journalist Gay Talese smirkingly noted their "resort-like atmosphere, lively cocktail lounges and Atlantic City-on-the-Hudson" atmosphere.

Knowing a good thing when he saw it, the always enterprising Mr. Maidman hoped to convert a couple of his own vacant buildings into motels, until the idea proved first too costly, then too difficult because of existing zoning restrictions. Searching for a way to make something work, he discovered a seventy-five-year-old legal loophole which had been inserted by the City Planning Commission that allowed for the conversion of vacant residential buildings into theaters. The law had been created so that the town houses originally built by John Astor on 42nd Street and that later became brothels could be reclaimed by the city and sold to legitimate theater owners. Maidman was able to use this law to turn one of his vacant properties into the eponymous Maidman Playhouse, for the entertainment and edification of the moteliers to his immediate west.

In 1959 this low-rent Hammerstein christened his theater with a production of *Sketchbook,* a play by Russell Patterson, who also happened to be one of the designers of the new playhouse. Although the show was a flop, the critics, to the surprise and delight of Maidman, raved about the physical layout of the new playhouse, which helped ignite his pragmatic profiteering into the flash point for live theater's return to 42nd Street. He quickly opened two more legitimate houses in which he offered stripped-down versions of classic plays. Much to his and everyone else's surprise, both tourists and native New Yorkers hungry for an alternative to the increasingly expensive Broadway productions continued to go the extra mile to 42nd Street west of Ninth Avenue, braving the gauntlet of druggies, hustlers, and Arcade Archies to get to the suddenly popular row of theaters. Piggybacking on his own success, Maidman opened four more theaters and then used some of his new influx of cash to buy a piece of one of the neighboring motels.

Maidman's one-man midtown theatrical renaissance came to an abrupt halt in the wake of the Supreme Court decisions regarding

In the mid-1960s storefront windows began to display their previously under-the-counter inventory of newly legalized, over-the-counter smut alongside the "underground" literature the Supreme Court's decisions were intended to legitimatize. (Corbis-Bettman)

pornography. By the mid-sixties, the would-be impresario saw his bourgeoning empire collapse when he joined the jaded jamboree and converted two of his legitimate theaters, the Maidman and the Garrick (in the Village), to movie theaters and pinned all his remaining legitimate hopes on the Mayfair, where his most successful midtown venue continued to pack them in. *This Was Burlesque* starred Ann Corio, an enduring name from the street's glamorous past. Maidman was able to keep the popular show open by dancing around the city's thirty-year-old ban on burlesque, a statute left over from La Guardia, claiming his was a historical look at the genre, rather than an actual revival of it.

By 1966 Maidman, finding his 42nd Street theaters increasingly surrounded by the proliferation of sex shops, quietly threw in the towel. He sold off much of his midtown real estate holdings to a new group of investors, as did most of the motels (the Sheraton was eventually purchased by the People's Republic of China to house its first consulate in the United States, where it stood facing the friendly museum antiaircraft guns of the USS *Intrepid*). Thus began a merry-go-round of turnovers that resulted in the emergence on the street of a new scourge: organized crime in the presence of the Gambinos, one of the five infamous New York City–based Mafia families,* whose specialty at the time was a three-card monte of porn, prostitution, and drugs.

By 1968, under the new Supreme Court guidelines, Maidman had leased his few remaining theaters to the Gambinos, who immediately converted them into pornographic bookstores selling peep shows, sexual services, and drugs.

B EGINNING IN 1965, twice a week every week one nondescript fellow wheeled a huge steamer trunk along West 42nd Street, stopping to collect quarters from the peeps. When he had a full load, usually about $10,000, he would then take it over to the Chemical Bank at the corner of Eighth Avenue. The quarters were deposited in the account of Martin Hodas, a propietor on the street known to the other shopkeepers as the King of the Peeps, a tribute that quickly caught the attention of organized crime.

Hodas had gotten into porn because of a handful of discarded nickelodeons he'd bought at an auction in 1965. He soon had the idea to fix them up and restock them with old stag films, placed them in various storefronts on 42nd Street, and a year later was pulling in an estimated $40,000 a week of pure profit. "Show me a man who doesn't admire a nude beautiful woman," he often boasted, "and I'll show you a degenerate."

To John "Sonny" Francese, one of the made men of the Colombo family, Hodas's message eventually came through loud and clear. Having already installed Leroy "Nicky" Barnes as his drug kingpin in Harlem, in 1970 Francese wanted to move in on the midtown porn action. Joe Colombo, Sr., the godfather of the Colombo family, was seriously wounded by the hired guns of rival mob leader "Crazy" Joey Gallo on June 28, 1971, while attending a

---

*The Gambino, Colombo, Bonanno, Genovese, and Lucchese families.

As West 42nd Street continued to decline, its amusement halls became, along with the bus terminal on Eighth Avenue, the favored pickup spot for pedophiles. (Ms. Vivenne Maricevic)

"unity rally" in Columbus Circle. Gallo was killed less than a year after that while eating clams in Little Italy, leaving the field all that much clearer for the Gambinos, who then made their move for a piece of the street's action. They made Hodas an offer he couldn't refuse. Hodas said no. A few weeks later he was seriously wounded and several of his businesses were firebombed. After a series of legal skirmishes, he found himself forced off the street and out of porn. By 1973, the street belonged to the Gambinos.

According to Mr. X, a family member put in charge of production first of print and later 8mm porno films, "Forty-second Street was already a shithole when we got there. When the Supreme Court finally said dirty books were legal, *la familia* decided time to go big-time into the business.

"We chose 42nd Street as our beachhead for a number of very good reasons. First off, the space was the cheapest we could find

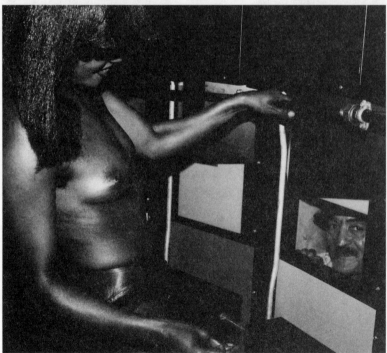

Toward the end of the 1960s, peep shows and live sex acts had replaced the once-burgeoning off-Broadway theater movement on West 42nd Street. (Ms. Vivenne Maricevic)

anywhere in the city and there was a lot of it. We needed space not just to shoot the shit but also to set up our own shipping drop where we knew no one would get curious or try to interfere, because no one gave a fuck. Back in 1969, 42nd Street was an anything-goes free-for-all. You could shoot your mother on the corner and people would step over her body without even noticing. And there were so many bars, game parlors, pimps, hookers, movies, we weren't going to stand out in that crowd.

"There was a little war that took place, but all we thought about it was that was the price for doing business. When the smoke cleared, we went out for two main types of customers: the vets who'd gotten their first whiff of real pussy in 'Nam and the nerdy college guys who couldn't get laid. They both came down to 42nd Street looking for action. We knew if we showed 'em some, they'd want more. We also knew we couldn't do it all at once, but if we did it in stages we could get away with anything.

"We started off selling stuff in storefronts because the Supreme Court said we could. We took every vacant place available, then painted the windows yellow which was like an immediate invitation to anyone looking for action.

"The step plan came from the lawyers. They told us some story about a guy, he gets caught for speeding doing eighty in a thirty-five-mile zone. You do eighty, you're gonna get pulled over. But do thirty-six and chances are you won't be. Or thirty-seven. Maybe even thirty-eight. They told us we could start pushing porn past the limit to thirty-six and gradually increase our speed up to the flow of traffic. Then, if everybody is doing fifty in a thirty-five zone, who are they going to pull over? Everybody? No. *The flow of traffic dictates the limit.* Somebody pulls out and does eighty, that's the fuckin' guy they'll go after. So don't be the fuckin' leader and don't do eighty and you'll be fine.

"Around 1970 we start shooting actual bush, then split the beaver with some little girlie holding herself open and showing pink. We put it all in our magazines, stacked them on the tables in the center of the bookstore, and moved the other shit to the wall racks. Of course, all the traffic went right to the magazines, sixteen-page jobs, four-page inserts, color photography, and the prettiest young girls who for fifty dollars would show you, shit, *liked* to show you everything. Where'd we get them? Easiest thing in the world. We'd put an ad in the *Village Voice* and get two hundred calls from girls wanting to do it.

"We graduated from semi-hard dicks to full fuckin' frontal hard-ons. We had specific publication dates when we figured we could increase the angle of stiffness on these guys. Then we moved to full penetration and showed everything, blow jobs, then cummin' on the fuckin' girls' faces, then girls takin' it in the ass. Then taking it from other girls. Then takin' it from other girls up the ass.

"I took a lotta the pictures myself, with my own camera. A Nikon. I didn't know too much about lights, lenses, anything like that, but I knew what pretty pussy looked like. I'd throw a silk sheet up behind the girls and shoot a hundred fuckin' pictures. By the time it was over we'd both be so fuckin' horny, for another fifty bucks, sometimes for nothing, I'd fuck the shit out of them. Right there.

"After a while, we'd get these Broadway yo-yos coming down to picket outside our porno stores because we sold pictures of naked girls for five dollars, while they were offering the same bare-ass shit up there on Broadway for forty-five dollars a ticket. The high-priced spread, we called it. At least what we put out got you off. The way we saw it, *we* were the real thing and *they* were the rip-off. *They* were the con guys. They didn't want to believe it, but the truth was, the street belonged to us now, and we intended to keep it.

"Then we found out something that changed everything. Dirty books and magazines did okay, but there was a lot of work involved in the production. There was printing costs, and hiring a million fucking writers and the girls and all that shit. The real fast-and-easy money was in drugs. It didn't take us all that long to realize that these losers coming to the street looking to buy a picture of some naked pussy most of the time were also looking to score some pot, maybe a little coke. The black dudes who hung out at the movies all day, they were all into full-card bingo heroin. We looked around and found ourselves in the middle of one great big ready-made market-place. If we could get them to come down to see naked girls, we could also sell them drugs.

"The big money was in product. Pot, coke, heroin. We used

42nd Street as our main point of distribution for dealers all over the city, Harlem, the Bronx, Queens, Brooklyn, and of course, New Jersey. We were in for the long run and we figured we could move a million bucks of drug merch a week.

"Turned out of course we were wrong. We wound up doing much, much more."

GERALD SCHOENFELD IS BALDING and roundish, decidedly unostentatious in look and manner. He is also the chairman of the board of the legendary Shubert Organization, the modern-day theatrical empire whose holdings include seventeen beautiful show palaces in New York City, substantial holdings of prime midtown real estate, and the most prestigious playhouses in Philadelphia, Washington, D.C., Boston, and Los Angeles. "The Shuberts," as the company is almost always referred to, is the largest and most powerful organization in modern American theater.

Schoenfeld spent the first half of his professional life in the pin-striped work of corporate law before joining the Shuberts in 1957 as its lead attorney. The organization had recently lost a six-year battle to defend itself against a major antitrust suit brought by the federal government in 1950 to prevent the Shuberts from continuing to refuse to allow competing national road tours of Broadway shows renting theater space in any of the national Shubert-owned houses.* The lawsuit was settled in 1956 when the entertainment organization agreed to stop the practice, a holdover from the early pre-movie days, relinquish some of its theatrical holdings and sign a consent decree prohibiting it from building or acquiring additional

*USA v. Lee Shubert et al.

In 1968, to the shock of many New Yorkers, the famed Astor Hotel was torn down to make room for a high-rise office building given generous tax abatements for including the new Minskoff Theater.
(Photographer unknown)

theaters. Although seen by the other Broadway producers and the-ater owners as a significant victory against the long-hated Shuberts, the settlement also cleared the way for the emergence within the organization of its newest rising star.

The Shuberts' offices were (and still are) located in the Shubert Theater building in Shubert Alley. The famed midstreet alley was created in 1904, when the city, concerned with the growing num-ber of horseless carriages in Manhattan and the need to keep the streets clear and clean for pedestrians, required an ample walking space behind the brand-new Astor Hotel, which took up the entire eastern half of the block.

One morning in 1972, as he did every day, Shoenfeld drove past Duffy Square, the triangular plot of land in the middle of Broad-way, part of the northern end of the Times Square "bow tie" just above 46th Street. And, as he did every day, he saw the same dozen or so homeless people pushed up against each other at the base of the statue of George M. Cohan, looking like nothing so much as the famous tableau of World War II soldiers raising the flag at Iwo Jima. In a final flap of haphazard irony, a single puffed-up pigeon nestled atop the bronzed head of one of the greatest theatrical tal-ents of all time.

It was an already simmering Schoenfeld who reached his boil-ing point later that morning when he saw all the neighborhood's wet and overflowing garbage bags. Then, suddenly, a Department of Sanitation truck came grinding up the street. Schoenfeld watched as the men slowly got rid of the bags. It must be some kind of national holiday, he thought to himself, and went on to his office. It was only then he realized that was *exactly* the reason all the garbage, which usually stayed on the streets for days, was now being collected.

"It was the third week of November 1972," Schoenfeld later recalled, "and from the Monday of the Thanksgiving holiday week on, for the sake of the tourists, or more accurately the tourists' money, the Department of Sanitation suddenly became very busy cleaning up Broadway.

It was a cleanup, Schoenfeld knew, that never got close to the real mountains of dirt accumulating in Times Square. "The place

Gerald Schoenfeld, chairman of the Shubert Organization. Schoenfeld, considered by many to be the most powerful man in American commercial theater, has been a political as well as cultural force in the Times Square district for thirty years.

was chock-full of concentrated pornography and ground zero for wall-to-wall hookers. Things had gotten so bad," Schoenfeld recalled, "they began lining up day and night along Eighth Avenue, barely a half a block away from our biggest and most famous theaters, harassing our patrons, and they became bolder the later it got into the night. We finally had to advance our curtains to seven-thirty so people could get out earlier. And the more I complained to the city about it, the more painfully obvious it was that either no one in a position to do anything had any realistic comprehension of how bad the problem really was, or else they just didn't care."

INDEED, THE PROLIFERATION of sex and drugs in the theater district was a diamond-clear reflection of how serious the latest twenty-five-year deterioration of New York's once-glamorous theater district really was. By 1965, nearing the end of his twelve-year reign, Mayor Wagner, in an interview, publicly prided himself on having never once, the entire time he'd served as mayor, set foot in Times Square west of Broadway, an area he often referred to with a combination of fear and disgust. The *New York Times* agreed, more than once describing the single street between Seventh and Eighth Avenues as "the single worst block in the town."

After a brief post–World War II flurry of activity, the boulevard, which had never fully recovered its theatrical splendor, fell victim to two seemingly unrelated events that, when combined, placed it into profound decline. The first was the series of Supreme Court decisions that liberalized the legal definition of obscenity. The second was the upzoning of the West Side of midtown Manhattan. For purely economic reasons, shortly after being elected, Mayor Lindsay called upon the City Planning Commission to take steps to commercially upzone Midtown West and create a "Times Square Special District."

Beginning in the fifties and lasting for nearly a decade, the East Side of Manhattan from 42nd to 89th Streets had experienced an excessive burst of high-rise construction that threatened to turn the entire stretch of the sunny, genteel Madison Avenue above 59th Street into one long, dark corporate alley. The East Side had long been designated for commercial development, since the mid-nineteenth century when Boss Tweed in the post–Civil War building boom that hit the city, openly favored corporate expansion on the side of the city nearest to where he operated from, the Tammany Hall district, as a way to keep a short leash on his many related industry kickbacks and to maintain the high values of his private commercial property holdings. It was a decision he justified with studies, for the most part true, which determined that the natural subterranean turf on the East Side was flatter than on the West Side and had fewer unstable rock formations, making it safer to build tall business buildings there. He exempted low-rise theaters hoping to keep "show business," and all the sex and street crime with it, as far away as possible.

In 1966, the first year of his administration, Mayor Lindsay believed rezoning Midtown West was the best way to shift commercial development from the overcrowded East Side to the largely underdeveloped Times Square area. In the twenty-year period after the end of World War II, while the East Side of Manhattan had undergone yet another round of corporate redevelopment, exactly one new commercial building had gone up in the vicinity of Times Square—the New York Telephone Company's headquarters on the Avenue of the Americas between 41st and 42nd, an ugly, impractical structure all but hidden by the long shadow of the street's great public library.

Because of the hundred-year-old zoning limitations, which made even the most rudimentary improvements nearly impossible to get approved by the city, property values on the West Side of Manhattan either stagnated or deflated, and nowhere more than on 42nd Street. This led to periodic sell-offs of existing properties.

Even the venerable *New York Times* fell victim to the restrictions. It took nearly forty years for the paper to get rid of its turn-of-the-century namesake tower, which it had outgrown by the early twenties (except for a few fourth-floor offices it maintained to operate the news "zipper" that flashed headlines around the building's exterior), in favor of larger and more practical space on 43rd Street between Broadway and Eighth Avenue. When Allied Chemical finally purchased the old tower from the *Times* in the early sixties, it somewhat optimistically announced plans to convert the space into a "showcase for chemistry," and although it had been encouraged to make the move by the Wagner administration, Allied, too, failed to overcome the severe zoning restrictions and finally gave up after managing only to get approval from the City Council to cover the exterior of the building with a windowless, pale marble that made it look like nothing so much as a bad crown in the middle of a crooked smile. A frustrated Allied finally emptied out the few remaining tenants and turned the once-beautiful building into one gigantic billboard filled with ads (which barely paid its mortgage) until the mid-seventies, when the corporation was finally able to unload its costly albatross.*

---

*The building was sold to Metropolitan Life. Allied took a $1.37-million loss in exchange for an outstanding $700,000 tax liability. (*New York Times,* June 17, 1976)

The Times/Allied Chemical debacle accelerated the cultural as well as economic devaluation of the area's real estate. As Jud Strunk, a topical songwriter of the early sixties, suggested in one of his tunes, celebrating New Year's Eve in Allied Chemical Square just didn't have the same sense of New York excitement about it. "They used to call it Times Square," he sang, "but oh how times have changed!"

Indeed they had. In 1965, two years after the *Times* left the building that had given the square its name, came the closing of the legendary Crossroads Café directly south of the tower. That was followed the same year by the demolition of the Franklin Savings Bank Building on Eighth Avenue and 42nd Street, one of the few nineteenth-century corporate structures still in use. The barren site became a rat-infested favorite for junkies to shoot up, and remained otherwise unoccupied for the next eight years before—in what some hailed as a sign of great progress—the city allowed another, bank to be built there to serve the local citizenry. By the time of Lindsay's election in the fall of 1965, real estate values in Times Square had fallen so low that the once-glamorous Knickerbocker Hotel, already having been unceremoniously converted to commercial space (for a time in the fifties it served as the home base of *Newsweek* magazine), was sold by its current owners for a dollar.

Lindsay believed the old zoning restrictions were the primary reasons the Broadway district and industry had fallen into economic decline, and sensed the key to revitalizing both lay in the physical redevelopment of the Times Square area.

The mayor's thinking may have been well intentioned, but it was flawed. His essential misunderstanding of how the industry (as opposed to the art) functioned began with an erroneous view of the relationship between the existing midtown zoning and the business of Broadway. It was, in fact, precisely those limitations that had allowed the low-rise Broadway houses and the Times Square "bowl" they sat in, to remain essentially unchanged—"undeveloped" in real-estate parlance—for as long as they had. No other commercial district in the city had managed to escape the wrecker's ball as long as Broadway. Going to the theater in New York City was, into the mid-seventies, very much the same cultural experience it had been for nearly a hundred years.

Theatrical pros like Schoenfeld understood the business of Broadway far better than the mayor. The Shubert Organization in its 1971–72 season (the last before Schoenfeld took over) lost more than $4 million in theatrical productions and was in danger of becoming insolvent. Schoenfeld's anger about the garbage and the hookers had, in reality, little to do with pride, respect, or even the need for proper appreciation by the city of his organization's continuing contribution to its culture. To Schoenfeld's way of thinking, the city's neglect wasn't just stifling Broadway's creative urge, it was helping to kill its ability to turn a profit.

However, those who most favored Lindsay's planned upzoning couldn't have cared less about Broadway's illusory bottom line. These were the area's nonindustry landowners who'd been sitting on undevelopable and therefore nearly worthless property. Believing, as Lindsay did, that rezoning would produce an influx of big-ticket developers, they decided to rent their venues, as is, to the one group of tenants not only willing to do business on the street but to pay big money for the dubious privilege, with the understanding they would immediately vacate when asked. These happened to be the operators of the newly legalized pornographic bookstores, movie houses, massage parlors, and peep shows, always desperate to find additional space to push their product. When the windows to previously empty storefronts began to fill up with lewd come-ons, and the street corners with hookers and pushers, the landlords simply and conveniently looked the other way.

Among them were some of the most respected names in New York real estate, including Seymour Durst, one of midtown Manhattan's most powerful and prolific builders, scion of the legendary New York real estate empire founded in the twenties by Joseph Durst. Durst, anticipating upzoning, willingly rented much of his available West Side space to the one tenant willing to pay the highest rent and ask the fewest questions—the porn merchants. So did lawyer Edward R. Finch II, the son of an appellate court judge who happened to also be Richard Nixon's uncle; members of the Association for a Better New York; several Park Avenue–based banks; even members of Lindsay's Times Square Development Council. Sol Goldman, of Goldman-DiLorenzo, one of the largest property owners (and tax delinquents) rented space to more than a dozen peep shows, massage parlors, and houses of prostitution on or near 42nd Street.

And so it was that Lindsay's plan to develop the West Side, combined with the Supreme Court's sex-related decisions, while bringing new hope to the long-suffering West Side landowners, in reality turned 42nd Street back into what it had been at the turn of the century—the city's most notorious tenderloin district.

T HE TONY Municipal Art Society (MAS) was founded in 1893 by a group of artists who painted murals on, and provided monuments for, New York's otherwise dreary public areas. By 1940 the organization had evolved into a formal committee whose goal was to try to get legislation passed that would prevent New York's landmarks in historic districts from being bought up by developers, torn down, and replaced by high-profit, low-aesthetic commercial structures. That same year, the MAS began a twenty-five-year campaign to gain passage of a Landmarks Preservation Act that was, after a long and bitter struggle, signed into law in 1965, which shifted the MAS's battle to the question of which structures in the city qualified as landmarks. This would become the essential issue of the mid-seventies fight to save Grand Central Terminal, among other familiar and historic New York City buildings, from being torn down and replaced.

Kent Barwick, the president of the MAS, is a tall, pleasant-looking fellow with a wide smile and an easy charm. By the age of thirty he had become a successful Madison Avenue advertising executive before shifting his professional gears and joining the MAS in the early seventies. After plunging into the complex world of politics versus preservation, one of the first lessons he learned had to do with the social and economic fallout from the Lindsay administration's decision to upzone Midtown West. "In fact, for all the self-kudos this mayor and his appointees gave themselves for finally having done something about the so-called problems in Times Square and on 42nd Street, his plan for upzoning led to a decade-long cycle of *dis*investment that in turn led to the further social, cultural, and real estate *de*valuation of the entire area. If you owned

Kent Barwick, president (and chief aesthetician) of the Municipal Art Society, often clashed with both politicians and the theatrical community over how to strike a balance between the billion-dollar planned redevelopment of 42nd Street and Times Square, and the preservation of the area's unique low-rise, turn-of-the-twentieth-century sunlit "bowl."

(Copyright Isiah Wyner, used by permission)

property on the street that you knew one day was going to be the sought-after site of a developer who wanted to put up an office building, why would you invest a penny of your money in any kind of long-term improvement, if you could get the city to allow you to, when whatever you put up is going to be torn down anyway. In the meantime, while you're waiting to make your big kill, someone comes along with a short-term month-by-month cash offer for your space, willing to take it as is. So what if he's a bit sleazy, you tell yourself, it's not forever, and meanwhile it pays the bills while you're getting ready to sell out to the big boys."

Lindsay, who never saw it coming, was shocked at the sudden, and to him, unexplainable increase of hard-core pornography that appeared on 42nd Street almost immediately after the City Planning Commission's fall 1966 approval of the first phase of his new West Side upzoning plan. In late December he appointed James Marcus of the Department of Buildings, Licenses and Traffic to see if there was anything that could be done about the mushrooming smut. After carefully studying the situation Marcus suggested to Lindsay that the city simply buy up all the available movie theaters on 42nd Street where the porn was playing, invest some money in restoring them to the legitimate playhouses they once were, and donate the space to nonprofit theaters that would bring the "right" kind of people back to the street.

Lindsay liked the idea so much that not long after he invited Louis Brandt, the head of the Brandt Organization, which owned the Apollo and the Lyric, both of which had recently added porn to their movie schedules, to accompany him on a tour of 42nd Street. Afterward, Brandt, who stood to make a fortune if the city (or anyone) bought him out, held a press conference during which he announced his good-faith intention to work with the city to turn both of his movie houses back into live production theaters. When asked by a reporter when that might happen, Brandt confidently replied, "Very soon."

Four months later, a smiling Lindsay accepted a special Drama Desk Award "for his efforts to save Broadway."

T HE MAYOR WASTED NO TIME in publicly attempting to woo potential corporate developers to Times Square, and was willing to put the public's money where his mouth was by dangling generous tax abatements in front of potential investors. Abatements, a lessening or forgiving of existing rates, are often used by government as loss leaders to stimulate development. In theory, new construction creates new premises that generate new property taxes, income taxes, occupancy taxes, sales taxes, and dozens of other related forms of income that eventually go to the government. Developed properties also increase the value of existing nearby structures. In commercial zones especially, all related businesses, from parking facilities to restaurants, enjoy increased earnings, which in turn generate still more taxable revenue. Finally, abatements sooner or later expire, while the properties they helped get built continue to generate taxes.

Nevertheless, Lindsay's newest plan sent caution flags waving in the hearts, minds, and purses of some of Broadway's biggest theater owners and operators. What particularly worried them was how Lindsay, who'd pledged to "save" Broadway, *their* Broadway, had suddenly given the green light to *outside* developers to come in and reconfigure Times Square into one more corporate alley.

It didn't take the mayor long to find his first money player, a choice whose first tangible result caused a new round of concern, not just along Broadway but among the general public as well: The city's newspapers reported that the legendary Astor Hotel was about to be torn down. The Astor had been, after all, one of the most familiar and beloved locales in New York City, part of the romantic iconography for countless young couples who had used the huge lobby clock as the place under which they met for first dates before having drinks, going to dinner, taking in a movie or a show, and falling in love. This grand hotel was as much a signpost on the road map for much of the first two-thirds of the American twentieth century as Yasgur's Farm would be for much of the last third. Tear down the Astor? Unthinkable. That would be like tearing down Grand Central Terminal.

Richard Weinstein, a young mover and shaker in the Lindsay administration, was a key player in the development intended to replace the Astor Hotel. He later recalled the capriciousness with which those who came into the area dealt with the issue of redevelopment. "Jerry Minskoff, the developer, balked at complying with one of Lindsay's hard-and-fast rules for any new development, which was that the builders had to include a theater built into the base of their buildings. His original primary tenant was going to be J. C. Penney, which wanted to put a department store in that space. Lindsay tried to force Minskoff's hand, and when push came to shove, Minskoff told the mayor to fuck off, that he wasn't going to spend an additional $5 million just to keep a bunch of Broadway crybabies happy. When Lindsay tried to explain how much more money he could make with a theater than a department store, Minskoff said, 'I'll make a fortune anyway. I don't have to make a fortune and a half.'

"But to his credit, Lindsay wouldn't take no for an answer. He really wanted this to go his way. He felt he owed it to the theater community. So he personally called Minskoff to make one final pitch. They agreed to meet, and the next night Lindsay and I went to see Minskoff at the Essex House on Central Park West. While going up in the elevator, Lindsay turned to me with a slight smile and said, 'I hope we don't go to jail for what we're about to do.' I had no idea what he meant.

"When we arrived, Minskoff took us directly into his living room and introduced us to his wife. There was a huge picture window, and the view was simply spectacular. It was winter, the lights were glistening in Central Park, the trees were covered with snow, an altogether bucolic scene. We were looking out the window when suddenly the mayor turned to Minskoff and said, 'You know, we're just so backed up in the Building Department issuing permits that I'm really worried, Jerry, you won't be able to meet your financing schedule. We'll do everything we can, of course, to expedite it, but I have to tell you it doesn't look good.'

"Of course I concurred. That's when I realized why I was there. I then related some bullshit story about how it looked like the backup could be as long as five years. Minskoff, nobody's fool, got our drift, and caved. Right then and there he agreed to put the theater in. 'I'll go along,' he said, 'just don't fuck me over.'

"We were just about to leave when Lindsay, who couldn't believe how beautifully this had all gone down, turned to Minskoff and casually asked him why he'd changed his mind. 'I'll tell you,' he said. 'My wife at one time was an actress and the Shuberts treated her so badly she wants me to build a competing New York theater the Shuberts will never be able to control.' That's when we knew we'd been had, that Minskoff had intended to build the theater from the start, knew Lindsay was trying to break his balls and decided to break his instead."

Things got worse when Gerald Schoenfeld came out publicly against the planned inclusion of a theater in the proposed new high-rise because he felt left out of the deal.*

Weinstein: "Our main support came from Harold Prince, who took the same position we did: that a new theater was a welcome addition to an industry that was slowly dying. At the time, he was the first one active in the theater who had the guts to go up against Schoenfeld, because everything Prince touched in those days turned to box-office gold.

"The Shuberts, meanwhile, focused much of their position on trying to quietly prevent what a lot of people didn't realize was going to take place as a part of the deal—the demolition of the Astor Hotel. He did that as a way to stop the construction of the building and therefore the theater. And although Schoenfeld talked a lot about tradition and landmarks and all that, his real motives were purely economic. Schoenfeld didn't want the competition building any more theaters. To offset Prince's influence, Schoenfeld brought in his biggest gun, the legendary producer David Merrick.

"Merrick and Schoenfeld forced a public hearing to see if there was any way they could prevent the Astor from going down. They tried to explain how important a hotel was in the middle of Times Square, how its occupants were nearly all tourists who went to the theater, while a new office building would generate nothing but nontheater-related jobs. The other side then pointed out the chronically low occupancy rate of the old hotel."

As it happened, the hearing took place the very day Cardinal Spellman died. Spellman was one of the most beloved and respected religious leaders the city had ever had. Everyone expected the hearing to be postponed, but it wasn't. The first to speak was Harold Prince, who stood up, went to the microphone, and said, "We are all saddened by the death of Cardinal Spellman, and in deference, I'm simply going to read the list of those here who would have testified today in favor of the building of the new theater." As each person's name was read, he or she stood up and received a quiet,

---

*The Shuberts had a 39,000-square-foot property that was not granted any of the rezoning benefits which required a minimum of 39,000 square feet.

dignified round of applause. Arthur Miller, Elia Kazan, Angela Lansbury, Diana Sands, and so on. The biggest names on Broadway. At that point, Lindsay, who was on the dais, started to weep.

Weinstein: "Merrick was scheduled to speak next, but he took one look at the crowd, knew it was a lost cause, and didn't want to be on the losing side. So he stood silent for a moment, then said simply, 'How can I be against what my beloved community is so passionately for? I have nothing further to say.' And left Schoenfeld to hang by himself."

Not long after, in 1968, with the swiftness and efficiency of a smart bomb, the Astor Hotel simply disappeared off the face of the earth. It was replaced a year later by Gerald Minskoff's fifty-story skyscraper One Astor Place, which included a movie theater and a street-level playhouse and the eponymous Minskoff Theater, a cavernous eighteen-hundred-seater with poor acoustics and an interior design that one observer wryly noted more closely resembled a Hawaiian beach hotel than a classically ornate Broadway-style theater.

Still, it was the first new legitimate Broadway house to be built in nearly sixty years, a part of the development deal Lindsay had insisted on, and he saw it as making good on his promise that his administration was dedicated to preserving the theater district. However, what bothered everybody else even more than the aesthetically unappealing playhouse and building was the swiftness of the disappearance of the venerable hotel. Lindsay conceded the loss of the Astor had been a big price to pay, and reassured everyone who would listen that it was an isolated incident, with no more corporate development schemes being hatched for Times Square.

As it turned out, it was anything but.

Joe Franklin remembered the eerie speed of the many Times Square teardowns that followed. Not long after the demise of the Astor, he later recalled, "there was a movie theater across from it on Broadway that had once been a vaudeville palace called the Loew's State. I'd go there every single Thursday to see the new show and movie. I remember one Friday it was business as usual, and the next morning it was completely gone. *Overnight!* No announcement in the press, no closing ceremony, no plaque, nothing. Just a pile of rubble."

The demolition of Loew's State was followed by the tearing down of several more of the area's oldest and most beautiful buildings. The next to fall was Stern's, one of the city's major retail department stores for over a century, the last fifty-six years on the corner of Avenue of the Americas and 42nd Street. It was a favorite of shoppers who loved the charm and elegance of the old building. Once the store announced it was closing its doors, midtown real estate developer Seymour Durst snapped up the rights to the land it sat on and immediately announced his intention to erect a new skyscraper on the site.

DURING LINDSAY'S EIGHT YEARS in office, five more high-rises went up in the vicinity of Times Square, and three more legitimate theaters before the 1972 recession finally brought to a halt this cycle of demolition and construction. By then, the mayor, who'd barely survived the onslaught of his opponents to win a second term (with only 42 percent of the vote), and facing a financial snowstorm that blanketed the city with municipal debt, growing union disruptions, and increasing racial unrest, reluctantly put on the back burner what was to him the unfinished agenda for the redevelopment of Times Square. Moreover, despite all the new theaters that had gone up, attendance had continued to decline, while pornography, prostitution, and drugs maintained its dominance of Midtown West.

SCHOENFELD, MEANWHILE, after complaining to various city agencies about the worsening problem of prostitution and pornography and getting nowhere, in 1972 asked producer Hal Prince if he would intervene and help get him an appointment to see Lindsay. At the time, Schoenfeld knew no one in the city administration, but was aware of Prince's close friendship with the mayor.

Prince set it up, and on the appointed day, Schoenfeld went

down by himself to City Hall where he was escorted into Lindsay's office. There, sitting with a group of his commissioners, the mayor listened patiently to his guest's litany of complaints. "When I left," Schoenfeld recalled, "I saw him turn to one of his associates and say, 'Who was that fresh sonuvabitch?'"

One way or another, he had caught Lindsay's attention. Not long after, the mayor decided to put together something he called the Times Square Task Force, made up of people from various city agencies connected to the Broadway area, including the Department of Licenses (which later became the Department of Consumer Affairs), the Building Department, the police, and the Department of Sanitation. No one was quite sure what the actual function of the group was, beyond a vague mandate to help do something about the situation in Times Square. It wasn't much, but it was a beginning.

One day in the spring of 1972, Lindsay found himself stuck with an old campaign gift he dearly wanted to unload. No one at City Hall could remember exactly where it had come from, or think what to do with it. Someone came up with the idea of using it as a discount theater ticket booth. The idea wasn't entirely new. Gray's drugstore in midtown had been selling discounts and "twofers"—two tickets for the price of one—on an informal basis ever since the Depression. The mayor decided to call Gerald Schoenfeld. With the campaign for reelection to a third term a year away, Lindsay thought it might be a good time to begin finding some new political allies.

So it was that the familiar patrician-smooth voice greeted Schoenfeld through the receiver. "Morning, Gerry."

"Mr. Mayor."

"Look, I want to run something by you. What do you think about a discount theater ticket booth over there on Broadway, right in the heart of Times Square? Would you support something like that?"

"Yes, I would."

"That's good, because I have a trailer sitting here at City Hall all ready to go and I'll be happy to donate to the cause."

Schoenfeld asked Lindsay where he thought it should go, and

the mayor suggested Gray's Pharmacy on 43rd and Broadway just north of the Times. "That is not the place," Schoenfeld said. "Duffy Square is much better. It happens to be the biggest outdoor flophouse in New York City, where every vagrant goes to sleep on the warm subway gratings and every hooker plies her trade under George M. Cohan's nose. Put the booth there and it will serve two purposes. It'll get rid of the bums, and will prove that people can safely come into the middle of Times Square."

Lindsay agreed that that was where it ought to go. Schoenfeld also urged the mayor to have it run by a nonprofit agency so no taxes would have to be paid, and offered a Shubert grant of ten thousand dollars to get the ball rolling.

He thanked the mayor, hung up the phone, and immediately dialed Phil Smith, vice president of the Shubert Organization who provided the logistics for the head of the Theater Development Fund (TDF), a not-for-profit organization whose job it was to help schools, hospitals, and other groups get the opportunity, through group discounts, to see Broadway shows. Schoenfeld told Smith about the mayor's offer and suggested TDF was the perfect organization to run the ticket booth. Schoenfeld got all the theaters to agree, and within weeks, the redecorated trailer appeared, parked east-west on the north side of Duffy Square, offering out of its windows same-day, cash-only, half-price tickets to most Broadway shows on a no-fee, first-come, first-served basis. The booth, identified by its signage as "TKTS," proved an instant hit, selling hundreds of seats every day that would otherwise have remained empty.

Schoenfeld was so thrilled he began taking midday walks from his suite of offices in Shubert Alley to the square just to see the people waiting on line. Yes, sir, he had to hand it to Lindsay. As far as he could see, for the first time in a long time, someone in city government had actually done something to *help* Broadway.

Thus encouraged, Schoenfeld helped set up a "Special Projects Division" within the League of New York Theaters and Producers (a Broadway alliance) and agreed to chair the Committee on Urban Environment to deal with the problems in Times Square. A neighborhood meeting was planned for that fall, in the rectory at Father

Rappelyea's Holy Cross Church, which was and still is located in the heart of "Hell's Kitchen," the neighborhood slang term for the West Side district officially known as Clinton that included many of Schoenfeld's theaters.

An unexpectedly large number of people showed up, claiming to represent most of the 133,000 Clinton residents. Schoenfeld was astonished to discover the number of people who actually lived in what he believed was an essentially commercial area, and quickly realized they were an influential voting bloc waiting to be organized. Schoenfeld spoke that night and asked those present to help get a law passed against loitering for the purposes of prostitution. "I'd called up Fred Ohrenstein, our local state senator, and Richard Gottfreid, our assemblyman, and neither would take our calls. I told the group about this, and they said the same thing had happened to them! Fine, I said, let's call them up and tell them goodbye, because they won't be here after the next election. A few weeks and a couple of thousand phone calls later, Ohrenstein introduced a bill in the assembly, and so did Gottfried, and, despite some First Amendment reservations, managed to push it through and make it into law."

The local police were especially grateful to Schoenfeld for helping to take the cuffs off their own hands, and he made it his business to get to know the police on duty, the men in the streets and the commanders in the precincts. He supported the Midtown North precinct putting wooden barriers along the west side of Eighth Avenue so that hookers could not approach men in their cars.

Word of Schoenfeld's actions eventually reached Lindsay, who called to reassure Schoenfeld he was solidly on Broadway's side. "And don't worry," the politician in him told the head of the Shubert Organization, "there'll be no more corporate towers with theaters in them going up on Broadway during my watch."

What he didn't tell Schoenfeld that day was that a new plan had already arrived at his desk, a proposal by an Atlanta, Georgia, developer for a new hotel to be built in the center of Times Square one block north of the site of the old Astor. That was the good news. The bad news was that this would, unfortunately, necessitate the demolition of at least four existing Broadway theaters. At this early stage, Lindsay saw no point in mentioning it to Schoenfeld or anyone outside the inner sanctum of City Hall. Who would believe him anyway? Another high-rise in the theater district was about as likely to be built in midtown as Disney was to open a souvenir store in Times Square.

NINETEEN SEVENTY-THREE was an election year in New York City. A nationwide recession had settled in, New York was particularly hard hit, and Lindsay knew his bid for a third term was in trouble. That January the mayor quietly intensified his involvement with two new Midtown West projects. He announced both at a press conference, hoping to squeeze enough good economic juice out of them to invigorate his shaky campaign. One was a residential high-rise west of Eighth Avenue, just beyond the main drag of the porn-and-drug-infested West 42nd Street. The other was a fifty-story hotel on Broadway, one block north of the new Minskoff skyscraper and theater. The developer behind that project was John C. Portman, Jr., a fifty-year-old Atlanta-based architect with a desire to get ahead of the real estate boom the mayor had assured him was about to hit Times Square.

To make room for Portman's proposed high-rise, Lindsay knew that several Broadway theaters were going to have to be demolished, at least two of which might raise a few eyebrows. The Gaiety was a no-brainer, a former Broadway burlesque house that had long ago been converted to an also-ran movie theater. There would be a general good-riddance over that one. The Astor, between 45th and 46th (one block north of where its namesake hotel had been located),

Grand Central Terminal's beautiful Main Concourse, with sunlight streaming through its arched windows onto the shining marble floor. In the 1970s, the dramatic day-to-day battle to save the landmark from the wrecking ball was played out publicly on the front pages of the city's newspapers and nightly on the local news, especially after Jackie Onassis became personally involved. (Corbis-Bettman)

was also a no-sweat deal. Like the Gaiety, it, too, had gone from a live performance house to showing half-dead movies, after which it became a low-rent tourist-targeted Ripley's Believe It or Not!, then a discount dry-goods outlet with shampoo, soap, toothpaste, and feminine hygiene products "for sale cheap," before finally going out of business, its windows covered with plywood, the plywood immediately tattooed with graffiti. Its marquee went permanently dark, turning the entire block into what Gerald Schoenfeld described as "the black hole of Calcutta." The vacant Bijou in the small, outdated, and already condemned Piccadilly Hotel, also between 45th and 46th, suffered from a lack of sufficient fly space (backstage area) to accommodate modern productions. It was the last two, the mayor knew—the elegant but technically outdated Helen Hayes and the glorioiusly intimate Morosco—that would not go down without a fight from the theater industry's most powerful movers and shakers.

The Helen Hayes was still a dish, aging gracefully with an air of regal intimacy. Called the Fulton before it was renamed to honor the legendary actress, it had been designed by the legendary team of Herts and Tallant at the turn of the century in what had become their signature belle epoque Times Square style, set off by a gorgeous terra-cotta facade meant to glow like a soft candle in the late afternoon sun.* The interior had what many performers considered the best natural acoustics on Broadway. As for the Morosco, Tennessee Williams had called it his favorite theater, not just on Broadway but in all the world.

Word that Portman wanted to build a midtown high-rise had originally come to Lindsay by way of Peter Sharpe, the mayor's campaign manager. Portman first proposed the project not long after the Minskoff building had been completed. Lindsay responded with a generous package of benefits and abatements and after several preliminary trips to the city in 1973, Portman was all set to move forward when the recession deepened, and he reluctantly pulled out of the deal. It had been a major disappointment for Lindsay, who'd counted on the Portman project to kick-start the

---

*Other jewels in the Herts and Tallant theatrical crown included the New Amsterdam, the Lyceum, the Booth, the Shubert, and the Brooklyn Academy of Music.

next round of corporate construction in Times Square and reinvigorate the city's economy enough to carry him to victory in the next election.

With Portman out, Lindsay pinned his reelection hopes on a seventeen-hundred-apartment complex being developed for Ninth Avenue and 42nd Street. While less flashy than the Portman project, the mayor believed Manhattan Plaza could still serve as the anchor for the residential revitalization of the far west end of 42nd Street. Seymour Durst had inherited the proposed building site from his father and in 1973 made the deal to build housing on it in partnership with Richard Ravitch, a private developer (and future chairman of the New York State Urban Development Corporation). The Durst and Ravitch partnership was buttressed by Lindsay with a good-faith $100-million construction loan to Ravitch from the city's operating budget.

Not long after ground was broken, the project, despite Lindsay's strong political backing, sank into a mire of municipal red tape that, combined with the deepening recession, caused its builders to halt construction. Like Portman, Manhattan Plaza looked as if it, too, had fallen victim to the economic hard times. Both appeared to be dead. That fall, Lindsay was soundly defeated in his bid for a third term.

ABE "SPUNKY" BEAME was a loyal Liberal/Democratic functionary whom Lindsay chose in 1965 to be his city comptroller. Lindsay knew he needed a good numbers man on his team, and when it came to balancing the books, there was no one better than Abe Beame. The tall, charismatic leader and his stubby, backroom white-maned money manager had developed a solid camaraderie during Lindsay's eight years as mayor, until the city was overwhelmed by recession and Beame decided only he could save it. Campaigning on a pledge that he would dedicate himself to saving the city from where Lindsay and his predecessors had brought it— to the brink of bankruptcy—the sixty-six-year-old Beame won the '73 election.

His victory allowed little time for celebration. He knew he faced an uphill battle to bring the city back to fiscal solvency, a bat-

Mayor Abe Beame in his later years, with the author. (Rebel Road, Inc.)

tle that dominated his first three years in office. Early in 1976, the short, square-headed Beame, five feet two in his stocking feet, began to look around for some single positive achievement with enough pizzazz to carry him to a second term as mayor.

Like a lot of little men, Beame wanted something big and sexy to grab hold of. Someone on his staff ran the old Portman deal by him. Beame said he'd never heard of it or Portman and, besides, he didn't like the idea of outsiders building in the city. Someone else brought up the Manhattan Plaza project, which Beame also rejected. He saw little advantage to being associated with anything happening on the west side of 42nd Street (he was already somewhat involved in the ongoing struggle to save Grand Central Terminal). As far as he was concerned, that part of town was nothing more than a depraved den of sex and drugs. Someone else then suggested going after the street itself. Everyone in New York knew that 42nd Street was a festering pimple on the face of their city; pop it and you were a hero. Perfect, Beame said. It didn't get sexier than that.

Borrowing a page from the La Guardia playbook, Beame's advisers mapped out plans for hizzoner to make a public "raid" on

West 42nd Street. Unfortunately for Beame, this ill-advised stab at front-page dramatics resulted in making him less like Fiorello and more like one of the Katzenjammer Kids (whose misadventures the Little Flower used to read to kids on Sunday nights over the radio during a Depression-era newspaper strike).

As Beame would later recall, "These were hard times, and the last thing on my list of priorities was 42nd Street, until someone suggested it might make me look good in the upcoming reelection if I took a stand on the situation down there. Mind you, as far as I was concerned that street had turned into a sinkhole of immorality, and for all I cared it could stay that way. What was the point in trying to do something about an area overrun by pornography, drugs, and street crime?

"In 1976, with the recession beginning to ease, I was able to get the Democrats to bring their convention to the city, and then of course we had the great bicentennial celebration in the harbor. The rest of the world was starting to notice us again, and that meant the possibility of fresh tourist dollars, which appealed to me.

"About that same time I had a conversation with Gerald Schoenfeld, who told me the reason the industry of Broadway was still in such financial straits and now was in danger of being totally dismantled, theater by theater, was that 42nd Street had become the porn capital of America. This disturbed me quite a bit and that same year I asked Schoenfeld to chair a new organization, the Mayor's Midtown Citizens' Committee to help me revive the area.

"Next, I came up with the idea to 'raid' 42nd Street. I felt something big needed to be done, some public demonstration to show the voters of New York City that I meant business. So I called a meeting with Gerald Schoenfeld and his new committee and invited a couple of reporters to observe it. One of them, Dick Oliver of the *New York Daily News,* said, 'Mr. Mayor, you've got to do something dramatic in order to focus everybody's attention, some kind of demonstration to show the city just how awful things have gotten down there.' I called all the newspapers and told them I was planning to go down to the Show World, on Eighth Avenue and 42nd Street, the biggest and most popular porno house in the neighborhood, with nude dancers and dirty books and all that went with it. The next night I stuck a notice on their front door saying this place was hurting the city and urging people not to support it."

The Show World Center had gained a reputation as the raunchiest sex show on the street. Not long after it opened it became 42nd Street's (and America's) first supermarket of porn. Every conceivable adult toy was for sale there, every category of porn magazine on display, every sex act imaginable available on film, even the newest craze—$250-a-pop videos. On the second floor were cages surrounded by small rooms that reeked of Lysol and Clorox. Inside them, windows were covered with wooden panels that for twenty-five cents would lift up to reveal a minute's worth of a live show of naked women playing with themselves and each other; the customer was then supposed to show his appreciation by slipping a tip through a one-way slot. Often, the glass was missing, and for the right price direct contact was available. A roll of toilet paper and a wastebasket sat conveniently in the corner of each room. The third floor's centerpiece was a live, in-the-round stage, where, for twenty dollars it was possible to watch couples, either male-female or the far more popular female-female, perform every conceivable sex act, with the climax of the performers the climax of the performance.

In 1976 this sex emporium clocked more than four thousand paying customers a day. It was then (and still is) owned by Richard Basciano, a five-foot eleven-inch, 185-pound former boxer whose private office above the emporium was built to the specifications of a full-size athletic gymnasium. In the seventies the Show World, as it was popularly known, was only one of several Manhattan porno operations in which Basciano held a financial interest, among them the glittery, East Fifties "upscale" massage parlor known as Plato's Retreat. The Show World and Plato's became the favored hangouts for the Studio 54 set, marking the birth of porno-chic, which, at the time made smut the mainstream's lateste pop-culture diversion.

Beame's "raid" took place on March 28, 1977, and to his surprise and subsequent dismay it was initially taken by the press to be nothing more than a cheap campaign tactic: a whole lot of orchestrated commotion over what was perceived by the general public to be of little importance. Typical of the type of coverage it received was a report by Mary Alice Williams, a young, blond, attractive local TV correspondent, in which she treated the whole

The Show World Center, on Eighth Avenue and West 42nd Street, in the 1970s. It remains in operation to this day, although its sexual presentations and inventory have been all but eliminated.

(Ms. Vivienne Maricevic)

event as if it were a joke. As she ended her piece, the camera pulled back to reveal she was reporting from directly in front of the Show World. "It's eleven o'clock at night," she said with a smirk. "I'm alone in Times Square, where my mother told me never to be."

The next day, the *Daily News,* the very newspaper whose reporter had suggested the raid in the first place, ran a lead editorial that called Beame's actions politically motivated, a "gimmick" played out by a La Guardia wanna-be, meant to distract voters from the very real problems the city still faced.

Beame was angered by the media's negative reaction, but utterly bewildered by the *Daily News* editorial, so much so that the next day he called Mike O'Neill, the paper's editorial director, to find out why he'd been set up. O'Neill insisted he didn't know that Dick Oliver had been involved, and the next day published an apology to the mayor that he'd written himself.

Which, like the original editorial, was met with indifference by a generation of New Yorkers, for whom 42nd Street had become the cool place to go to buy porn, see live naked women, get laid or get stoned. What was the big deal? To them, fuddy-duddies like Beame who still got upset about it were the ones out of touch, not the porn merchants.

Beame, who couldn't believe what he'd seen during his raid, didn't give up trying to do something about smut on 42nd Street. He conducted another dozen porn shop raids, none of which received any coverage in the local press, during which the police confiscated material from bookstores that dealt with everything from bestiality to pedophilia. Each time the stores were padlocked, and reopened for business the next day.

In the last months of what would be his single term in office, Beame managed to get the federal government to underwrite the cost of the Midtown Enforcement Project (MEP), a police division specifically mandated to investigate any possible link between the proliferation of drugs, prostitutes, and porn on 42nd Street and organized crime. Beame had brought in Sidney Baumgarten to head the MEP. After a brief stint, he was replaced by Carl Weisbrod, who had a strong background in law enforcement. Weisbrod then left to join Koch's 42nd Street project, and Bill Daly took over. Daly, a tough native New Yorker and former special agent in military intelligence, had spent two years in Germany working counterespionage before returning to the States, to head up the MEP.

According to Daly, "By the mid-seventies Beame was under extraordinary pressure, not from the public, which was for the most part indifferent, but from local businesses, and particularly Gerald Schoenfeld and the whole theater industry, to do something about the ugly situation spreading out from 42nd Street. Unfortunately, because Beame had to constantly trim his overall budget to get the city through its financial crisis, cops were being laid off in huge numbers. That's when he decided to turn to the feds for aid to start the Midtown Enforcement Project. He applied for a half-million-dollar grant, got it, and we were eventually able to occupy some Crossroads building directly south of the Times Tower, which had sat vacant for years before becoming a porn shop, which we were able to convince to move out. As a result, for the first time the police force had a permanent physical presence on 42nd Street."

Chief Alan Hoele, a thirty-nine-year veteran of the police force, also worked in midtown in the seventies and was one of those

*Chief Alan Hoele, executive captain of the Midtown South
Precinct of the New York Police Department in the 1970s.*
(Courtesy of Chief Alan Hoele)

assigned to the street's local precinct, Midtown South. "I was the
executive captain," he remembered. "I worked in one capacity or
another there for twenty years, until I became the second-in-com-
mand of everything below Central Park. When I first arrived,
Times Square was the anus of the country, a particularly wild, dangerous anything-goes place, sex stores, prostitution, stores that sold
weapons, narcotics, peep shows with live sex acts, everything from
threesomes to guys having sex with other guys, young girls having
sex with girls, even girls having sex with monkeys.

"Of course, most of the initial resistance we met came in one
form or another not from the hookers and the hustlers and the nickel-
and-dime boys, but from the citizens of the city who frequented the
street and thought we were giving them too hard a time, and
organized crime, the leaders of which knew why we were there and
what we intended to do, which was rid the area of them.

"Because the mob was so slippery, they were difficult to nail.

We'd start targeting massage parlors, mostly along Eighth Avenue and some between Ninth and Tenth, and were able to close a few of them down. They would then simply move to another locale, rent another storefront, and continue doing business. Beame even tried putting the names of the landlords in the papers. Well-known people like Irving Maidman, Sol Goldman, and Seymour Durst. Durst owned a whole lot of places, including the Luxor Hotel, a little north of 42nd Street, right in the heart of the theater district, which operated as a twenty-four-hour brothel."

The Luxor was one of the many older hotels in the area that had once catered to the theatricals—actors, musicians, dancers—until it became an SRO (single-room occupancy—"quick-stay"), where hookers and johns could rent a place for as briefly as twenty minutes. When Durst's ownership of the Luxor was exposed in the press, he quietly resigned his position as board member of Schoenfeld's Midtown Committee.

"A 'Superfly' mentality developed on 42nd Street," Daly later recalled. "There were the pimpmobiles, the women in very short hot pants, blond wings, and big platform shoes, the pimping foot soldiers for the mob—all of it was very out in the open and very, very dangerous. They were the ones who'd threaten people and use intimidation against legitimate businesses. The atmosphere was very threatening, and tourists were scared shitless about coming into the area. On the surface, to the public and the politicians, 42nd Street may have looked harmless, but the most serious problem was, without question, the street crime that came along with it, most of which we could trace to organized crime's growing drug operation."

According to records kept by the MEP, in 1977, the same year as Beame's "raid," more than eight thousand civilians frequented porno-related businesses on 42nd Street in a single hour on any given weekday evening. At the same time, because of Beame's budget problems, a maximum of sixteen patrolmen could be assigned to the single block between Seventh and Eighth (the "Seven-Eight" in police jargon), with just two mounted officers and fewer than a half dozen patrol cars left to cover the rest of the neighborhood. Out of necessity, the majority of local police actions were street summonses issued to hookers and blatant pot smokers. The standard policy of the day was not to arrest anybody if it could be helped, and keep the street traffic moving.

Still another police captain assigned to 42nd Street in the seventies related, "There was, in fact, little we could do, short of knocking the whole block down or blowing it up. The problem was, the mayor didn't really have his arrows lined up with his targets because porn, as bad as it was, was not the real problem. Drugs were fueling the craziness, and because we couldn't stop it, the craziness got crazier."

Statistics kept by the Drug Enforcement Administration and the New York State Commission of Investigation show that by 1977, for every two dollars 42nd Street civilians spent on pornography or prostitution, they spent five on narcotics and marijuana. And while the Gambino family was in control of both the sex and the drug businesses, it was nearly impossible for the MEP to trace any of the action directly back to them because they owned no property in Times Square and were careful to avoid direct contact with the nickel-and-dime dealers and twenty-dollar pimps who worked the streets. As one police officer put it, "They had more local stops between them and the street than the D train had between the Bronx and Coney Island."

This was also the height of the public's idealism of the mob, romanticized by the two *Godfather* films, a time when organized crime, both in the movies and in real life, was at the peak of its power and popularity. The press for the most part kept its distance as well, focusing instead on the more titillating aspects of the new permissiveness. Pornography, if seriously examined at all during this period, was almost always looked at as a social phenomenon rather than an instrument of organized crime. Every major news publication in New York City and the country put a journalistic microscope on the new commercialism of sex while turning a blind eye toward the career criminals who profited from it. For instance, instead of looking at the reasons why porn had proliferated on 42nd Street, the *Village Voice* published an endless stream of graphically illustrated pieces detailing the goings-on behind the forbidden doors of the boulevard's sex palaces.

Even the *New York Times* fixated on the street's funky, often dangerous atmosphere rather than the money trail. One article it published during this period described the lack of law enforcement without going beyond the moment to examine the methods of either the criminals or the police. In vivid, cinematic detail it described the sounds of 42nd Street at midnight, the contrapuntal thump of car tires crushing empty bottles and cans in the street with the continual whispered chant of small-time drug dealers: *"Joints, coke, acid . . . joints, coke, acid . . ."* One dealer the newspaper interviewed claimed to have received more than one hundred summonses and still managed to return every night to the same subway entrance on Seventh and 42nd Street, where he would do his business within ten feet of the same uniformed police officer. The cops eventually became fed up with the bureaucratic merry-go-round that always resulted in the offender being able to leave the station house before the arresting officer and simply took themselves off the ride.

O N THE EIGHTH AVENUE end of the street, the Port Authority Bus Terminal, which cost $24 million and took ten years to build, beginning in 1940 and ending a decade later (delayed by a World War II steel shortage), was New York City's surface link to the nationwide interstate highway system. It was seen at the time as one of the most modern facilities in all of Manhattan, with its dozens of ramps, escalators, and elevators giving passengers a futuristic sense they were gliding rather than walking. Conceived as a city within a city, it offered consumer services that included a bakery, a bank, a couple of bars, a barbershop, a beauty parlor, bookstores, candy stores, a twenty-four-hour chiropodist, and dozens of newsstands and coffee shops. The terminal was the transport equivalent of the fifties' favorite fast-food fad, the TV frozen dinner— sleek, fast, shiny, and cold, all held together in what appeared to be one giant aluminum container.

And, by 1977, Beame's last year in office, suffering from chronic poor management and an undermanned security staff, the terminal had become, with its numerous halls and stairwells, the destination of choice for the gay netherworld of teenage runaways who gathered there from all across the country. Young hustlers met in designated areas of the main concourse near the two main departure gates, then known as the Meat Rack and the Minnesota Strip. And, because New York and New Jersey shared responsibility for the terminal, neither side had the singular power, the necessary funds, or the political motivation to do anything about the worsening situation. Caught in a bureaucratic nightmare, the once-glamorous terminal had turned into a multimillion-dollar sex and drugs emporium for predatory pedophiles and teenage runaways.

John F. Ryan, a police lieutenant who worked for the terminal's small police force for more than twenty years, remembered how bad things had gotten by the time Beame left office. "The crime problem was so pervasive, it was a joke to try to effectively fight it. Every day I'd see some businessman on his way home, passing through the terminal, and he'd get 'wolf-packed,' attacked by a group of young toughs like hyenas in a jungle. By the time we could get to him they'd have ripped off his pants so that along with being robbed he'd have to suffer the humiliation of standing in the middle of the terminal in his underwear."

Chief Hoele recalled the futility of trying to convince the public of the seriousness of the situation, not just in the terminal but all along West 42nd Street. "There was a house of prostitution across from the bus terminal. We used to have a cop stand in front of the entrance telling the would-be patrons that if they went inside, they were certain to be robbed. That was the house scam. They'd usually say thank you, go in anyway, and a few minutes later come running back into the street without any pants on, having been taken down. We became so frustrated we had a sergeant whose assignment it was to go into all the bordellos and rip out their wiring with his bare hands. In response, the operators got together and kept an electrician on twenty-four-hour call."

Limited by the vagaries of the law, a misconception as to the nature of what the real problems were and who was causing them, and an overall reluctance on the part of the general public to have its tax money spent on closing down dirty bookstores, in 1977 Manhattan District Attorney Robert Morgenthau threw his hands up in defeat, admitting that Beame's ongoing battle against 42nd

Street had resulted in very few significant arrests, and most of those produced "prosecutions that were lengthy, expensive and often pointless."

In the ten years since Lindsay had succeeded in getting the West Side rezoning started, 42nd Street between Seventh and Eighth Avenues had been completely taken over by organized crime. Porn, drugs, and prostitution engulfed the very neighborhood Lindsay had believed would blossom under redevelopment. Instead, the unexpected economic downturn scared the big money away, and by the time Beame managed to turn the city's finances around real estate developers were no longer interested in the sex-and-drugs drenched west side of 42nd Street. Instead, they turned their focus and their money back toward the east.

O ONE OF THE GREAT truisms of New York real estate is that, for better or worse, "built to stand forever" means an average of about fifty years. On an island as small as Manhattan, no matter what the state of the economy, land rights are always more valuable than the properties built on them.* Redevelopment supports both the construction and the demolition industries, and the resale of surface and air rights are perpetual profit-generators. For these and other reasons, including the need for every generation to rebuild the city in its own image, structures are erected and torn down in New York with a rhythmic regularity that, if viewed in long-term stop-frame motion photography, would resemble a concrete garden where cement plants grow, bloom, and are then replaced in the blink of an eye.

The delicate balance between aesthetic preservation and profitable redevelopment pitted those who believed in the inherently

---

*The Coliseum on Columbus Circle is a good example. Built in 1956 by Robert Moses out of concrete and steel on the condemned ruins of thirty buildings, New York's master builder for the first half of the twentieth century envisioned a structure that would endure as long as its Roman namesake. However, in 1998, just forty-two years after it went up, it was sold by the Metropolitan Transportation Authority to developers as New York's next great commercial site. Among its scheduled future tenants are AOL Time Warner, a hotel, and a new jazz concert hall, at a construction cost starting at $345 million. The sale ended a fourteen-year battle over what to do with the long-vacant, awkwardly designed, and poorly situated building originally intended as New York's premiere convention site. Standing, the structure was worthless; torn down, the land it sat on was worth nearly a half billion dollars.

priceless value of the city's great landmarks against those who looked to put a price tag on the land they sat on. Such was the essence of another ongoing crisis of 42nd Street: the battle for Grand Central Terminal.

For much of the first half of the twentieth century, it had been the city's main artery of rail transportation. When it was operating at its peak in the 1940s, 63 million passengers a day either boarded or disembarked from trains in the cavernous terminal. To accommodate subterranean rails, nearly half of Grand Central, including its glorious main concourse, sat below street level. By 1920 a highway bridge snaked around the building's great facade, making Park Avenue a single uninterrupted automobile thoroughfare that weakened the terminal's mighty visual impact, a physical and symbolic obscuring of one of the city's most instantly recognizable structures. Covering it up in a very real sense buried it even further, and made it easier for many to accept a plan that included tearing the great terminal down.

After World War II, a new generation of American real estate developers arrived on the streets of Manhattan. Many were returning veterans who'd experienced firsthand the human horrors and property destruction of war, and in doing so lost whatever awe they may have once had for nonliving monuments. Having learned the hard way that survival, not sentiment, was the only road that led to the future, these postwar professionals set about modernizing "old" New York, refitting Manhattan in row after row of functional (and profitable) high-rises cast in angular steel and glass. To this generation of developers, relatively low-rise structures like Vanderbilt's terminal were nothing more than money-losing white elephants whose time had come and gone.

Indeed, by the early fifties, many of those who'd once traveled cross-country in the splendor of the sleek and legendary Twentieth Century Limited now preferred long-distance travel by one of the newly affordable perks of postwar prosperity, the family automobile. Air flight, too, dramatically increased with the introduction of relatively inexpensive commercial jet travel. The terminal's very existence, once considered crucial to the transportation of goods, services, and people in and out of the city to points anywhere, USA, no longer seemed so vital, especially when, in the late forties, the

New York Central, Grand Central's owner, was losing an average of $30 million a year.

Once the crown jewel of 42nd Street, the terminal that fifty years earlier had inspired the construction of a dozen new hotels and apartment buildings within walking distance had, by the late fifties, outlasted most of them. The elegant twelve-story Montana Apartment complex, for example, built on Fiftieth and Park for its proximity to the terminal, was demolished in 1958 and replaced by the forty-story Seagram Building, whose owner, Samuel Bronfman, head of the family distillery operation, insisted his skyscraper/monument, with its postmodernist sleek high-rise design, complete with an expansive street-level plaza, was the area's new "crowning glory."*

In 1954 Robert R. Young, an up-and-coming investment speculator from Texas, bought a majority interest in the failing New York Central that made him the nominal owner of Grand Central Terminal. What he was really after were the air rights above it. To stop the Central's financial bleeding, he immediately opened merger talks with several of the rail line's major competitors. Three years later, when Bronfman announced his intention to tear down the grand Montana Apartments and replace it with a new corporate skyscraper and was met with little or no resistance from the city, Young took that to mean he, too, could now tear down and build whatever he wanted. He decided to demolish the entire granite and limestone street-level facade of the terminal and replace it, over the remaining tracks, with a 108-story office tower, which would be the tallest building in New York City. To his surprise, the plan was met with strong opposition from the rest of the Central's stockholders—they were against the cost, not the concept—and a few months later he voluntarily reduced the projected tower's size to a mere fifty-five stories.

Young's opportunistic disregard for the history and sentimen-

---

*The Seagram Building at 375 Park Avenue was completed in 1958. Its architects were Ludwig Mies van der Rohe, one of the leading German Bauhaus visionaries; Philip Johnson, who did the lobby; and the firm of Kahn & Jacobs. The building is notable as the first fully modular office tower designed to accommodate standardized interior partitioning, permitting unobstructed views through floor-to-ceiling windows, and a permanently heated outdoor plaza.

tal value of the terminal set off a competition among dozens of speculators who insisted Young's ownership of the New York Central didn't automatically include the air rights to the terminal. These challenges resulted in numerous lawsuits that dragged on for years, during which time Young, anticipating victory and the subsequent demolition of the terminal, ignored its expensive upkeep. By the late fifties whole chunks of plaster from the world-famous and wondrous Paul Helleu constellation of 25,000 stars ceiling mural were routinely dropping onto the heads of passengers crossing the main concourse.

The sky was falling on Young as well, and he knew it. In 1958, while still defending his claim to the terminal's air rights, a merger between his New York Central and the Pennsylvania Railroad, which he'd been negotiating for more than two years and which he desperately needed to help lessen his increasingly heavy financial load, completely fell apart. The collapse of the merger devastated him. Suffering enormous and ever-mounting financial losses and facing several more years of legal battles he would have to win before he could tear down his terminal, Young committed suicide.

His shocking death threw the future of the terminal into an even deeper state of uncertainty. The New York Central continued to operate without clear leadership, while the land around the terminal underwent more redevelopment. In 1963 another new highrise went up on Park Avenue, this one directly behind Grand Central. Walter Gropius's Bauhaus-influenced Pan Am Building all but obliterated the northern, or rear, view of the terminal. It was described by some as a "seven-league monster," a "fatal blow" to New York's Park Avenue (it was voted by readers of *New York* magazine in 1987 as the building most city residents would like to see torn down).* The public uproar over the forty-nine-floor ornate tower further complicated the situation concerning the terminal's air rights. It also renewed the fear among preservationists that Grand Central would soon be completely surrounded by modern glass-faced skyscrapers.

Ironically a solution of sorts came in 1966, eight years after Young's death, when the federal government, looking to strengthen

*It was subsequently sold and became the Met Life Building.

the nation's increasingly troubled rail system, forced a merger between the New York Central and the Pennsylvania into the Penn Central Corporation. Unfortunately, the shotgun-marriage organization proved nothing short of a disaster. With the Pennsylvania Railroad's home base remaining in Philadelphia and the Penn Central's (along with the New York Central's) in New York, there was little in the way of any real consolidation. Instead, relations between the branches worsened over the unresolved issue of what to do with Grand Central's air rights. The Pennsylvania Railroad was in favor of tearing the terminal down and selling the air rights (as it already had with its own Penn Station), while the New York Central wanted to keep it intact. With financial pressures mounting, Penn Cental agreed to sell the air rights to a third party, British developer Morris Saady, who in turn hired famed architect Marcel Breuer to design what was to be 42nd Street's newest, tallest, and grandest skyscraper.

To prevent this from happening, on September 21, 1967, the two-year-old Landmarks Preservation Commission designated Grand Central Terminal an untouchable municipal landmark, an action the rail company immediately rejected, insisting the city no longer had any jurisdiction over property that, due to the forced interstate merger, fell under the jurisdiction of the federal government.

Further complicating matters was the fact that many New Yorkers actually favored demolition of what had to them become an embarrassment to the city and a danger to themselves. Besides a further drop in ridership and a parallel rise in commuting in and out of the city by car, the homeless and the druggies had turned Grand Central's main waiting area into a communal bedroom. Muggings inside the cavernous Grand Central dramatically increased to a point where the police actually had to warn the general public to avoid the terminal during nonrush hours. Things got so bad that after being continuously open twenty-four hours a day for more than sixty years, Grand Central Terminal started locking its doors at night, leaving the homeless and the druggies its only occupants between one-thirty and six in the morning.

After several failed attempts by the City Planning Commission to get Penn Central to accept alternative sites to transfer the air rights above Grand Central Terminal, in 1973 an acceptable site was agreed to by both sides. The city had offered the small street commonly known as the "Biltmore block" on Vanderbilt Avenue between 43rd and 44th Streets, to Penn Central, and the Planning Commission went so far as to rezone it to allow the skyscraper that the rail company wanted. However, before groundbreaking could begin, the recession hit, and Penn Central pulled out of the agreement, claiming it could no longer raise the necessary financing to build, and reverted to its original position of wanting to build above the site they already owned, even if it meant tearing down much of Grand Central Terminal to do it.

I N 1974 NEW YORK STATE elected Democrat Hugh Carey as its next governor. One of his biggest campaign contributors (and also his opponent's, Baggies-fortune inheritor Howard Samuels) was a hitherto-unknown real estate developer by the name of Donald Trump, whose father had built several residential, mostly middle-class outer-borough housing developments. Trump wanted into the big money world of Manhattan real estate, and got his break when the newly elected Carey named him among the first appointees to a new blue-ribbon task force on housing, even though the young Trump had yet to lay a single brick anywhere in the city.

Carey had his election victory party in the old Commodore Hotel, directly to the east of Grand Central Terminal, named in honor of Vanderbilt and built to serve his station's many passengers. Like Grand Central, the hotel had suffered from neglect and fallen into general disrepair, and after a city inspection it was declared in danger of imminent collapse. Most of the upper floors were sealed off after being evaluated as unsafe to occupy. The average rate of occupancy had fallen below 50 percent, and much of that was short-stays by prostitutes and their johns, either before or after the men took a turn in the resident massage parlor.

When Trump arrived, he took a look around and thought it the perfect place for him to establish a beachhead in Manhattan. He knew all about the tax-abatement deals Lindsay had offered Minskoff and Portman. The next day Trump set up meetings with the Hyatt Group, at the time one of the most powerful commercial hotel operators in the city, convinced them to underwrite his planned redevelopment of the hotel, and, when they agreed, sought Carey's help in getting the state-administered HUD (the Department of Housing and Urban Development) to condemn the Commodore and sell it to Trump's newly formed conglomerate. Trump also sought condemnation to rid the property of an outstanding tax debt of $70 million. By committing $9 million up front toward rebuilding, money that came not from his own pocket but from Hyatt's, Trump asked for, and got, a lease agreement with the state, in effect a clean financial slate, with all past tax burdens simply erased off the books. The bottom line to the deal was that Trump negotiated for and got the Commodore for nothing and received tax abatements for the first forty-one years of the renovated hotel's new lease on life. The deal was the beginning of what would come to be known as the Trump Dynasty. It forged the template for all future real estate deals in midtown.

Except for the embattled terminal. Trump's cleverly structured deal also prompted Penn Central, which took the occasion of the hotel's 1975 "reopening" to offer the city what it considered a similar deal for itself. If the Commodore Hotel could be torn down and rebuilt, the railroad company asked, why couldn't Grand Central, especially if they guaranteed uninterrupted rail service during construction of a high-rise built on top of it. The city said no. So did the state. In response, Penn Central then vowed to continue its legal challenge to the granting of landmark status.

A few months later, Judge Irving Saypol of the New York State Supreme Court ruled on the side of Penn Central, agreeing with the company that the city had acted illegally when it granted landmark status to the terminal, not on jurisdictional grounds, but because it constituted a "taking" of private property for public use without just compensation or alleviation of economic hardship.

The decision shocked and angered the pro-preservationists, most vocal among them Ada Louise Huxtable, the highly literate and extremely influential architecture critic for the *New York Times,* a position the paper had created for her. (The first on any American newspaper. She would later go on to win a Pulitzer Prize.) Reacting to Judge Saypol's decision, Huxtable wrote, "The decision is, of course, a dreadful blow to the cause of landmark preservation in

Fred Papert, a former advertising man, played a key role in the successful effort to save Grand Central Terminal. (Rebel Road, Inc.)

New York. . . . The future of [the city's] best buildings is now extremely shaky, and what is involved ultimately is a significant part of the city's quality, amenity and style. . . . One realizes, of course, the city is broke; but one was not aware that this bankruptcy was moral as well as financial."

It was at this point that Mayor Abe Beame, sensing that the city was about to lose the terminal under his watch, and that if it did, his already slim chances for reelection were finished, went to the Municipal Art Society (MAS) for help, which was where he first met Frederick S. Papert. Papert, an elegant and savvy former advertising executive well connected to both the media and the tony MAS, had closely followed the ongoing battle waged by Penn Central for the right to demolish the terminal.

As Papert later recalled, "My involvement in saving the terminal came directly out of my association with the Municipal Art Society. When Penn Central announced it was going to try to tear down Grand Central, it was the first time I'd heard the term 'land use planning,' and also the first time I'd ever heard the word 'preservation' used in a political sense. I knew a bit about this kind of thing because my advertising background had been primarily political. The agency I'd worked for had done advertising for both the Republican and the Democratic National Committees and the U.S. Senate political campaigns for Arthur Goldberg, Jacob Javits, Charles Goodell, and Robert Kennedy. I'd been personally involved with Robert Kennedy's senatorial advertising and his presidential campaign ads."

Fred Papert was born and raised in Manhattan and grew up in the upper-middle-class section of Carnegie Hill, a neighborhood north of East 86th Street, near Gracie Mansion. He was still living there in the late sixties when the area was threatened with the erection of what was to be the first mid-block high-rise in that part of town. All of New York's residential neighborhoods had been zoned so that tall buildings could only be built on the avenues and low buildings in the middle of the block, to provide light and air for both.

Papert: "To try to prevent that building from going up, I organized the Carnegie Hill Neighbors. We came up against a quite influential real estate developer at the time by the name of Peter Sharpe, later Lindsay's campaign financial manager. Sharpe hired some topflight attorneys, and we went all the way to the state supreme court before we lost on some obscure technicality, which was a good lesson to me about how New York works—that money plus real estate equals political advantage."

Following his failed but spirited Carnegie Hill campaign, Papert was invited to join the board of the prestigious MAS. When those fighting to preserve the terminal lost their first round in court, Papert opened a temporary office in the Pershing Building directly across from the terminal, and, working under the auspices of MAS, formed the Committee to Save Grand Central Terminal.* From the committee's new headquarters, Papert coordinated a series of daily, celebrity-rich, "Save the Terminal" rallies. Although the committee got a lot of coverage in the local and national media, Papert, a veteran of these campaigns, knew the odds were not in its

---

*The Pershing Square Building, named after General John J. Pershing, commander in chief of the American Expeditionary Forces in World War I, sits on the site of the old Grand Union Hotel, torn down in 1914. For six years, the site was a park—Pershing Square—until a private developer built the twenty-three-story structure directly opposite Grand Central Terminal.

favor. After studying the situation strictly from the vantage point of the opposition's bottom line, which he believed the appeals court would do, he came to the conclusion that not only did it make good economic sense to tear down Grand Central, no one on the opposition had presented a single practical reason not to.

Papert then refocused his efforts. Rather than trying to save a single structure, he decided to force the issue and make Grand Central Terminal the symbolic line in the sand. On one side were the aesthetic preservationists, on the other the opportunistic progressives. According to Papert, "Not only was it still the most beautiful railroad terminal in the world and one of the greatest buildings left standing in America, it was also the sentimental heart of the city, and its preservation was vital. Losing the terminal would have put every single historical structure in the city in jeopardy."

Judge Saypol's decision clearly defined the positions of the opposing forces. On one side were the new kids in town, those who lived outside the five boroughs of the city, who preferred driving in, who never took the subway or used the services of the rails or went to the public library or attended a Broadway show. Their singular goal was to wrest "old" New York away from the fogies they saw as responsible for its decline, to tear down its faded symbols of the past century's dead to make room for a new generation of corporate cornerstones. On the other were those fogies, led by Papert, the small but fiercely loyal group of moral preservationists trying to save what they considered one of New York's greatest monuments.

A feisty, if increasingly desperate, Papert now made his money move. Having become friendly with the Kennedy family through his earlier involvement with Robert's Senate and presidential campaigns, he'd maintained close ties with Jacqueline Kennedy Onassis, and had made himself emotionally available to her following the assassinations of her husband and brother-in-law.

On February 24, 1975, one month after Saypol's decision, Papert played his trump card. He paid a visit to Ms. Onassis and asked her to join the terminal cause. Without hesitating, the normally publicity-shy former First Lady sat down and composed an impassioned handwritten open letter to Mayor Beame that elegantly captured the essence of the dilemma:

February 24, 1975

1040 FIFTH AVENUE

Dear Mayor Beame

I write to you about Grand Central Station, with the prayer that you will see fit to have the City of New York appeal Judge Saypol's decision.

Is it not cruel to let our city die by degrees, stripped of all her proud monuments, until there will be nothing left of all her history and beauty to inspire our children? If they are not inspired by the past of our city, where will they find the strength to fight for her future?

Americans care about their past, but for short term gain they ignore it and tear down everything that matters.

Maybe, with our Bicentennial approaching, this is the moment to take a stand, to reverse the tide, so that we wont all end up in a uniform world of steel and glass boxes.

Old buildings were made better than we will ever be able to afford to make them again. They can have new and useful lives, from the largest to the smallest. They can serve the community and bring people together.

Everyone, from every strata of our city, is wounded by what

Dear Mayor Beame,

I write to you about Grand Central Station, *with the prayer that you will see fit to have the City of New York appeal Judge Saypol's decision.*

Is it not cruel to let our city die by degrees, stripped of all her proud monuments, until there will be nothing left of all her history and beauty to inspire our children? If they are not inspired by

1040 FIFTH AVENUE

is happening — but they feel powerless — hopeless that their petitions will have any effect.

I think of the time President Kennedy was faced with the destruction of Lafayette Square, opposite the White House. That historic 19th century square was about to be demolished to make way for a huge Eisenhower-approved Government office Building. All contracts had been signed. At the last minute he cancelled them — and as he did so, he said "This is the act I may be most remembered for."

Dear Mayor Beame — your life has been devoted to this city. Now you serve her in the highest capacity. You are her peoples' last hope — all their last hopes lie with you.

It would be so noble if you were to go down in history as the man who was brave enough to stem the tide, brave enough to stand up against the greed that would devour New York bit by bit.

People now, and people not yet born will be grateful to you and honor your name.

With my admiration and respect

Jacqueline Kennedy Onassis

(Copyright Kennedy Schlossberg/John F. Kennedy Library)

the past of our city, where will they find the strength to fight for her future?

Americans care about their past, but for short-term gain they ignore it and tear down everything that matters.

Maybe, with our Bicentennial approaching, this is the moment to take a stand, to reverse the tide, so that we won't all end up in a uniform world of steel and glass boxes.

Old buildings were made better than we will ever be able to afford to make them again. They can have new and useful lives, from the largest to the smallest. They can serve the community and bring people together.

Everyone, from every strata of our city, is wounded by what is happening—but they feel powerless—hopeless that their petitions will have any effect.

I think of the time President Kennedy was faced with the destruction of Lafayette Square, opposite the White House. That historic 19th century square was about to be demolished to make way for a huge Eisenhower-approved Government office building. All contracts had been signed. At the last minute he cancelled them—and as he did so, he said, "This is the act I may be most remembered for."

Dear Mayor Beame—your life has been devoted to this city. Now you serve her in the highest capacity. You are her people's last hope—all their last hopes lie with you.

It would be so noble if you were to go down in history as the man who was brave enough to stem the tide, brave enough to stand up against the greed that would devour New York bit by bit.

People now, and people not yet born will be grateful to you and honor your name.

With my admiration and respect,
Jacqueline Kennedy Onassis

"Without the slightest doubt," Papert later said, "Ms. Onassis becoming involved was the reason the MAS and the rest of us were able to continue the fight to save Grand Central. And not just because of her celebrity. She was a smart political thinker, much smarter than her strange voice and good looks might allow you to believe. There might not have been an appeal of the decision at all if it weren't for that letter and her decision to take an active role in the fight. It's why Beame, who thought it was all over after Saypol, decided to appeal the court's decision. He would never have done it otherwise because of the timing and precarious state of the city's finances. To continue the fight and lose again would kill his political future. As it was, Penn Central was threatening the city with a

1975

Free Noontime Concert

Tuesday, April 15, 12–2PM, rain or shine. Overhead ramp at 42nd Street.

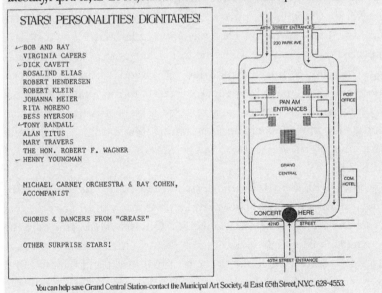

STARS! PERSONALITIES! DIGNITARIES!

- BOB AND RAY
  VIRGINIA CAPERS
- DICK CAVETT
  ROSALIND ELIAS
  ROBERT HENDERSEN
  ROBERT KLEIN
  JOHANNA MEIER
  RITA MORENO
  BESS MYERSON
- TONY RANDALL
  ALAN TITUS
  MARY TRAVERS
  THE HON. ROBERT F. WAGNER
- HENNY YOUNGMAN

MICHAEL CARNEY ORCHESTRA & RAY COHEN, ACCOMPANIST

CHORUS & DANCERS FROM "GREASE"

OTHER SURPRISE STARS!

You can help save Grand Central Station-contact the Municipal Art Society, 41 East 65th Street, N.Y.C. 628-4553.

separate lawsuit for damages in the range of $80 million if it made any further attempt to hold up the sale of those land rights."

The ironies were difficult to miss. Landmark designation had made Grand Central Terminal eligible for federal funding, something Penn Central accepted and then pointed to as justification for its legal position. At the same time, the recession, which had worsened the financial condition of the railroad, also scared off most of the big-money developers from investing in new construction, which in turn further delayed any move toward actual demolition. This helped buy time for Papert and the MAS to take their case to a further appeal without fear of a surprise midnight wrecking ball.

In the weeks following Saypol's decision, the committee, now fronted by Ms. Onassis ("Jackie will save us!" architect Philip Johnson declared to the press) and former mayor Robert F. Wagner, put together a group of private attorneys to file an *amicus curiae*, or "friend of the court," motion, a highly detailed brief arguing the case against demolition, insisting that because it had benefited from a federal tax exemption, the terminal's owners could not now tear down the terminal and rebuild it for profit.

While the appeals court pondered its decision, the committee intensified its campaign. Each day another famous New York face appeared on the local news or the front page of the dailies, protesting the "impending" demolition of Grand Central Terminal. Alongside Ms. Onassis, Mayor Abe Beame, former mayor Robert F. Wagner, and Fred Papert came a parade of stars of radio, TV, nightclubs, and film, and an up-and-coming Manhattan congressman with a wide grin and a clever way with sound bites by the name of Ed Koch.

That April, Mayor Beame hosted a huge rally that the *New York Times* called "a galaxy of Broadway stars" directly in front of the terminal and led by the impassioned Ms. Onassis. That same day, the newspaper's editorial made note of Penn Central's latest counterproposal: to keep the lobby of the terminal intact and merely build over it. The editorial quickly rejected the idea. "There are more ways to destroy a building than with bulldozers. In the case of Grand Central Terminal, the bankrupt Penn Central Railroad is [proposing] to mutilate it by erecting a 50 story tower above a subtler, but equally effective kind of landmark destruction."

On December 16, 1975, in a 3–2 decision, the Appellate Division of the New York State Supreme Court reinstated the landmark status of Grand Central Terminal, concluding that the plaintiffs had not sufficiently proved that landmark status had deprived them of all beneficial use of the property, and denied Penn Central the right to tear down the terminal. It was a major victory for Papert, the MAS, Beame, Ms. Onassis, and the Landmarks Commission, but even as champagne corks were being popped, everyone knew the battle was far from over.

Penn Central vowed to take their fight all the way to the United States Supreme Court, where, three years later, on June 26, 1978, by a 6–3 vote, it finally and irrevocably lost. Justice William Brennan, writing for the Court's majority, once again validated the position of the MAS and the preservationists by noting that "over the past fifty years, all 50 states and over 500 municipalities have enacted laws to encourage or require the preservation of buildings and areas with historic or aesthetic importance." The decision said that New York City's landmark laws were "typical" and that there was no evidence the property had actually been "taken" by the city. Finally, Brennan wrote, "An owner does not have a constitutional right to destroy a designated landmark in order to realize a greater economic return."

The Court also stated that the private owner of a piece of property must forgo his right to make a better, more profitable use of it, for the greater benefit of the public. Normally, public funds had to be used to compensate the owners for that right. In this case Brennan agreed that early on, when the city had offered Penn Central the Vanderbilt Street site on which to transfer their air rights, and the rail company rejected it, the city's obligations for due compensation had been met.

Not long after Brennan's decision, Penn Central fell into bankruptcy, and control of the terminal passed to the city's Metropolitan Transit Authority, which immediately began to raise funds for what would be one of the most magnificent restorations in the history of New York City.

The city's victory did more than save Grand Central Terminal. It succeeded in awakening the sleeping passions of its citizens, changed the lives of those who'd put their careers on the line for it, and helped rotate the power wheel of New York politics. Catapulted into the spotlight during the demonstrations that helped keep the terminal from destruction during the long appeal of the

Saypol decision, Ed Koch became the city's newest and favorite media mensch. Rubbing shoulders with the celebrity elite, always available to the press with a wry smile, a shrug of his shoulders, and a sharp if whiny comment aimed at the absurdity of the opposition's arguments, Koch was now perfectly positioned for his successful 1977 run for mayor.

In the weeks following the Supreme Court decision, Fred Papert worked to reconcile the differences between preservationists and the developers. The challenge, he tried to make both sides understand, was to be able to maintain as much of the history of the area as possible while also allowing a necessary next phase of industrial-level real estate development to proceed, a combination of restoration and rebuilding that, he reassured them, would benefit everyone.

He renamed "The Committee to Save Grand Central Terminal" "the 42nd Street Development Corporation," persuaded the Ford Foundation to underwrite it, and set his sights on restoring and rebuilding the rest of the boulevard.*

"One day," Papert recalled, "Ms. Onassis and I decided to take a walk to the West Side, to see what was happening on the other end of 42nd Street. It was supposed to be a relaxed, nostalgic look at what we both remembered as the heart and soul of the city. After all, the block between Seventh and Eighth Avenues had been at one time the most famous street in the world. It was at the New Amsterdam that Ziegfeld had produced his *Follies*, at the Apollo where George White gave the city his *Scandals*. George M. Cohan had played the street, *Abie's Irish Rose* had run on it for years, first in the Fulton and then in the Republic. Later on there were offbeat but fun attractions like Huberts' Flea Museum. Whenever you felt lonely at three o'clock in the morning, you could always come to 42nd Street.

"When we crossed over past Sixth Avenue, we were shocked

---

*Papert's Ford Foundation grant was a mandate to fulfill the committee's stated objective: "To rescue West 42 Street from four decades of misuse and neglect . . . and create a river-to-river grand boulevard that would become a magnet for private investment, visitors, jobs and tax revenues, and have a major impact on the economy of New York City." The committee's original board of directors included Papert, Jacqueline Kennedy Onassis, Gerald Schoenfeld, and Father Rappleyea, the pastor of Holy Cross Church on West 42nd Street.

and horrified by what we saw. Drug dealers were operating out in the open, half-naked prostitutes were everywhere, and old men were propositioning young kids in front of the amusement parlors, in broad daylight and plain sight. And, of course, there were the rows and rows and rows of peep shows and sex stores that seemed to go on forever.

"We both just stood there staring in disbelief, and I kept thinking to myself, over and over, my God, how did all this happen?"

ACT NOW!

On the occasion of NIGHT OF 100 STARS at Radio City Music Hall on February 14, 1982, the following petition was presented to Mayor Koch:

Dear Mayor Koch:

PLEASE — stop the demolition of the Morosco and Helen Hayes Theatres until the Broadway Mall issue is resolved.

There is intense opposition to the Mall even among Portman proponents. If the Mall is not approved Portman must re-design the hotel, since without the Mall the hotel would extend illegally onto Broadway. The existing build-over alternative could allow the hotel to go forward immediately, even without the Mall.

Today we are in a theatre that was almost destroyed by the wrecking ball. We, the undersigned, representing more than 100,000 public petitioners and 10 public interest organizations and theatrical industry Unions, call on you to give us your promise that there will be no demolition of the theatres until the Mall issue is resolved. (The petition was signed by, - in alphabetical order):

Jane Alexander	Clare Copley	Doug Henning	James D. Pinto
Steve Allen	E.A. Cortese	Judd Hirsch	Anthony Quinn
Don Ameche	Anthony Cortino	Celeste Holm	Charlotte Rae
Loni Anderson	Joseph Cranzano	George S. Irving	Tony Randall
Barbara Armstrong	Joseph Cuervo	Kate Jackson	Robert Reed
Lucie Arnaz	Arlene Dahl	Judith Jamison	Christopher Reeve
Beatrice Arthur	Elonzo Dann	Ann Jillian	Jason Robards
Edward Asner	Michael Davis	Van Johnson	Pernell Roberts
Lauren Bacall	Sammy Davis Jr.	James Earl Jones	Cliff Robertson
Catherine Bach	Lennard DeCarl	Debra Louise Katz	Mickey Rooney
Pearl Bailey	Annie M. DeMille	Howard Keel	John Rubinstein
Kaye Ballard	Robert DeNiro	Barbara Kelly	Donald Saddler
Martin Balsam	Colleen Dewhurst	Alan King	Farouk Salik
Priscilla Barnes	Placido Domingo	Jack Klugman	Isabel Sanford
Jewel Baxter	Alfred Drake	Frances A. Kolan	Nina Seely
Harry Belafonte	Sandy Duncan	Ted Knight	Mark Settembre
Jeanna Belkin	Nancy Dussault	Burt Lancaster	Werner Sherer
Tony Bennett	Patricia Elben	Frank Langella	Sylvia Sidney
Milton Berle	Alan Eisenberg	Linda Lavin	Alexis Smith
Jack Beutel	Douglas Fairbanks Jr.	Baayork Lee	Don Smith
Theo Bikel	Peter Falk	Michele Lee	John Springer
Pam Blair	Greg Fauss	Jack Lemmon	Maureen Stapleton
Tom Bosley	Irene Ferrari	Dorothy Loudon	Anna Strasberg
Danielle Brisebois	Jose Ferrer	Myrna Loy	Lee Strasberg
Jerome Brody	Peggy Fleming	Gavin MacLeod	James Stewart
Marlene Brody	Jane Fonda	Penny Marshall	Beatrice Straight
Candace Broecker	John Forsythe	Mary Martin	Donald Sutherland
Irving Buchman	Phyllis Frelich	Jerry Masarone	Willard Swire
Ellen Burstyn	Eva Gabor	James Mason	Daniel J. Travanti
Tony Cacciotti	Rosemarie Gardner	Maureen McGovern	Cicely Tyson
Candy Carell	Melissa Gilbert	Ethel Merman	Liv Ullmann
Diahann Carroll	Farley Granger	Dina Merrill	Peter Ustinov
Nell Carter	B. Richard Grant	Ann Miller	R. Van Perry Sr.
Dick Cavett	Charles Grodin	Liza Minnelli	Ben Vereen
Richard Chamberlain	Henry Grossman	Anna Moffo	Thommie Walsh
Cher	Arne Gundersen	Roger Moore	Jack Warden
James Coco	Harry Guardino	Jeanne Nicolosi	Allen Weisinger
Alexander H. Cohen	Robert Guillaume	Leonard Nimoy	Henry Winkler
Charles Honi Coles	Larry Hagman	Jerry Orbach	Iggie Wolfington
Alvin Colt	Valerie Harper	Al Pacino	Lynn Wood Wolfington
Barbara Colton	Julie Harris	Joseph Papp	Debbie Zehnder
Pamela Cooper	Helen Hayes	Hildy Parks	
Joan Copeland	Florence Henderson	Gregory Peck	

Join the petitioners above. Tear here and send now.

COALITION TO SAVE THE THEATRES:
Actors' Equity Association Committee to Save the Theatres,
(212) 869-8530 x 342

Lenore Loveman and Sandy Lundwall, Co-Chairs
Save Our Broadway Committee, Joan K. Davidson, Chairman
American Federation of Television and Radio Artists,
National & New York Local
American Guild of Musical Artists
American Guild of Variety Artists
Screen Actors Guild, New York Branch
Society of Stage Directors and Choreographers
Treasurers and Ticket Sellers, Local 751 IATSE
Theatrical Wardrobe Attendants, Local 764 IATSE

Mayor Edward I. Koch
City Hall,
New York, N.Y. 10007

Dear Mayor Koch
PLEASE — stop the demolition of the Morosco and Helen Hayes Theatres.

Name _____

Address _____

City _____ State _____ Zip _____

JOIN OUR READ-IN MARATHON.
STARTS TODAY, 12:30 pm,
MOROSCO THEATRE.
217 West 45th Street

ARLY IN 1976 Gerald Schoenfeld received a call from real estate developer Richard Ravitch, who wanted to have a meeting about his moribund Manhattan Plaza apartment project.

Schoenfeld: "I had never met Ravitch before, but I agreed to meet with him now and his partner, Irving Fisher, as a representative of the Special Projects Division of the Theater League. They knew I had testified in favor of the project, because I believed a new, middle-income residential complex on 42nd Street would be a great help to the whole area, that good uses drove out bad uses, while bad uses attract other bad uses.

"So we got together, and that's when Ravitch told me he and his partner could no longer meet the payments on their $95-million mortgage, and was there any way I could help them out? I understood the implications of what he was saying. Should he default, the city would lose the entire $95 million. Then he dropped a bomb on me when he said Manhattan Plaza was therefore going to be converted by the state into unrestricted Section 8 housing, which happens to be the lowest level of subsidized public housing there is.

"I quickly had some studies done and every one came back with the same conclusion: Section 8 housing always brings down the neighborhood it is put into. I then called Richard back, who suggested I talk to another one of his partners, real estate developer Seymour Durst. I got Seymour on the phone. He listened politely to my objections, said no thank you, and hung up."

Fred Papert had also found out about the impending default on

Manhattan Plaza from Ravitch. He had already begun to focus his 42nd Street Development Corporation on the deteriorating situation on West 42nd and, like Schoenfeld, was disturbed when he heard what the city had in store for Manhattan Plaza. Ravitch had called Papert to see if he had any ideas about how to save the complex if the new state-funded housing deal fell through. If so, according to Papert, Ravitch was ready to pledge $2 million of his own money to Papert's committee.

Ravitch sounded a bit anxious, and Papert thought he knew why. Ravitch and Durst's original deal with the Lindsay administration had included a 5 percent private developer's fee to come out of the city's designated $95 million, payable to Ravitch upon completion. The designation of that fee had also made him, by law, personally liable for all accrued costs if for any reason the project wasn't finished. At the time, the trade-off appeared to Ravitch a low-risk way to make $5 million. Now, after being stalled for five years, should the Section 8 plan fall apart, it was his neck on the chopping block.

Papert agreed with Ravitch that Manhattan Plaza needed to be completed, but for different reasons than the developer and Schoenfeld. Papert saw it as the potential anchor for the revitalization of the old Theater Row west of Eighth Avenue that had briefly flourished under Irving Maidman before the sex merchants had moved in and converted all the theaters into peep shows and massage parlors. Papert knew that any new, nonporn development would help attract new, legitimate development money and maybe drive some of the porn out. He told Ravitch he would see what he could do.

As Papert later recalled, "Seymour Durst was a dear friend of mine, a really terrific guy, with a definite opinion about the situation. What was funny to me about the whole thing was that Seymour had at first believed strongly that the government should stay completely out of it and not bail Ravitch out. Ravitch and Durst were classic capitalists and believed in the risks as well as the rewards of private enterprise. Of course, that didn't prevent them from taking the $95-million construction loan and the completion bonus from the Lindsay administration. That's the way business is done in the big city. It did, however, leave both of them seriously exposed. If the project went into bankruptcy, which now seemed a very real possibility, in addition to Ravitch's $5-million bonus, all those tax breaks that Durst had taken up front would have to be paid back, immediately and in cash. That's why they both suddenly changed not just their positions regarding the deal but their entire political philosophies. Durst and Ravitch had both gotten involved with Manhattan Plaza as private investors, and now suddenly were pushing the government to impose Section 8, just to save their own financial asses.

"At the same time Schoenfeld, who had recently joined the board of my new 42nd Street Development Corporation, was vehemently opposed to the unrestricted Section 8 plan because he thought it would further bring down the economy of whatever was left of the neighborhood. He feared it would turn Broadway into a slum, and worse, the Shuberts, who owned a lot of midtown property, into slumlords. So there I was, in the middle of two completely opposite points of view in a situation that needed to be reconciled, and at the moment I didn't have a clue how to go about it."

Schoenfeld, meanwhile, supported by Durst, decided to take matters into his own hands: "I couldn't wait any longer, so I went to see a fellow by the name of Roger Starr, the city's representative for HUD [the state-run Department of Housing and Urban Development]. I told him Section 8 was a bad idea and he needed to come up with a new plan to keep it as a middle-income project.

"'I don't have to do anything of the sort,' he said in a rather high-and-mighty tone that made me furious. I decided to try to push him a little. 'Well, if you don't,' I said, 'you're facing lawsuits from the Shubert Organization, the Broadway Association (of which Durst was President) and Papert's 42nd Street Development Corporation. You'll spend the next ten years of your life in a courtroom.'

"'Yes, well, you know what? Nobody cares,' he told me, still calm and disinterested. 'Everybody's already written off the west side of 42nd Street.'

"I couldn't believe what I was hearing. I leaned forward, lowered my voice, and said, 'Well I haven't. I can't believe to save a hundred million dollars' worth of subsidies the city might or might not get back, you people are willing to destroy not only whatever is left of the Broadway theater district but the entire west side all the way to the waterfront.' I didn't wait for his response. What could he say? I got up and walked out.

"A few weeks later I was having dinner with Alexander Cohen, the famed theatrical producer, and eventually our conversation turned to Manhattan Plaza, and after listening to the problem, he said matter-of-factly, 'You know, that place would make a great actors' bedroom.'

"I put my fork down and stared at him. 'That's the answer,' I said excitedly. 'Leave everything to me.'

"The very next day I went to the office of Actors' Equity, the performers' union, secured their cooperation, and went to work to bang out a deal that would bring peace to all the warring factions. Upon completion, 70 percent of all housing in Manhattan Plaza was to be given to those directly involved with the performing arts, 15 percent was to go to the Clinton residents—people already living in the neighborhood—and 15 percent was to be set aside for the elderly and the poor."

The new plan was presented to the city, which held the outstanding mortgage, and was given the green light. Construction resumed, and by the middle of 1979, Manhattan Plaza was ready for occupancy. Under the terms of the agreement, rents at the Plaza were strictly controlled by the government, with most tenants paying a maximum of 25 percent of their arts-related income, up to fair market value, with any negative difference to be made up by federal subsidies.

Although the plan was designed to help three groups that desperately needed housing—starving artists; local residents, whose economics could be defined by the area they lived in, Hell's Kitchen; and the elderly on fixed income—as it turned out, politics, not poverty, became the decisive qualification for admittance. One of the Plaza's first occupants was Tennessee Williams.

Having heard about the new complex, he applied for and was given a spacious one-bedroom apartment that overlooked the Hudson River. On his application form he checked the special eligibility box and wrote in the explanation section that he felt he was entitled to one of the apartments because of a combination of his theatrical credentials and the existence of a chronic infirmity. The smell of bougainvillea and hibiscus rising from the Plaza's gardens, he claimed, would be a great comfort to his ailing back.

When Rodney Kirk, the original managing director of the Plaza, was asked by the *New York Times* to explain why Williams had been pushed to the head of the long line of applicants, he replied, "What the community said to me was, don't create a slum." Angela Lansbury was the second occupant.

There may have been a far more practical reason for the early celebrity stacking. According to Gerald Schoenfeld, "We had a problem getting people to move in. No one wanted to walk across 42nd Street between Seventh and Eighth Avenues to get to their apartments. They felt it was too dangerous, and surrounded by all that porn and filth, even if at the other end was a gorgeous two-bathroom apartment with air-conditioning, a health club, and tennis and handball courts. It took a while to get filled, and Tennessee's presence certainly helped legitimize the place."

Finally, according to Papert, although Schoenfeld was a board member of the 42nd Street Redevelopment Corporation, "We never got two cents from Richard Ravitch, let alone $2 million."

E ARLY IN 1978, as the Manhattan Plaza crisis was slowly getting resolved, newly elected mayor Ed Koch, who'd kept his distance from the West 42nd Street subsidized housing development, teamed with Governor Hugh Carey and came up with a revised package of city and state incentives worth a total of $21.5 million and an additional $18 million UDAG (Urban Development Action Grant) from the federal branch of HUD, as the first step in their plan to lure Atlanta-based private developer John Portman back to the city for another go at building his hotel in Times Square. The new package was sweetened with a proviso that would allow Portman to turn the three blocks of Broadway from 45th to 47th Streets into an enclosed pedestrian mall, for which his hotel, built on land to be donated by the city without cost to him, would then serve as its central, unifying structure.

Koch's proposed revival of the Portman deal made the front page of the *New York Times* and, as Lindsay had always known it would, set off a divisive firestorm of protest within the Broadway community that split it into two opposing factions when it was revealed that the new hotel necessitated the demolition of those four Broadway theaters—the Astor, the Bijou, the Helen Hayes, and the Morosco. The fact that Portman also promised, as part of his abatement deal, to build a theater in his hotel the same way Minskoff had in his office building meant little to either side.

Kent Barwick, president of the Municipal Art Society, spoke out against the plan. He was vehemently opposed to the destruction of the Helen Hayes and Morosco, theaters that both he and his organization considered worthy of immediate landmark status. Barwick's aesthetics meant nothing to Koch, who was even more eager than Lindsay had been to see Portman succeed, believing the new hotel and pedestrian mall were exactly what the financially strapped city needed to give it an enormous and much-needed kick start out of the red. Barwick and MAS pushed for public hearings on whether the two theaters should be designated as landmarks, which, if granted, would not only have prevented their demolition but once and forever put an end to the Portman project.

To his surprise, Barwick was met with rigid opposition from those he had assumed would be among his strongest supporters, among them Fred Papert. Whatever Papert's true feelings may have been he had his own reasons for not backing Barwick. He did not want to get on the "wrong" side of an issue the mayor felt so strongly about—a mayor whose cooperation on the redevelopment of West 42nd Street was going to be crucial.

When Papert backed Koch over Barwick, many of those involved on both sides immediately suspected it had more to do with politics than preservation. Then, again to Barwick's surprise, the MAS itself backed off. Joan Davidson, at the time a member of the MAS board of directors, later blamed "a lack of unity" (presumably Papert's reluctance to go up against Koch) as the reason "the Portman Hotel [became MAS's] one major lapse. There was a moment when, had all the major forces joined, I think then we could have forestalled everything that [followed]. Nobody got the point except a few theater people. . . . The {New York} Times didn't help; Ada Louise Huxtable was late [with her editorial support], and the MAS was concerned not to duly antagonize the big players."

In truth, everyone even casually involved in the situation had "gotten the point." Both the Helen Hayes and the Morosco, despite the impracticality for modern production that had resulted in recent years in their being dark more often than not, would easily have qualified for landmark protection. Nevertheless, not so much as a single hearing was ever held. Instead, Koch, reportedly angered by Barwick's strong opposition, became more determined than ever to stand behind Portman, even when the developer's 1978 budget doubled from his original 1973 estimate of $150 million, an increase Portman passed on to the city, which Koch immediately approved for payment.

In the spring of 1978 Koch delivered on the promised land-site grant to Portman, worth in the vicinity of $21.5 million. His pockets now filled with municipal money and commitments, Portman had no trouble finding additional private investors and tenants. Several new corporate players eagerly wanted in to the project, cash in hand, including a group of midtown's bluest-chipped players, most notably the Equitable Life Assurance Society (the venerable company that had funded the *New York Times* seventy-five years earlier), Metropolitan Life, Manufacturers Hanover Corporation, and the Marriott hotel chain.*

The only group (besides Barwick) willing to openly oppose Koch was what Joan Davidson had dismissed as those "few theater people" who believed the mayor had sold out Broadway. To those opposed, Portman's building a high-rise meant more than the loss of four theaters; it also threatened to destroy one of the last of the

---

*The details of Lindsay's rezoning of midtown west made investing with Portman all that much more desirable. The commercial zone line zig-zagged through two major plots, allowing for the construction of the Uris Theater (now called the Gershwin) on 51st–52nd Streets between Broadway and Eighth Avenue and Portman's project, what would eventually become the Marriot Marquis hotel and theater. The zone lines specifically exempted these two structures from the adjoining building limitations, and allowed for the addition of plazas, arcades, vehicle lanes and ports and, for Portman, because of his theater, even more square footage and height "bonuses." In the end, Portman was able to build approximately twenty-five times his initial "footprint," or designated raw footage, nearly a third more than the rezoning initially allowed. Schoenfeld then demanded equal concessions from the city for some of the Times Square Shubert property in need of renovations and was denied permission. His organization wound up having to share the boundaries of Shubert Alley with the rear of the Minskoff building, in what amounted to a jarring clash of turn-of-the-century eloquence (the Shubert and the Booth) with the contemporary look of black glass and steel.

low-rise areas in Manhattan that still enjoyed the luxury of having sidewalks and windows bathed in morning and afternoon sunlight. In one last-ditch desperation effort to stop Koch and Portman from burying midtown in seventies skyscraper-black, Actors' Equity, the players' union, formed an ad hoc committee called Save Our Broadway.

Unfortunately for them, even within this tight pocket of resistance there was dissension. Not only was Papert noticeably absent, so was Gerald Schoenfeld, who only a few years earlier had been one of the strongest opponents of the Minskoff project. This time around, the head of the Shubert Organization was among Portman's most vocal supporters. "I was for the project," Schoenfeld later said, "because I had come to the conclusion that the key to saving everything was a viable strategy to protect our economic borders. I thought an investment of $300 million in the center of Times Square was the best way to show that the neighborhood and its theaters were alive and well. That's why I came out in support of Portman, even if it meant the demolition of the Helen Hayes and the Morosco. Yes, they were the equivalent of theatrical houses of worship, but temples without congregations are empty and therefore worthless."

According to Broadway actress Celeste Holm, "Schoenfeld didn't care if they tore down those theaters because they weren't his. He was prevented by law from building any new ones, so getting rid of a little bit of the competition was just fine with him." (Schoenfeld: "Celeste is a dear friend, but was no more aware of my motives than the man in the moon.")

Anti-Portman sentiment was also expressed by Robert Brandt, Louis Brandt's son and at the time vice president of the Brandt Organization. The Brandts were another of the family dynasty landowners in Times Square who, like the Dursts, favored private enterprise over what Brandt defined as government "interference." A year earlier, in 1977, Brandt had finally carried through on his promise, first made to Lindsay in 1973, to reconfigure one of his many Times Square holdings back to its original legitimate stage proportions. The Apollo Theater on 43rd and Broadway became the "New" Apollo, where *Bent* opened with Richard Gere in the starring role. *Bent,* about imprisoned homosexuals during the

Holocaust, managed a respectable, if not blockbuster, run. The point was, according to Brandt, the conversion had been done, and a legitimate theater was brought back to (or in this case around the corner from) 42nd Street, and, as Brandt was quick to point out, "without any financial assistance from the city, the state or the federal government. However, after *Bent*'s brief run, the Apollo turned dark again.

The stage was now set and the opposing forces gathered for what promised to be a major showdown. On one side stood those in favor of government-funded corporate redevelopment and economic stimulation of Midtown West. On the other, the city's physical and creative preservationists. Each saw its side as saviors forced by the other to become soldiers in what looked to be the definitive turf war over property, profit, culture, and political power on these sidewalks of New York.

F RED PAPERT WAS ALWAYS more effective as the coach who called the plays from the sidelines than as the quarterback who ran them on the field, one of the reasons he had been able to sidestep a direct confrontation with Koch over the continuing conflicts of the Portman project. Even as the battle continued to rage a few blocks to the north, Papert, with Koch's political support and the Ford Foundation's open checkbook, quietly but determinedly kept his focus on the far west end of 42nd Street.

In 1979, under the auspices of his committee, he began acquiring whatever 42nd Street properties became available. He was able to get office space in the old Crossroads building directly south of the Times Tower, after which the city ousted its only other tenant, a street-level peep show (a space it then donated to the MEP, Beame's federally funded midtown police force).

Although his committee wouldn't hold any ownership in them, Papert helped broker a deal for several new apartment houses to be built west of Eighth Avenue believing their street levels would attract new, upscale restaurants. He also managed to find a new home on West 42nd Street for Playwrights Horizons, a performance group that had lost its original Theater Row site in 1974 when the space was rented to a peep show. Papert also rescued designer Raymond Hood's legendary blue-green Art Deco tower, the McGraw-Hill Building, which had stood empty for years awaiting demolition, by working on the successful campaign to get

A detail from an artist's rendering of "The City at 42nd Street." (Courtesy of Richard Weinstein)

it declared a landmark. Soon after, he relocated his committee's headquarters there.

Encouraged by his run, Papert began to formulate a larger plan. The biggest problem he'd faced so far in trying to restore 42nd Street was having to do it piece by piece, which meant having to start from scratch with each parcel, each tenant, each fund-raising campaign. A better way to go, he now believed, was to use the same effort to take on an entire block in a single sweep, and the one he wanted was the Seven/Eight that had been so savaged by porn, prostitution, and drugs. Papert knew better than most that this raunchy strip had once been the crown jewel of 42nd Street. With its eight historic but rapidly deteriorating turn-of-the-century theater palaces—the New Amsterdam, Victory, Liberty, Lyric, Harris, Selwyn, Times Square, and Empire—Papert believed it was the perfect block to be retrieved in one sweeping act of reclamation and then properly restored to glory.

He thus focused all his efforts, talent, and skills on the Seven/Eight corridor and fully expected the city to support him. Sure enough, Ed Koch, grateful for Papert's having stayed out of the Portman situation, assured him that when the right time came, he would have the city's full support.

Koch's word was good enough for Papert, who wasted no time in setting up a series of meetings with Roger Kennedy, the vice president of the Ford Foundation, his longtime friend and business partner (and whose foundation continued to provide financial support for Papert's committee), to come up with a workable plan. Kennedy's office was on East 42nd Street in the foundation's lavish New York City headquarters. One day, after spending much of the morning with Papert discussing possible ways the committee might take back Seven/Eight, Kennedy decided to take a walk over to West 42nd, a neighborhood he consciously avoided, to see for himself what the once-glamorous New Amsterdam Theater, which Papert had so enthusiastically described, actually looked like.

When he got there, he was stunned by the dramatic, tattered and torn but still-there beauty of the grand old playhouse, made even more vivid by the yellow-windowed storefronts selling porn and peep shows that surrounded it. While staring at the entrance, he had the flash of an idea. Why couldn't the Ford Foundation, which was always being approached by small, underfunded, non-tax-exempt dance companies for grants, help Papert's committee simply buy the New Amsterdam, then give it to all the dance companies to share, a strong first step in taking back the rest of the street?

The next day Kennedy had a little research done for him on the once-grand Art Nouveau showplace and discovered that in its prime, the New Amsterdam was often referred to as Broadway's "House Beautiful." That in its better days, Eddie Cantor had once performed on its legendary stage, Fred Astaire had danced on it, W. C. Fields had cracked wise from it, Fanny Brice had musically charmed from it, and Flo Ziegfeld's hot, leggy chorus babes ("The Glorification of the American Girl," as the great producer described it) had high-kicked across its luxuriantly wide proscenium. Then, in the 1950s, after years of being a second-run movie house, the theater had been sold to New York radio station WOR-AM, which turned the once-magnificent roof garden into its prime broadcasting studio. The New Amsterdam was sold again a few years later and in the seventies reduced to a porno flick emporium before going completely dark.

Kennedy phoned its present owner, Mark Finkelstein, to see if the theater was available for purchase. Finkelstein eagerly took the call. He was losing $500,000 a year in maintenance and taxes on the empty and decrepit theater, so when Kennedy asked about its availability, Finkelstein assured him it was *very* available. He even arranged to give Kennedy a private backstage tour.

A few days later, standing on its legendary proscenium confirmed Kennedy's belief that a refurbished New Amsterdam would be the perfect site for a Ford Foundation–funded dance-troupe cooperative. The next morning he called to ask how much Finkelstein wanted for the theater. Eight million dollars, he replied without hesitation, and quickly added it was nonnegotiable. Kennedy told him the figure was probably too high, but he'd see what could be done.

He then approached the mayor about the possibility of the city sweetening the deal for the foundation with tax abatements and other incentives similar to the Minskoff and Portman packages. A few days later Koch came back with an offer of a loan from the city to Papert's committee for $1 million to be put toward the purchase, and no tax incentives. Kennedy thanked the mayor and said he would let him know what the committee decided. He then considered bypassing the city completely and going directly to the Ford Foundation to have them make what would be for them a rare outright "retail," that is, "unsweetened" purchase, something no nonprofit organization liked to do. However, even before he could put a deal together, the dance companies he had contacted about the possibility of using the New Amsterdam began feuding with each other over things like access, individual creative control, and financial autonomy. That proved the breaking point for Kennedy. Fed up with Finkelstein's high asking price, the mayor's stinginess, and the dance companies' hostilities, he told Papert to forget about the deal.

Not long after, the *New York Times* ran an editorial, on March 18, 1979, that indirectly criticized Koch's lack of enthusiasm over trying to save the New Amsterdam:

> *Right now, 42nd Street is a stalemated mix of squalor and splendor . . . looked at purely for its physical attributes, it is a fabulous street, with a magnificent assortment of superior structures and spaces, and what would ordinarily be considered an ideal urban mix. . . . The stretch between Seventh and Eighth, dominated by adult movies and sleazy pornography, is actually a nearly continuous row of some of the world's most beautiful theaters built in the first decades of this century. . . . This incredibly undervalued block has been thrown away as a cultural resource . . . no other city could, or would, let this all go down the drain.*

The piece caught the attention of Don Elliot, deputy mayor and city planning commissioner under Lindsay. He and Papert had also been talking for a while now about the idea of a total-block reclamation of the Seven/Eight. Still, Papert, who had been surprised and disappointed by Koch's low offer to Kennedy, decided it might be better if he remained, for the time being, involved but firmly in the background.

The next person Elliot contacted was his onetime cohort from the Lindsay days, Richard Weinstein, who, a few years earlier had

Richard Weinstein (left), a Lindsay administration alumnus who, along with fellow Lindsay man Dan Elliot, helped develop the original plan for the City at 42nd Street. (Courtesy of Richard Weinstein) *Don Elliot (right) believed Koch's resistance to the City at 42nd Street was based on the mayor's longstanding personal animosity toward Lindsay.* (Courtesy of Don Elliot)

gotten the Ford Foundation to underwrite the original design of the Minskoff Theater, and who'd accompanied Lindsay the night the mayor went to visit the developer to convince him to include the theater in his high-rise.

Weinstein, like Elliot, had been part of a group of young New York sixties intellectuals so inspired by the election of John F. Kennedy that upon graduating from college they did volunteer work on political campaigns before beginning their "real" careers. Lindsay particularly liked Weinstein's youthful energy and fresh New Frontier attitude and, shortly after being elected mayor, offered him a paying job in his new administration. Weinstein was assigned to work with Don Elliot, Lindsay's chief policy guide before becoming deputy mayor. Working side by side, Elliot and Weinstein found they shared an ability to travel with relative ease between New York's highly competitive corporate world and its cultural movers and shakers. Weinstein made good use of these connections, and when Lindsay left office at the end of 1973, Weinstein took a position with the Rockefeller Foundation to study design applications for possible future projects, which is where he was when Elliot called him.

Weinstein: "My office was on the fifty-fourth floor in the building next to the Museum of Modern Art. He had been running the reclamation idea by me, and as we tossed ideas back and forth I realized I was looking out the window and down into the museum's garden. I started drifting. He asked me what I was doing. I told him, and out of nowhere he asked me the size of the garden plot. Not much, I told him, then pulled up the exact size of the parcel, to which he replied that it was big enough to build a fifty-story building on top of. I then asked him what the annual revenues would be from a building like that. He thought about it for a second and said about $4 million. 'Not enough,' I said, and laughed. 'You'd need at least $6 million to make that space work.'

" 'You could get it and maybe more,' he said without laughing, 'if you worked the right tax deal with the city.'

"I hung up the phone, started thinking about what he said, and quickly realized he was exactly right. I did a little research and discovered that in 1976, the bicentennial year, when Beame first began to turn the fiscal crisis around, he had formed something called the New York State Trust for Cultural Resources, whose sole purpose was the issuing of bonds against revenues from joint cultural/commercial developments. The kicker was that taxes from these developments were to be used to retire the bonds. This, of course, was where Koch had 'found' the money to lure Portman back to New York. I knew there must have been plenty more of that kind of designated revenue lying somewhere in a closet that Koch probably didn't even know was there.

"Don and I got together that weekend and kicked around the germ of a notion of building a new high-rise on top of an existing, even open structure on 42nd Street, maybe one of the old theaters that would be restored in the process, and using city bonds and taxes to pay for it. It was kind of a combination of the Grand Central Terminal plan and the Portman deal. That was the real beginning of what eventually became 'the City at 42nd Street.'"

Elliot brought the idea to Papert, who refined it, suggesting the new committee try to make a deal with Koch for the city to buy the old theaters with bonds and tax abatements from Cultural Resources, after which the air rights would be sold to private developers, with a portion of that money used to pay for the restoration of the theaters.

Koch's reaction to Elliot's and Weinstein's presentation, according to several witnesses at the meeting, was distant and formal, but in the end he agreed to consider the project if and when the group produced sufficient letters of intent from legitimate private developers for the air rights. It was enough for Elliot and Weinstein to take the project to the next level. The two then approached Kennedy's Ford Foundation, which loved the idea and agreed to join the project's committee.

To acquire the letters of intent, the three needed to bring in at least one power developer with enough experience to be able to put down on paper exactly how the finished project would look. During a brainstorming session they agreed that the man with the best creative vision and practical know-how to do the job right was Paul Reichmann, co-owner with his two brothers of Olympia and York, the giant and powerful Toronto-based real estate development firm that had recently made several successful high-profile moves into Manhattan.

Reichmann, an Orthodox Jew, was still largely unknown—some felt unknowable—to most of the longtime power brokers and politicians of New York City. Yet, when the committee approached him, he proved surprisingly amenable, and after their first meeting, Reichmann told Elliot how much he wanted to be involved in the redevelopment of West 42nd Street. (What he didn't tell Elliot was that he, Reichmann, believed that if successful, the redevelopment would dramatically increase the value of all properties in and around the Times Square area, including Reichmann's most prized and to him drastically undervalued New York City possession, 40 million square feet of the fourteen-building Rockefeller Center complex.)

The group came up with a proposal for what it called the City at 42nd Street, a 6-million-square-foot carnival of culture, with events, exhibits, theaters, showcases, and amusements in the middle of a matrix of restored theaters alongside new theaters, office buildings, and hotels. Two new high-rises would be built at the northwest and southwest corners of 42nd Street and Seventh, and a third would replace the Times/Allied Chemical Building. An IMAX theater, a series of dance arenas and concert halls, and professional, working film, television, and radio studios would all operate twenty-four hours a day. One of the passenger "tubeways" was to lead out of the Fashion Hall of Exhibits directly to a giant fashion mart that was to extend from 42nd Street to 40th. All of it was to be linked by various walkways and those modernistic tube tunnels into one gigantic, urban theme park stretching from Seventh to Eighth Avenues, from 41st to 43rd Streets. As they stated in their formal proposal, the City at 42nd Street would be "a celebration and investigation of urban life, a panoply of praise to the life and spirit of a great city."

The committee had no difficulty in finding nonprofit organizations eager to be included. Columbia University's Film School, which had been searching for a permanent off-campus location, quickly agreed to relocate to the City at 42nd Street, where the public would be welcome to observe students learning their craft and to view their works in progress.

To fund the fashion mart, they went to New York real estate tycoon Harry Helmsley, who already owned most of the buildings on Seventh Avenue immediately to the south of 42nd Street, in the city's Garment District. The mart would bring buyers from all over the world to a single gigantic showroom where they could gain exposure to every major garment and textile house in the world. Helmsley loved the idea and signed on.

Weinstein: "We envisioned a promenade of restaurants and retail shops, a modern communications and information center, and towering over the entire complex, three brand-new high-rise office buildings and several hotels. We wanted to have Disney-like three-dimensional figures everywhere that used projected animation to make their faces look real. For instance, we were going to have a Leonard Bernstein exhibit in which it appeared that Bernstein himself was narrating your look-behind-the-scenes at the Philharmonic. And one with Pavarotti singing, and then explaining what an opera production was all about. We planned on converting the old Victory Theater into a mini-Met, a place to put on small-scale operas that are never performed in New York, a La Scala two-thirds reduced in size.

"Everything was to be content-rich and scripted by New York's best writers. Perhaps my favorite thing of all was the gigantic 'slice of the apple,' one long, continuous peel, a concept not unlike the Guggenheim, where, as you walked along starting from a hundred feet below New York's streets, you viewed one long progressive, life-size cutaway of the infrastructure of the city—the water, electricity, gas, and cable systems—until you reached the top of the World Trade Center. At each hundred-foot-high level the view of the actual city would change, so that as you'd pass by, you could, for instance, see *through* the rose window of St. Patrick's Cathedral. That was the beauty of this exhibit. What does the city look like at a hundred feet up? At two hundred feet? When you got to the top, you were ready to go on a four-hundred-foot Ferris wheel at one end of the development that curved out over Seventh Avenue as it went around. If you were on it facing north, you could see straight up to Central Park, and south down to the lower tip of Manhattan."

"By the end of '79 we had letters of intent from Olympia and York and Helmsley-Spear," Elliot later recalled. "The two strongest developers in New York City had put in writing that they were ready to build on 42nd Street."

Preliminary estimates for the cost of buying back the Seven/Eight's seventy-three individual parcels from its fifty-eight separate owners came in between $70 and $143 million. *If* they could convince everybody to sell; a big if, especially once they discovered how difficult it was to find out exactly who owned what property. Layers and layers of leases, subleases, subcontracts, and assignments blurred the facts of actual ownership. This process alone, Elliot realized, would take years, unless Koch put some of the city's political muscle behind the project.

While Papert continued to offer guidance, he remained firmly planted in the project's background, while Elliot smartly filled his committee with New Yorkers whose very names exuded power, money, and influence, all of whom would be difficult for the mayor to ignore or turn down. He chose John Gutfreund of Salomon Brothers, the leading investment banker in New York City, to head the group that now included, besides Elliot, Weinstein, and Kennedy, NBC News anchor John Chancellor; Broadway director Hal Prince; Howard Clark, the retired chairman of American

Express; John Ganz Cooney from the Children's Television Workshop; James Hardy, the president of the Dreyfus Fund; Al Zeigner, chairman of the Port Authority; businessman Martin Stokes; James Trees, a highly successful bond salesman; and I. W. Barnes, all of whom promised to support the project in any way they could.

With this high-caliber roster in place, Elliot went back to Koch and was able to convince the mayor first to petition the Urban Development Corporation (New York State's Economic Development Corporation in charge of condemnation and reclamation of any and all land in the city and state) to condemn every parcel on the Seven/Eight block by invoking the state's right of eminent domain, and then to have the city grant the committee a first payment of $40 million to begin the buyout of the property owners.

Elliot: "We did a detailed evaluation of the block, and eventually found that, in fact, the largest amount of space we were dealing with was vacancies. Most of the buildings were old, one story or two, with porno in the storefront and either small theatrical family businesses above, barely able to hold on, or just empty rooms filled with boxes of porn, warehouses for the retail outlets. Also, we discovered there was virtually no money coming to the city from what should have been an incredibly profitable street. Under our plan, we would actually tear down much less than we would build up. And because we were so far ahead of the market, the land was going to be evaluated by the courts as not worth very much, which we believed would make the project that much more attractive to the city, especially in terms of the potential for future profits. As hard as we tried, we couldn't find a downside to the plan."

Elliot's committee had already raised $1.5 million in private seed money and acquired the support services of one of the street's oldest and most influential investors, the Equitable Life Assurance Society, which donated both money and staff for the committee and also hired Holloway and Schlager, two of the best real estate financial managers in the country, to oversee the entire operation.

"Our strategy was the same that Disney had so successfully used at Epcot," Elliot said later. "Once the core money was in place, the idea was to use that credibility to attract other major corporations to the project, to finance their own exhibits. On the strength of Helmsley, Kennedy, and Olympia and York, Coca-Cola was set to come in, and a dozen other major companies were already knocking on our door. As far as we could see, we were poised for a much bigger success than even Disney had achieved in Florida.

"And we had the numbers down cold. Our research had told us that the projected number of people who would visit the City at 42nd Street annually was 40 million, 13.5 million of which earned more than $25,000."

The meeting with Koch was set, and Elliot made his presentation. After quietly sitting through it, Koch dropped a bomb on the committee, calmly informing Elliot, Weinstein, and Kennedy that theirs was not the only plan for West 42nd Street on the city's table. At least two other groups of private investors, Koch told them, had also submitted redevelopment proposals. Moreover, Koch said, there was already the rumble of growing opposition among the present landowners on 42nd Street over the threat of eminent domain. However, he told them, he was still interested in their plan and would get back to them. The three left, disappointed but hopeful.

T HE MAYOR HADN'T BEEN blowing smoke. The property owners on the Seven/Eight block of 42nd Street, following the Lindsay administration upzoning, had been waiting for years to sell their parcels to deep-pocket developers for big profits. Having sat through a long recession, during which the battles over Manhattan Plaza and the still-unresolved Portman project had taken center stage, they now faced the possibility of having their property taken away by the state for a fraction of what they believed they could get in an openly competitive market. They had quietly informed the mayor in no uncertain terms they would fight any plan that included government reclamation.

Metropolitan Life, the current owners of One Times Square, also opposed the plan, fearing the old Times Tower would face mandatory demolition at a buyout price far below what they knew the building, and more important the land it sat on, were worth.

Also opposed to the plan was the Brandt Organization, already at war with the city over Portman. Robert Brandt knew that eminent domain could seriously devalue all his various 42nd Street properties, even those not on the Seven/Eight, and, besides, he objected on philosophical grounds to any form of government claim on the private ownership and businesses of hardworking tax-paying citizens. Writing a guest editorial for the *Wall Street Journal,* Brandt labeled the City at 42nd Street nothing more than "a thinly disguised land grab for developers."

Mark Finkelstein, the owner of the New Amsterdam, who'd originally turned down the million-dollar offer from Kennedy, and who now faced the possibility of losing his theater for an amount likely to be far less, called the project a public disgrace. In his opinion, the best way to help the theater and its environs was to beef up police protection around Times Square and simply force the police to drive out the porn and the drugs.

Seymour Durst thought it outrageous that the mayor would even *consider* asking the state to force him to sell his parcels at what would surely be a considerable loss.

Gerald Schoenfeld also came out against the plan. The problem for him was Elliot's insistence on the inclusion of landmark status to all eight theaters on the street, restoring them and then bringing in nonprofit, city-subsidized shows to compete with the Shuberts' privately financed productions. Schoenfeld remained steadfastly against any form of public subsidies for professional theaters and considered landmarking an indirect form of just such an endowment.

Even the *New York Times*'s Ada Louise Huxtable had her doubts. In a column she wrote for the paper, she questioned whether West 42nd Street was even eligible for condemnation, citing the Times Tower and its news zipper among the many other legitimate businesses that were as much an indigenous part of the neighborhood as the porn parlors. What would really be accomplished, she asked, by an across-the-board condemnation?

In April, Elliot, believing that in spite of the many public denunciations of the project, his committee was still the front-runner, confidently told the press that the City at 42nd Street intended to return all eight of the city's once-great 42nd Street theaters between Seventh and Eighth to "their former glory *and then some.*" On the basis of that statement, director Hal Prince came out in support of Elliot's plan and announced his desire to personally supervise the Lyric's renovation with an eye toward using it as an experimental performance space. He was warmly welcomed by the committee as Elliot believed Prince's involvement lent enormous prestige and credence to the project.

Interviewed on April 3 by labor leader and writer Victor Riesel on his WEVD radio program, Elliot used the broadcast to try to pressure a still-undecided Koch to approve the plan. He walked Riesel's considerable listening audience through the outline of the plan, assuring the audience that the way the plan was laid out, in the end it would wind up not costing the taxpayers a cent. "The problem in the past," Elliot told Riesel, "was that the government tried to find ways of spending the public's money to improve things, when in fact the heart of this city's development should come from private investment." Most of the money for his project was already in place, Elliot said, from three primary sources: Harry Helmsley of Helmsley-Spear, Roger Kennedy of the Ford Foundation, and Paul Reichmann of Olympia and York.

Nevertheless, Koch, who never liked to be publicly pressured, considered Elliot overconfident and arrogant, and remained undecided about whether to throw his support behind the City at 42nd Street.

Things then became a bit more complicated when organized protests were staged in front of City Hall by several minority coalitions claiming the planned "gentrification" of 42nd Street would destroy what had become, over the years, the city's only legitimate, if de facto, black and Hispanic entertainment "zone."

"It was amazing," Weinstein said. "In response we hired an anthropologist who spent three months riding around in a police squad car on 42nd Street to get a firsthand look at what was actually happening. It turned out this was the most crime-ridden block per square foot in the city. Ironically he produced irrefutable data that clearly showed it was, in fact, black children who were among the street's biggest victims. These 'chickens,' as they were called, were hung out in the arcade game rooms until they were picked up by older men, taken back to hotels, and molested. Also, it turned out that more black adults were being robbed and stabbed and in some cases raped on 42nd Street than any other group. This is what they were protesting to save."

According to Bill Daly, the MEP at the time strongly suspected that the Gambinos, to protect their own interests, had hired some of the so-called protesters. And still others looking at the situation believed one or more merchant organizations on 34th and 14th Streets had also secretly funded several "protests," fearing that if blacks and Hispanics were displaced from 42nd Street, they would make those streets their next favorite "hood."

IN APRIL 1980 KOCH appointed Herbert J. Sturz, tall, gangly, jocular, and articulate, to be the new chairman of the City Planning Commission. Sturz had been deputy mayor for the first two years of Koch's administration and was a savvy politico who knew how to get things done. At Koch's directive, Sturz's top priority became the City at 42nd Street. On April 28 Sturz told Elliot he intended to "cut through the red tape" and that a decision from the mayor would be forthcoming.

Sturz, like Koch, in theory, at least, favored a broad-based cleanup of 42nd Street, particularly the Broadway/Eight corridor. "It wasn't so much the pornography," Sturz later explained, "as it was the drug dealing, solicitation, and robbery. People were being hassled in one way or another whenever they came near the street, just trying to get to wherever they were going." He just wasn't sure the City at 42nd Street plan was the best way for the city to go about it.

Then, in early May, after yet another month of indecision, word began to leak to the press (Sturz was almost certainly the source) that Koch was going to pass on the Elliot plan. On May 23 the *Daily News* made it official when it reported that the mayor had decided to "delay face-lifting 42nd Street," after one final, "heated session" that had taken place at the Ford Foundation between Elliot's team and the mayor.

That meeting had indeed taken place, one Papert considered so crucial he decided to attend it in person, his way of reminding the mayor that favors were owed. It was, in every way, a disaster. As he later recalled, "We'd made up a model of the entire City at 42nd Street, twice as big as a typical dining room table. The thing was

Herb Sturz, Mayor Koch's City Planning Commissioner, advised against going forward with the City at 42nd Street. (Rebel Road, Inc.)

full of glitz, lots of gold and silver and shiny lights, because we wanted to capture the theatrical, fabled, legendary spirit of the Seventh–Eighth Avenue block, and get the point across that this was the cultural center, really, of the world.

"We showed it to Koch at the Ford Foundation's headquarters on 42nd Street, which, in retrospect, was probably one of our biggest mistakes. The place was way too 'Wasp' for him. He was obviously uncomfortable and made no secret of the fact he hated being there."

Weinstein agreed. "Just being summoned to the Ford Foundation to see that mock-up of the project made Koch a nervous wreck. He was out of his element in the Wasp establishment's premier house of culture. Roger Kennedy was a remarkable man, without question, but probably a bit too elitist for Koch's taste, and at the meeting, for whatever reasons, his mere presence rubbed the mayor the wrong way."

The main sticking point at the contentious meeting became Koch's refusal to have the city go along with the condemnation of all the property along the street. What was the point, he wanted to know, of taking it out of the hands of one part of the private sector, which had admittedly let it go to seed, only to give it to *another* part of the private sector?

There was precedent for this kind of deal, Elliot reminded the mayor. Lincoln Center had been created from a similar arrangement in the sixties, and a nine-block parcel in Greenwich Village made up of private housing and merchants had been condemned in the fifties by the city and then sold to New York University. The land that Rockefeller Center sat on had been acquired in a similar manner. The essential difference with the 42nd Street plan was the notion of private investors taking over the condemned property directly, rather than the city, buying out the existing landowners out of their own pockets, and then using abatements to help restore the existing properties and finance the building of new ones.

The meeting ended with Koch telling Elliot he would have his answer in a few days. The mayor waited a full week before calling a press conference at City Hall to announce his administration was officially severing all ties with the City at 42nd Street. Standing before a battery of microphones, cameras, and lights, Koch angrily referred to Elliot's well-publicized plan as "junk" and "a monstrosity." Making his famous prune face and raising both arms, he shrugged his shoulders and declared that the main problem with the project was "too much orange juice and not enough seltzer." Laughter rippled through the reporters. "They want to build Disneyland between Seventh and Eighth Avenues!"

Elliot and Weinstein were devastated by the mayor's vicious dismissal and couldn't understand where they had gone so wrong. The only thing they could come up with was that Koch's rejection had less to do with the quality of the plan than it did his own agenda of political vengeance. Koch was known for holding professional grudges (according to one close associate, "forever"). Both Elliot and Weinstein had been key players in the Lindsay administration and now convinced themselves the problem was personal, that Koch's longtime hatred for the former mayor was at least part of the reason he had pulled the plug on them.

According to Elliot, "There had been bad blood between Lindsay and Ed Koch that lasted a long time after Lindsay left office. Koch had been furious at Lindsay ever since he first ran for mayor way back in '65. Koch was then the district leader of the Independent Democrats of Greenwich Village, which was the southern-tip contingency of the Seventeenth Congressional District, which had also been Lindsay's district when he was a congressman. Koch desperately wanted Lindsay's congressional seat and broke ranks, crossing party lines to endorse him even though he was a Republican. Koch figured when Lindsay was elected, he would pay Koch back by helping him get it. Lindsay was elected but didn't support Koch's bid for the seat. Koch then turned around and attacked Lindsay over the Queens housing controversy. Lindsay then supported Cuomo over Koch in the '77 mayoral race. Koch never forgave Lindsay for any of it."

Weinstein: "We completely underestimated the bitterness that Koch still harbored. I think Koch feared that the worst-case scenario would be that if successful, because so many of us were Lindsay administration alumni, the project would ultimately be remembered as that mayor's legacy to the city and not Koch's."

"What nonsense," said Herb Sturz. "One of the first major policy decisions I had to make when I became city planning commissioner was what to do about Don Elliot's proposal. What I discovered early on, for better or for worse, was that Koch had never been particularly enthusiastic about the project. What Elliot apparently doesn't remember is that from the beginning, I thought the mayor should entertain other plans, or else throw the whole thing open to a public bidding."

One week after Koch's press conference, the *New York Times* published an editorial with the heading "Starting Over in Times Square." It called for Koch to waste no time in revealing his alternative plan for saving 42nd Street, urged the mayor to get on with the redevelopment of Times Square, and gave him a light spanking for "allowing sponsors to push their hopes and campaign so far" before tossing it out.

In an editorial on July 10, 1980, the *Daily News* came out wholly in favor of Koch's decision. It said that "Koch pulled the rug from under the 'City at 42nd Street' [and] these misguided amateurs [who] want the city to work with the current owners of porn palaces to improve the area. Talk about inviting the fox to guard the hen coop!"

According to one observer close to Koch at the time, "They [Elliot and Weinstein] got what was coming to them. They were a bunch of spoiled elitists thrilled with their own 'brilliance.' They wanted to turn midtown into some kind of joyride that almost certainly would have bankrupted the city. Koch may have had his own reasons for killing the project, but instinctively he was right on the money."

Kent Barwick summed up the situation this way: "Weinstein and Elliot, even when they were still with the Lindsay administration in the early seventies, had the careless arrogance of the very young and treated everybody, including then-Congressman Koch, as if they were all nothing more than footmen. These were a group of supersmart college hippies who loved flying around in David Rockefeller's Learjet in an administration led by a mayor who looked like a movie star surrounded by guys fifty-five and overweight. They thought they knew 'who was who'; at the time Ed Koch was most definitely not on that list, and they treated him accordingly. Koch remembered each and every one of them, I'm sure, and when the time came to make his decision, he knew exactly who it was he was dealing with."

There may have been some truth to Elliot and Weinstein's suspicions that Koch had sabotaged them just to get back at Lindsay, and Herb Sturz's job was to justify the actions of his boss. Still, it was difficult to come to any conclusion that did not take into consideration the fact that Elliot, Weinstein, and the rest of their committee might have seriously overestimated their own influence and power, and by doing so let slip from their fingers a golden opportunity to take control of the city's destiny and their own.

The defeat so devastated Weinstein, a lifelong New Yorker, he permanently relocated to Los Angeles, where he began a new career in education. Elliot withdrew from public service and went into private law practice. Kennedy returned to his duties at the Ford Foundation and for the rest of Koch's time as mayor had nothing more to do with 42nd Street. Papert also withdrew from the Seven/Eight project and once more refocused his energies on the revitalization of off-Broadway theater activity farther west, and his newest goal for the crossroads of the world: the restoration of long-gone trolley service on 42nd Street river-to-river, to make the boulevard more sociable. Trolleys, he insisted, were great places for people to meet and make new friends.

Koch, meanwhile, having cleared the field, that August announced a new plan that called for the state and federal governments to come up with $600 million—the same amount Elliot's original buyout projection had wanted—to help him turn Times Square into "the world's greatest entertainment district." The money, Koch explained, was to begin the payout to property owners after condemnation, which he now favored as the first step in his plan to rebuild the Seven/Eight. He estimated that the time from groundbreaking to completion would be five years.

The *Times* reacted quickly, calling Koch's broad-stroke strategy more of a "plan for a plan, hurriedly devised over the past two weeks."

In response, Koch announced he was already actively at work with HUD, on a revised set of operational guidelines, and shortly after issued an official RFP—request for proposal—from any and all private developers who might want to be involved with the project.

What particularly struck a lot of people about Koch's new guidelines was how closely they resembled the ones for the City at 42nd Street—the physical layout, the square footage, the enforced collective buyout.

Indeed, if the plans may have been similar on the surface, the key difference was in the vision. Rather than creating some kind of touristy theme park, or artificial-looking world's fair, Koch shifted the emphasis to restoration, his way of keeping most of the theater district people happy and, more important, in line. The other major difference was the increased amount of privatization. His plan called for four corporate towers instead of the original three, one at each of the corners of Broadway, Seventh, and 42nd Street. What was unique and brilliant about it was the inclusion of an idea that originated with Herb Sturz: to transfer the air rights above the restored theaters to the four corners as a way to finance both the restorations *and* the corporate towers.

He did it by having the City Planning Commission, which he

headed, amend Lindsay's original and severely limited upzoning provisions to allow for the "transfer of bulk." Lindsay's plan had been conceived to kick-start commercial redevelopment via tax abatements and bonus footage for the inclusion of new theaters. Sturz's allowed for the air rights above existing theaters to be transferred to the four corners as a way of justifying the condemnation of those properties, the right to build with private funding, and the simultaneous protection of the architectural integrity of the existing theaters. Without these key moves, there was simply no motivation other than cultural or P.R., which in reality meant no motivation at all, for private, corporate investment to buy into the redevelopment of the street.

Sturz's plan allowing for the transfer of rights was what the city had offered to do for the Penn Central Corporation during the Grand Central battle. It was an altogether brilliant way to get private investors to pay for the restoration of 42nd Street's theaters to their original beauty, because it allowed those who paid for it to build a high-rise for their trouble. In other words, to restore the street's cultural past, Sturz had provided the essential ingredient missing from Elliot's plan—a profit incentive to ensure its financial future.

Sturz still needed to find a way to legally develop the four corners while ensuring the rezoning did not leave the area's privately owned theaters vulnerable to redevelopment projects that would ultimately destroy Broadway's unique, low-rise theaters. While formulating his new program, Sturz conferred with Schoenfeld, and together they came up with the idea of a "special demolition permit" that would be required before any theater in the city could be torn down. While he supported the plan in theory, Schoenfeld would soon regret its existence, because he found it too restrictive. It not only made it impossible to sell a theater without the buyer agreeing to continue operating it as such, it also severely restricted unapproved remodeling and technical upgrading of any existing Broadway house.*

---

*Schoenfeld believed, as did many others, that the Reagan administration would be less inclined to regulate private enterprise. In 1982 the Shubert Organization submitted a formal motion to the federal courts that went uncontested, and as a result, that same year all limitations on the company building and expanding were permanently lifted.

W ITH THE WHEELS of his project turning, Koch turned his attention toward trying to finally resolve the Portman situation, whose progress had slowed to a crawl.

During the height of the City at 42nd Street crisis, on March 6, 1980, the *Times* had published another in its extraordinary series of unsigned editorials (many believed they were written by Ada Louise Huxtable) that took a longer view of what to do about the problems of midtown Manhattan. The editorial surprised and angered those in the theatrical community who remained against the project:

> *Broadway is currently casting the Portman Hotel as the bad guy in a municipal melodrama of greed and destruction. . . . It is particularly sad to see this script playing so well to the acting profession, which has a large stake in the survival and therefore revival of the Times Square theater district. . . . The project, which New York needs more than ever, was conceived seven years ago as a kind of dramatic and useful new construction that could spark a reversal of Broadway's long decline.*
>
> *That decline would not cancel out the loss of three {sic} theaters on the hotel site. But at least one adjoining theater, the 46th Street, would be restored, a new 1,500 seat theater {which would be called the Marriott Marquis} would be built as part of the hotel, and Shubert Alley would be extended another block. Theater people should also consider the long-term benefits of 2,000 first-class hotel rooms. . . . What the protesting artists are really telling us, correctly, is that New York cannot afford to lose its smaller, older theaters . . . but they have gotten their targets and heavies mixed . . . lovers of Broadway should concentrate on what they can gain, not on what they can stop.*

Theater impresario Joseph Papp had formed a committee to protest the project. It was led by some of Broadway's biggest stars, including Celeste Holm, Colleen Dewhurst, Irene Worth, Mildred Dunnock, Jason Robards, and Geraldine Page, all of whom wanted to know why the mayor they'd helped elect, one of the so-called saviors of Grand Central Terminal, had targeted a street on Broadway with two cherished theaters for demolition, while so many others in the neighborhood that had already been stripped bare by prostitution, crime, and open drug dealing remained untouched.

The answer, as the Municipal Art Society's Kent Barwick well knew, was not in the stars, but in the real estate. "Long before Joe Papp arrived on the scene, the upzoning of the Wesr Side had doomed the neighborhood. The devastation was far more serious than immediately apparent at the time, certainly to the demonstrators who, for all their sincerity, really didn't get the bigger picture. Portman was the final test case to see if Times Square could actually be turned into one more ugly but highly profitable corporate alley. All along 42nd Street were run-down low-rises whose ground floors were being rented to pornmongers, but whose second, third, fourth, and fifth floors housed hundreds of small, family-owned theatrical businesses that made their living from Broadway. If Portman were allowed to continue, they would surely be the next to go.

"The real endangered heart of the theater district was not the Helen Hayes or the Morosco, but the nondescript hundred-year-old office buildings on 42nd Street, which housed agents, managers, rehearsal halls with guys with cigars in the sides of their mouths playing old upright pianos while auditioning pretty girls singing 'Give My Regards to Broadway,' script services, wigmakers, makeup companies, violin bow makers, scenery people, prop people, costume makers, and cleaners. In truth, the entire underpinning of the theater industry was right there, in those crummy buildings, mostly craftspeople whose skills had been passed down from generation to generation. If Portman succeeded in opening the floodgates, they were all in danger of being displaced by a city administration desperate to corporately reconfigure midtown Manhattan, the point being, if and when the neighborhood went, they went. And once they were gone, along with their talents and their abilities, they were *gone,* and along with them the talent, training, expertise, and vitality of a hundred years' worth of theatricality. Portman was their collective death certificate."

The Atlanta developer remained openly defiant in his public dismissals of the theatrical community and its concerns. He referred in interviews to how he was the one who was going to save "the goddamn corny image of Times Square. . . . Maybe before the Helen Hayes and the Morosco there were a few little dry-goods stores there. Maybe they should have kept those li'l ol' buildings because they, too, had some historical context."

Two weeks later the actress Helen Hayes announced to the press her refusal to allow Portman's new theater in the base of his hotel to bear her name.*

O N JANUARY 14, 1982, nearly four years and countless delays, demonstrations, and denunciations after the hotel project had been revived, and nine years after its original conception, demolition finally began on the first of the theaters. The wrecking ball smashed headlong into the front of the Bijou, its marquee still advertising its final production, Barbara Perry's *Passionate Ladies,* and then continued on to the Astor. The Helen Hayes and Morosco avoided a similar fate only by their supporters obtaining one final last-minute stay from a federal appeals court, which they had asked to declare the two theaters *automatic* landmarks.

On March 5, during a blinding snowstorm, Papp, Lauren Bacall, James Earl Jones, Jack Gilford, Martha Scott, Jose Quintero, Elizabeth Ashley, and Christopher Reeve all stood together atop a makeshift platform outside the Morosco and read aloud from eight Pulitzer Prize plays, seven of which had been presented at the Morosco and one at the Helen Hayes. It was intended as a celebration of Supreme Court Associate Justice Thurgood Marshall's last-minute order that had once more prevented demolition at least through the weekend. After each of the celebrities read, he or she shared personal sentiments with the crowd. However, as the day went on, the snow fell harder, the wind blew colder, and the tone of

---

*It became the Marquis. Helen Hayes's name still graces a Broadway theater. The Little Theater, on West 44th Street, was built in 1912 and enlarged in 1920. The smallest Broadway theater, with 499 seats, in the fifties it was used as a popular TV studio, from where Dick Clark and Merv Griffin, among others, regularly broadcast. It was refurbished in 1987 to once more accommodate live theater, immediately designated a landmark, and soon after rechristened the Helen Hayes Theater. Hayes, considered by many to be the First Lady of American theater, died in 1993.

the speakers turned fatalistic. Arthur Miller characterized the demonstration as "either a funeral or a rebirth." Jason Robards (after reading from the scene in *Long Day's Journey* where the father tells his younger son that surrendering to commercialism had ruined his life) told the crowd, "I'm so heartsick. I feel it's the end of everything." Christopher Reeve said he wished he really were Superman so he could "stand there and just catch the wrecking ball and tear it apart." Joseph Papp called the proposed hotel and mall project a "cesspool." Alexander Cohen, who'd split from Schoenfeld over Portman, called the Portman hotel deal "corrupt all the way down the line."

The two-day stay stretched into two weeks before time finally ran out the morning of March 23, hours after the Supreme Court finally lifted Marshall's temporary restraining order. Dozens of celebrity onlookers watched in horror and dismay as two bulldozers tore into the facades of the Helen Hayes and Morosco Theaters. At the last minute, thirteen protesters, among them Celeste Holm, tried to block the heavy machines from continuing their destruction by putting themselves in the doorways of the two playhouses. All were arrested. "As I was standing in the rubble," Holm later recalled, "I looked up and could see the exposed shells of the dressing rooms that had once been used by Fanny Brice, Bob Hope, Fred Astaire, all the legends that had played there. That's when I realized all over again that decades of joy, humor, fun, excitement, and drama had been swept away in a flash. Just then, a policeman took my arm and said, 'Now don't get hurt.' I stared at him, wondering how I could possibly be any more hurt than I already was."

It was a chilling defeat for the protesters and a total victory for the mayor, who once again had demonstrated his private toughness and resolve, while continuing to smile into the lenses of the cameras as he ridiculed the protesters' attempt to halt something that was good for the city and therefore good for them. As one who was close to the scene later recalled, "Koch may have come across as a humble sentimentalist to the public, but those who dealt with him on a one-to-one basis knew they encountered a hard-edged, strong-willed manipulator. He'd managed to convince a lot of people, including many in the press, that what he was doing was actually

The Helen Hayes Theater (along with the Morosco and several lesser venues) was torn down in 1982 as part of the Portman high-rise hotel deal with the city. (Ms. Vivenne Maricevic)

The Marquis Theater, a tax-abatement compromise establishment lo-cated on the second floor of the hotel, has no Broadway marquee. The theater is accessible only through the hotel's mid-block entrance (the street-level box office is obscured here by construction). (Rebel Road, Inc.)

good for the city. This was a mayor with two faces, who worked behind the scenes to put his name on every street corner and then appeared in public moved to tears by such a tribute."

The idea for a pedestrian mall disappeared,* but the Portman hotel didn't, and in 1985, after a particularly long and difficult period of construction, it opened as the Marriott Marquis, complete with a fully equipped Broadway theater built into its base. It quickly became the most financially successful hotel in America. Whatever the actual cause and effect may have been, not long after Portman's new hotel opened, attendance at Broadway shows significantly increased, as Schoenfeld, from the start, had predicted it would.

However, so did the proliferation of porn shops, prostitution, and drug dealing all along West 42nd Street, from the Avenue of the Americas to Eighth Avenue and points west. No problem, Koch insisted. Just leave everything to him. From here on in, he told one and all, it was going to be nothing but smooth sailing. After which, the smiling, gesticulating mayor, the ever-loquacious captain of the good ship *New York,* led himself and the city straight into the worst political storm of his career.

*According to Schoenfeld, "Nobody except Koch ever really wanted the mall. It was a ridiculous and unworkable idea. However, if we had openly opposed the mall at the time, it might have very well killed the hotel. Once the federal grant money was in place, the site couldn't be moved, and that's when we voiced our opposition to it. It really had no support, and quietly disappeared from the drawing board."

PART THREE

WHEN YOU WISH UPON A STREET

B Y SEPTEMBER 1, 1980, Mayor Ed Koch had received dozens of proposals from several of the city's largest and most powerful private developers, including the Reichmann brothers and Harry Helmsley. Despite the official and, some felt, humiliating public dismissal of Elliot's plan for the City at 42nd Street, in which they had been major players, both still wanted in on whatever Koch had in store for 42nd Street. The slow selection process stretched into the following May, when to everyone's surprise, Koch divvied his plan into several smaller ones and handpicked new leaders for each.

To develop the four office towers and rejuvenate the subway stations, the mayor chose a relative newcomer to Manhattan development, George Klein, the head of relatively unknown Park Tower Realty. Klein's third major building in New York City, and only his first in Manhattan (the other two were in Brooklyn), had gone up a year earlier. Nevertheless, he suddenly found himself in charge of the key segment of Koch's 42nd Street project.

According to *Forbes* magazine, Park Tower Realty "had landed one of the great real-estate plums in New York City history: four giant office towers around a reborn Times Square, in the heart of Manhattan, with 4.1 million square feet of office space and generous incentives from the city that could make [Klein] one of the richest men in America."

What everyone wanted to know was why Koch had chosen

Ground zero. A pre-redevelopment view looking west from the southeast corner of Seventh Avenue at 42nd Street. Nedick's is in the foreground, and behind it are many of the retail establishments long associated with the street. In the midground is the Candler Building. In the background the McGraw-Hill Building. Note the New Amsterdam's iconic vertical marquee, a sign of the chronic shortage of commercial display space on the city's streets. The marquee would be retained during the theater's extensive renovation. (Corbis-Bettman)

The northwest corner of Seventh Avenue at 42nd Street in the 1970s, with the corner cigar store still in operation.

someone as little known and inexperienced for such an important, not to mention potentially profitable, assignment. Who was he, anyway, people wondered, and how had he managed to dance over the city's ready-to-rhumba real estate heavyweights?

George Klein was the son of Viennese immigrants who'd fled their native country in 1939, just before the Nazis began rounding up its Jews. Soft-spoken, bright, and articulate, Klein eventually took over the Barton's candy company his father had begun in New York City in the forties, a local retail chain with stores throughout the five boroughs (including, in the fifties, one on the south side of 42nd Street a few doors from the New Amsterdam Theater). Upon his father's death, Klein sold the Barton's chain, and with an initial investment of $25,000, founded Park Tower Realty. The fledgling company won its first major project in 1973 when the Lindsay administration awarded it a federal grant that funded several urban-renewal projects. Klein's assignment was to rebuild what had become a run-down derelict cross street in downtown Brooklyn (the intersection of Flatbush and DeKalb, site of the old Fox movie theater).

Notwithstanding the success of that venture, downtown Brooklyn was a million money miles from midtown Manhattan, and when chosen by Koch, Klein was still for the most part an outer-borough builder. Why, then, had Koch chosen him? For one thing, it didn't hurt his chances that Klein was, like Koch, a Jew born of European immigrants, and an outspoken supporter of Israel. Both men had an interest in Holocaust research, and both

The southeast corner of Broadway at 42nd Street—the site of the Knickerbocker Hotel, one of the so-called four "elephant legs" of the new 42nd Street. Built by the Astor family in 1902, the hotel, seen here in the early 1930s, fell into serious decline during the Depression. At one time the headquarters for News-week *magazine, the Beaux-Arts beauty was saved from the wrecking ball by the Landmarks Commission and is now being restored to its original splendor.* (Museum of the City of New York)

were members of a task force that would eventually lead to Klein's heavy involvement in the building of Manhattan's Holocaust Museum and Memorial. Without question, Klein was a full case of the "seltzer" Koch had claimed was missing from the Ford Foundation–funded City at 42nd Street project.

Klein also had strong connections to the Municipal Art Society, whose involvement with the saving of Grand Central Terminal had helped position Koch to make his successful run for mayor. Finally Koch believed Klein was well-thought-of by the new governor, longtime Koch adversary Mario Cuomo, whose cooperation in the administration of HUD's condemnation of all the land parcels of West 42nd Street was going to be not only necessary but absolutely crucial to its happening, as the agency operated at the state level and needed the governor's approval. Despite the chilly atmosphere that had lingered between the two politicians since the 1977 mayoral race, Koch knew he was going to need the governor on his side, and figured Klein might serve as the perfect go-between, if not an actual peacemaker.

According to Kent Barwick, "George Klein was a brilliant choice on Koch's part. Although he hadn't actually built very much in Manhattan, it was obvious early on from his accomplishments that he was special. His structures in Brooklyn had established him as being among the most talented and sophisticated of the new crop of up-and-coming developers. Also, Klein was an extremely religious person, an Orthodox Jew, which was important to Koch because Klein's personal aesthetic was infused with a deep morality that made him perfectly suited to the 42nd Street project. Both he and Koch were, on a spiritual level, totally against everything that was then endemic to the street—not just the porn, the drugs, and the crime, but all of it combined into some sort of a perverse urban carnival. Klein was exactly the right choice for a mayor determined to clean up 42nd Street. He was not someone who was going to fight to preserve the 'nostalgic atmosphere.' Quite the opposite."

There was, finally, one more reason. According to Koch, in his 1984 autobiography, *Mayor,* George Klein, whom Koch described as a very close friend, was not only one of the earliest donors to the mayor's already considerable war chest for the upcoming reelection campaign, he was also, by Koch's own admission, its single biggest contributor.*

Klein's appointment sent a clear message to the existing property owners on 42nd Street that the mayor intended to move ahead with this plan to invoke and enforce the power of eminent domain to reclaim all the properties between Broadway and Eighth Avenue.

Barwick: "Remember, the rezoning of the West Side of midtown Manhattan had been an article of faith for a long time. In theory, here's a neighborhood in the city that was a natural for development, and if you had property, the smart thing to do was to wait for the right time to name your price. What none of the property owners figured on, after the recession had delayed any real movement for so

*From *Mayor:* "[Klein was] at the very top of my list of campaign contributors when I ran for reelection in 1981 . . . and at the top of my list of contributors in 1982 when I was running for governor." In an interview with the author, Klein, although admitting to having been a "generous" supporter of Koch's reelection campaign, called Koch's claim "hyperbole" and said his records showed his contributions to the mayor's 1981 reelection campaign totaled only $4,100.

many years, and all the turmoil going on in Times Square over development, was what eventually became the primary reason nobody could get anything going. Not long after Klein's appointment, the long and bitter fight over the issue of condemnation resumed. With eminent domain there was not even any room for negotiation over the true value of their land because according to the law the court sets the value of state-appropriated land, and that's it. Game over. The property owners regarded what was happening to them as legally sanctioned theft at the highest and most corrupt level.

"As for the mayor, instead of sanctimoniously complaining about the proliferation of all this pornography as a reason to go in and take these people's land away from them, it might have been a bit more productive if he had stopped acting like he was doing them and the people of New York City a favor, and just for a moment tried to understand how and why it had all gotten there in the first place. Unfortunately developers and politicians aren't particularly skilled in that kind of thinking. Koch was, therefore, totally not only unprepared for but genuinely shocked by the reaction of the property owners on the street. He actually believed he was doing these 'struggling' landlords a favor by taking the burden of their low-rent properties off their shoulders, when in fact they were the ones who'd brought porn to the street in the first place in anticipation of the big payoff Koch was about to deny them.

"Believe me, nobody who owned property on that street saw Koch as their savior."

Once Klein was in place he suggested to Koch that he bring aboard Dallas-based billionaire and formidably successful real estate developer Trammell Crow to build a revised, closed-to-the-public version of the City at 42nd Street merchandise mart. Koch, however, split that contract between the New York-based Tishman-Speyer Properties, one of the city's most prestigious real estate firms, and Harry Helmsley. Larry Silverstein, like Crow a name not well known in New York, was given the air rights to three Eighth Avenue corners (the fourth was the Port Authority Bus Terminal).

However, the most shocking and bizarre action of all was Koch's choice of Michael Lazar, the head of a small financial management firm, the Cambridge Investment Group, to oversee the restoration of the eight historic theaters. Lazar, a member of the

City Council and former head of the Taxi and Limousine Commission, had no theatrical experience whatsoever. It was a puzzling appointment by any measure and one that would eventually come back to haunt the mayor.

Koch was now ready to approach the state to implement what he referred to as his 42nd Street Redevelopment Project. At first, Governor Cuomo appeared eager to work with Koch. Using *his* by-now-particular style of political hyperbole, he hailed the new plan to rebuild 42nd Street as "the greatest single private real estate development in the history of this great city, and state, and nation, *and probably beyond.*"

The private understanding between the two was a little more down-to-earth. They agreed that Cuomo would oversee HUD through the legal proceedings of formal condemnation, while Koch would supervise the Manhattan-based City Planning Commission (CPC). Koch would have final authority to resolve any and all disputes arising between HUD and the CPC. It was, at best, an arrangement certain to bring to the table a whole new set of problems.

It didn't take long. When HUD, with Cuomo's enthusiastic support, decided that before eminent domain could be invoked all the money to pay off the landowners had to be placed in escrow, Koch nearly hit his high dome on the one at City Hall. As Koch knew he would, and felt he should, Klein balked at having to suddenly come up with $600 million in cash. When the news of Klein's resistance reached Cuomo, whose relationship with Klein was not nearly as close as the mayor had assumed, the governor, ever suspicious of Koch's tactics and motives, began to suspect that what had been whispered about in the state capital was true. The word going around was that Klein was too much of a lightweight novice to handle such a key assignment and that Koch's awarding of it to him probably had less to do with professional credentials than political payback. Word soon came down to City Hall from Albany that the governor had serious doubts about Klein.

Koch responded by leaking word back to Albany that the following year, 1982, he might take a shot at the governor's seat as a stepping-stone toward a possible '88 run for the presidency. When Cuomo heard about it, he appeared to back off his criticism of Klein. The governor was too smart to be pulled into the Hudson on the losing end of another political power struggle with Koch. He still had the emotional bruises from their 1977 hardhead-to-hardhead confrontation in the race for mayor. A better way to go was to take a page out of Koch's own political playbook and wait for the right opportunity to flex his gubernatorial muscles, when it would do him the most good.

The chance to do just that didn't take long in coming. As soon as Klein complained about having to put up so much advance money, Harry Helmsley, still without a fully-defined role, sensing that he and all the other developers were at best about to be tapped for a hefty contribution, and at worst sucked into a deal that had insufficient funding to move forward, folded his cards and left the table. That was all Cuomo needed. As soon as Helmsley withdrew, the governor insisted the Morse family, a well-established upstate-based development corporation, replace Tishman-Speyer as the new head of the merchandise mart. Klein countered by putting Dallas billionaire real estate developer Trammell Crow's name into the mix, and quietly brought an apparently always ready and willing Equitable back into the scenario to underwrite the escrow fund account, thereby neutralizing Cuomo and everyone else on that issue.

The governor immediately challenged Texas-based Crow's qualifications, which infuriated Koch, who threatened to eliminate the state from the project completely. Not possible, a smiling and soft-spoken Cuomo reminded him, not if he wanted Albany to invoke eminent domain.

During these skirmishes, and in the wake of mounting pressure from the New York Times, the Daily News, and the New York Post, all of which were clamoring in print for Koch to get the project moving, in 1982 a closed-door meeting was arranged by Sturz. Both sides agreed beforehand they would either reach an agreement or call off the whole project. After a particularly acrimonious session, a compromise of sorts was reached, wherein all of Cuomo's chosen players and all of Koch's would have a role in the redevelopment project. To further protect the state's, and his own, interests, Cuomo insisted that someone from upstate, in this instance Vince Tese, chairman of the state-supervised Urban Development Corporation, be made chairman of the 42nd Street Development project and that Crow had to be removed from the merchandise mart.

Longtime rivals Mayor Ed Koch and Governor Mario Cuomo went elbow to elbow over who would control the redevelopment of 42nd Street and Times Square. (Corbis-Bettman)

Koch, realizing the future project hung on these two conditions, reluctantly agreed to both.

In 1983, after Koch made an unsuccessful bid to challenge Cuomo for the governorship, the MAS, under Barwick's leadership, and Gerald Schoenfeld officially distanced themselves from the 42nd Street project.

Barwick had grown increasingly dismayed at what he believed was about to happen to one of New York's most important streets: that it was going to be transformed by Koch into one more big-ticket corporate alley to benefit the city's fat cats and, no matter how the government tried to say otherwise, that it would be done at the expense of its taxpayers.

According to Barwick, "By 1983 it was clear the developers had lost sight of the historic side of the development. For instance, out of nowhere, Klein came out against maintaining any of the traditional lighted signs and billboards that were so much a part of the emblematic signature of Times Square. Why? Because he felt they were the 'wrong element' for the neighborhood. But signs and billboards also cut into valuable rental space. As far as the MAS and I were concerned, that 'element' was an invaluable part of the cultural uniqueness of 42nd Street.

"We asked Klein to consider a compromise, maybe setbacks built into the new high-rises as a place to put signage, which, in addition to being aesthetically pleasing, would allow more natural daylight to bathe the area. He was unresponsive. To make our point, we organized a demonstration one summer night where we had all the lights in the district turned off at the same time, to show what Times Square would look like if all these high-rises were actually allowed to block out the sun, and how pitch-black the entire theatrical area would be at night. We were trying to make the point that lighted billboards were not just unique and historic but *necessary*. What everyone sees in Times Square on TV every New Year's Eve is a huge, wide, unrestricted area filled with thousands upon thousands of people all standing in one big lighted bowl. That open, free look was what we were trying to prevent from being converted into another of the city's oppressively dark business districts."

"A toilet bowl," insisted Gerald Schoenfeld, "and I told Barwick so. The MAS's position, and that ridiculous lights-off demonstration, which, by the way, the Shubert Organization did not participate in, did nothing to help the situation. The MAS never did a single thing to help 'preserve' the theaters *already in* the theater district. Their record is zero to this day. They had no idea how appalling the conditions still were, not just in Times Square but throughout the district, or what the financial stakes were to those of us who actually made our living there."

Why, then, did Schoenfeld also pull away from the project?

"Fred Papert was making real progress with his Theater Row redevelopment on the West Side, in which the city had participated. All right, we could live with that, but when he began pushing Koch and his people to have the huge New Amsterdam Theater restored so it could become the home of regional, nonprofit theaters, and the mayor said he supported that idea, I drew the line. I reminded Mr. Koch that I had some credibility in my business and would not allow myself to be associated with something I knew simply couldn't work. I thought that had all disappeared with the City at 42nd Street, but when Koch's new plan intended to once again bring nonprofit theater to the restorations, I simply couldn't go along with it. Fred Papert, whom Koch had given all that city money to, stood with the mayor on this issue, so I promptly resigned from his committee and decided to have nothing further to do with the redevelopment of 42nd Street."

As far as Schoenfeld was concerned, Broadway's theaters were irreplaceable, but 42nd Street itself remained unsalvageable. "The Regional Plan Association was another alliance in the ever-more-crowded field of players to want to have a hand in the future of 42nd Street. They held a series of meetings and invited me to speak, which I did. However, I stayed out of the developments on 42nd Street. I felt it was something different than the rest of Times Square and the theater district. I just felt it couldn't be saved by anyone."

Barwick also suspected that Klein's reasons for opposing the lights, the billboards, and the building of frequent setbacks for signage into the four high-rises were less rooted in aesthetics than economics. Setbacks would significantly reduce the interior square footage of floor space and therefore cut into the potential rent profits of the buildings. However, after Barwick's dramatic lights-out demonstration (more successful than Schoenfeld expected or was willing to admit) and in response to the publicity and subsequent negative press brought about by the blackout, Klein agreed to reconsider his game plan. He hired the legendary, if controversial, Philip Johnson and another highly respected architect, John Burgee, to modify the design of his four buildings to allow for setbacks, signage, lights, and billboards.

The resulting plans recast the four "elephant legs," as the corner buildings were now being referred to by some in the press ("white elephant legs" by others), into typically postmodern New York City high-rises—tall, dark-windowed, and ugly but with setbacks. Despite everyone from the Municipal Art Society to Ada Louise Huxtable's strong criticisms of the revised blueprints, they were accepted without challenge by the city's Koch-controlled Planning Commission.

All that was left for ground to be broken was Klein and Equitable to put up the prerequisite $600 million earmarked for the condemnation payout fund. However, at the last minute, Equitable refused to front the entire amount, insisting instead that the high-rises' primary tenants should have to put up at least some of it. The only problem was, there were no primary tenants. With no actual ground having yet been broken, there wasn't any way to guarantee the buildings would ever actually get built, which made it extremely difficult if not impossible to get the kind of high-ticket good-faith investors Klein and Equitable needed to fulfill the state's financial requirements to begin construction.

For the next two years Klein searched, without success, to find a single primary tenant willing to put up so much as a dollar toward the properties buyout. During that time, nothing much changed on the street. Sex parlors, porn shops, prostitution, and drugs continued to flourish, with their landlords unwilling to evict them and lose that income, and the court refusing to grant eminent domain until Klein came up with the money to ensure the property owners due compensation.

Koch's great plan to redevelop 42nd Street slowly ground to a halt as he waited, increasingly impatiently, for Klein to come through. Then, on October 19, 1987, the Dow Jones Industrial Average dropped 508 points, 20 percent of its value, and plunged New York City and the rest of the country into yet another recession.

In the immediate aftermath of the market's collapse, none of Koch's original handpicked team of developers, with the exception of George Klein, were financially secure enough to fulfill their commitments to the city and the street and were forced to leave the project without having made or lost a single dime. Tishman-Speyer was the first to say good-bye, followed by Michael Lazar's Cambridge Investment Group. Lazar, originally put in charge of the theaters by Koch, was replaced by Larry Silverstine of Jujamcyn, the production conglomerate, who, after a very brief stay, also left. Equitable also joined the exodus, leaving George Klein as the last of Koch's original choices, and he was able to do so only at the last moment by managing to pull a very rich rabbit out of a very deep hat. Following a series of top-secret and extremely tense meetings, Klein managed to cobble together a new joint partnership with the Prudential Insurance Company, which had previously underwritten urban redevelopment projects in such difficult places as Newark, New Jersey, and the Embarcadero in San Francisco. Klein was able to convince Prudential that the stock market crash had, in fact, created a once-in-a-lifetime financial advantage that would allow them to build further below value and ahead of the inevitably rebounding New York real estate market than anyone had originally projected. Buy in on the dip, he urged them, and they'd make an even bigger fortune. Prudential said yes and agreed to put up the entire $600 million needed to keep the project alive.

Koch, anticipating a third reelection campaign two years down the road, and sensing political salvation in what appeared to be Klein's singular ability to save the 42nd Street project from becoming a major and lasting embarrassment, now offered him the chance to take over the entire project, including the restoration of the theaters. Klein took the deal to Prudential and got them to put up an additional $88 million as "seed money" for the development of the entire street and $25 million more, specifically for the restoration of the theaters. Prudential also agreed to become Klein's first and primary tenant, hoping to ignite a run by other companies. With this new and enormous financial base, and a partner with impeccable credentials, Klein was certain he would have no further trouble getting the courts to invoke eminent domain.

He was wrong. When the existing landlords realized Klein had met the legal requirements for condemnation, which no one thought he would ever be able to do, they refiled their class action into forty-eight individual lawsuits. Although the public, by virtue of the tabloid press, continued to see the issue as essentially the city versus the sex shops, in reality only a few First Amendment cases were brought by a relatively small number of porn-related businesses. Besides, eminent domain allowed for seizure and then a hearing to set the amount of the buyout. First Amendment issues were not going to decide or prevent that. The majority of the lawsuits were much more solidly based in individual challenges to the constitutional right of condemnation under the existing structure of eminent domain, a strategy that allowed the landowners to avoid immediate confiscation. Because they now had brought forty-eight individual lawsuits, their challenges could easily add years, perhaps decades, of new delays.

The lawsuits also destroyed any chance for Klein to find additional primary tenants. Things then got worse for him when the court directed that he and Prudential put up an additional 150 percent of the estimated value of the property to allow them to extend the time limit on their exclusive development rights while the lawsuits went through the system. Klein eventually worked out a legal compromise that limited the additional amount to $240 million, which Prudential then agreed to add to the escrow account, retrievable only after every last lawsuit was settled. In return, Prudential demanded and got from Klein the right to control all future deals of any kind related to the four high-rises, in effect taking control of that part of the project away from him.

Just when it seemed things couldn't get worse for the 42nd Street redevelopment plans of the mayor, political scandal huffed and puffed and blew down the Koch administration. Koch managed to stay above the ensuing fray, using every grimace and "oy vey" in his media-face repertoire to sell himself to the public as the helpless and unsuspecting victim of others in his administration, rather than a knowing participant in the most widespread network of corruption in New York City politics since the days of Jimmy Walker.

Things had first begun to publicly unravel as early as March, 1986, when Queens Borough President Donald Manes, the county's Democratic leader and a strong political ally of Koch, committed suicide. The investigation into his death eventually uncovered what amounted to an extensive network of municipal bribery, influence peddling, and various other forms of financial scamming that had included members of the Parking Violations Bureau, the Housing Authority, the Department of Environmental Protection, the General Services Administration, the Board of Education, the Taxi Commission, and sewer, electrical, and gas-line inspectors, all of whom had been appointed by the mayor and operated under his supervision.

It was difficult to see how Koch could not have known what was going on all around him. How else, for instance, could two key parcels on 42nd Street have been left out of the planned eminent domain seizure? One of these was where the legendary Candler Building sat, adjacent to the New Amsterdam Theater. Built in 1913 by Asa Griggs Candler, the man who made Coca-Cola a household name, the building, although not officially designated a landmark, was specifically, some thought suspiciously (because of its low occupancy and need for extensive repairs), omitted from the state's planned seizures of properties. In 1987, at the height of the investigation into the City Hall scandal, a journalist pointed out that Michael Lazar, already under indictment for his involvement in the Taxi Commission's part of a kickback scheme, was the same

Michael Lazar who had been Koch's original and—to everyone at the time—inexplicable choice in 1982 to lead the theatrical portion of the street's redevelopment. Lazar, as it turned out, happened to be the present owner of the Candler Building. The implications were devastating. By avoiding state condemnation, the inherent increase in value of the property after the development of the rest of the street would provide an enormous financial windfall for Lazar.

Worse for Koch, the former taxi commissioner had apparently bought the site at the beginning of the decade, well ahead of the market, not long before he had been made a member of Koch's hand-chosen development committee. This raised the very real possibility of conspiracy, deepened by the revelation that Lazar had made substantial campaign contributions to many of the elected city officials in Koch's administration still involved in the decision-making of the 42nd Street project.

Through it all, Koch was never legally charged with any wrongdoing, although many remain convinced to this day that because of his association with Lazar, he should have at least faced indictment on conspiracy charges. Lazar, meanwhile, was convicted for his part in the kickback scheme and went to jail.

AS 1987 CAME TO AN END, the future of West 42nd Street looked bleaker than ever. Hundreds of millions of dollars sat in untouchable escrow while Koch fought the taint of corruption and stared down the wrong end of at least another decade's worth of legal delays before any redevelopment might actually begin. It wouldn't take nearly that long before those untouched by scandal in Koch's administration began to put some distance between themselves and the mayor. Before the year was over, Herb Sturz, Koch's handpicked choice to head the City Planning Commission, resigned to join the editorial board of the *New York Times*. His departure was particularly difficult for Koch, as Sturz had given the administration its much-needed credibility in the theater community of Times Square, where he was well liked and his aesthetic sensibilities were trusted far more than the mayor's.

Koch replaced Sturz with Carl Weisbrod, from the Mayor's Office of Midtown Enforcement. With a background that included a stint working with the FBI, Weisbrod, unlike Sturz, was more enforcer than artiste. To some, Weisbrod's appointment seemed intended to send the message to the public, and the District Attorney's Office, that Koch was and always had been, an above-the-board, by-the-books law-enforcement mayor.

By 1989 the continuing fallout from the stock market disaster had decimated the city's real estate market and created a financial free fall among the city's developers. Even if every lawsuit connected to 42nd Street were settled in a single day, the economy was in such shambles it would have been impossible to find any company willing to invest anywhere in New York City real estate. In Midtown West, the half-dozen new office towers that had gone up to beat the expiration of certain abatements were suffering from large vacancies, with no hope in the foreseeable future of renting to capacity, even at deeply discounted rates.*

That same year, Ed Koch, the city's favorite uncle and self-proclaimed savior of 42nd Street, lost his bid for a fourth term and found himself out of politics, out of influence, and out of power, even as his protégé, George Klein, clung desperately to the hope of one day seeing ground break somewhere on 42nd Street. After nearly eight years, the public's perception of Koch had changed from that of the moral high-roader with wholesome chicken soup running through his veins to that of one more political has-been irrevocably tainted by scandal. He had wanted to remake 42nd Street into the ultimate monument to his own stature, historical importance, and moral character. Instead, as he disappeared from politics into the shadow of his own falling star, 42nd Street remained essentially unchanged from what it had been since the day he first took office: a neon nightmare of porn, drugs, and prostitution firmly in the grip of the Gambino family, whose new boss, John Gotti, the city's newest favorite son, was unmistakably on the make and irresistibly on the rise.

---

*Part of City Planning Commissioner Sturz's 1982 revised zoning plan had included a five-year "window," or limitation on new construction, included at the time to prevent unnecessary delays in commencing to build. Some felt Koch wanted this provision to ensure his plan for the redevelopment of 42nd Street was completed during his administration, guaranteeing his "legacy."

VEN AS KOCH'S ONCE grandiose plan to redevelop 42nd Street slid into political and economic free fall, a series of apparently unrelated events took place that, when added together, resulted in significant improvement of the boulevard's commercial redevelopment and redemption. Perhaps none of these was more crucial than the remarkable end of organized crime's hitherto unbreakable hold on the Seven/Eight strip.

By 1986, the height of Republican conservative Ronald Reagan's second-term popularity, pornography was more pervasive than ever in America. Ironically, during the eight years of "family values" politics, porn's ubiquitous over-the-counterculture had come completely out of the movie-theater closets of the raincoat crowd onto the bedroom VCRs of the cultural mainstream. And every op-ed pundit in the country thought he or she knew the reason why. In politically repressive times, "forbidden" pleasures become far more desireable. In an age of killer sex diseases, porn was as good a way as any to practice safe sex. Porn's popularity was a groundswell reaction to Reagan's embrace of the censorious Christian Far Right. Porn was guilt-free and therefore good. Porn was guilt-ridden and therefore great. In whatever permutation the balance of the truth lay, porn had become universal, a chic diversion for the young and wealthy, an obsessive dream in plain wrap for the working class, the miracle release for the pent-up passions of adolescence.

Mayor David Dinkins. Distracted by racial tensions for most of his one-term tenure, he proved ineffective in moving the redevelopment of 42nd Street forward. (Corbis-Bettman)

That same year, the Reagan administration began a nationwide double-edged assault against sexually explicit material. The primary thrust was geared toward the user, educating the public, as the administration put it, what many in the public took as intimidation. The war on smut became official when Edwin Meese, Reagan's attorney general, published his highly anticipated commission's report on pornography. Meese fiercely rejected most of the claims of an obscure (and bizarrely uncharacteristic) 1970 government study conducted during the Nixon administration called "The President's Commission on Obscenity and Pornography," which essentially claimed there was no significant cause-and-effect relationship between sexual crimes and what was then the relatively new phenomenon of widespread legalized pornography. Meese's report did not merely declare pornography "harmful"; it defined it as an evil cancer eating away at the moral fiber of the country.

It claimed the danger of a physical threat as well, using homophobically juggled AIDS-related statistics to blame gays for causing the spread of the new and terrifying disease. The extremists within the Reagan administration were quick to suggest that those who got AIDS deserved to get it and were suffering the retribution of a heterosexual, conservative God. The report called not only for legal reform of the increasingly liberal laws regarding pornography but also for a general outcry by the "public," the assumed monogamous heterosexual silent majority, with organized boycotts to be encouraged against the producers, distributors, and retailers of all (i.e., straight and gay) pornography.

Following Meese's report, *Time* magazine commissioned a poll and published its results that July. It showed that, in fact, 68 percent of all respondents believed pornography to be a "harmless fact of life," and 78 percent supported the public's right to buy it. The poll outraged the Christian Right, led by a suddenly ubiquitous Jerry Falwell, and fueled the antigay rantings of Lyndon LaRouche's extremist fringe, both of which called for and got the Justice Department to issue a ruling that allowed businesses to discriminate against workers with AIDS.

Meanwhile, in California a petition seeking to quarantine people with AIDS gathered nearly 700,000 signatures. Chain stores such as 7-Eleven and Rite Aid rushed to remove *Playboy* and

Penthouse from their shelves after receiving threatening letters from the Meese Commission that they might be liable and if so would be prosecuted to the fullest extent of the law for distributing pornography.

In the hope of restoring the pre-sixties parameters of the First Amendment, a series of federal cases was introduced in the fall of '86 to challenge the liberalized standards set by the Warren Court. In one of these cases the government gained the suspension of a student who gave a speech peppered with sexually explicit language. In another it was able to limit the distribution of sexually oriented material in certain instances on the grounds that it had become a public-health nuisance. Still another helped restrict what could and could not be openly displayed in bookstores. Social commentator Michael Novack told *Time* magazine that these latest skirmishes that ended with government victories, no matter how limited, marked the official end of America's expanding sexual revolution, which had begun with such a deep breath during the giddy, permissive sixties, and that the only hope for the country's moral future lay in its outright banning of pornography. "The coming theme for the liberal society is virtue and character," he stated. "In its youth America could claim that the sex shops on 42nd Street represented emancipation. Adulthood means learning to choose, and above all, to say no." It was a sentiment with resonance, supported by the Reagan administration, repeated over and over again in the eighties, and used as part of Nancy Reagan's "Just Say No" antidrug campaign.

The second thrust of the Reagan administration's antiporn campaign was aimed at its manufacturers and wholesale distributors in the guise of the New York Gambino organized crime family. In the fall of 1986 the FBI, working with the New York State Organized Crime Task Force, declared war on the heads of the city's Five Families and won convictions against several of them on various charges of racketeering. Sent away for long stretches were Anthony "Tony Ducks" Corallo of the Lucchese family, Anthony "Fat Tony" Salerno of the Genovese family, Carmine Persico of the Colombo family, and Aniello Dellacroce of the Gambino family. After what the *New York Times* called the "Waterloo" of mob rule, a generation of aging Mafia rulers had finally lost control of their respective organizations, which created a mob leadership vacuum that made possible the rise of the next generation of "bosses," among them John Gotti.

Sensing an opportunity, Gotti made a grab to take over as head of the Gambinos by putting out a contract on Paul Castellano, the assumed heir to Dellacroce. Castellano and Gotti had disagreed over the direction of the mob's financial interests. Castellano wanted to keep the family business firmly rooted in the past, in its lucrative concrete and road building operations on the other side of the Lincoln Tunnel in New Jersey, and sanitation extortion in Nassau County, while Gotti was anxious to expand the family's interests in its drugs and porn operation, both of which operated out of 42nd Street. In 1985 Gotti buried Castellano and became the new *capo di capi* of the Gambinos. His immediate goal was to intensify the family's involvement on 42nd Street by increasing the output of hard-core magazines and videos and stepping up the street distribution of coke, heroin, and marijuana. However, even as he was busy reorganizing the family's interests, the feds were closing their net around him.

The first of three consecutive New York–based trials of John Gotti (one federal, two state) began in 1987 but failed to deliver a legally sustainable smoking gun, and for the rest of the eighties, despite the government's best efforts, Gotti remained a free man. His acquittals, movie-star charisma, and romanticized lifestyle helped gain him the nickname the Teflon Don, as well as the support of the public, nowhere more so than in New York's blue-collar outer-borough population, where he cruised in style along the highway of organized crime, giving the finger to the government, which came off as nothing more than the ultimate motorcycle cop. To his adoring fans, the Teflon Don was just one more guy caught speeding times-a-thousand trying to get out of paying the fine. As his popularity rose, both his major products—pornography and drugs—particularly along 42nd Street, were more in demand than ever.

However, even as the nation's generals were hitting a brick wall in the courts, they kept the pressure up on New York City's street soldiers with threats to cut off federal funding for the Midtown

John Gotti, leader of the Gambino crime family in the late 1980s and early 1990s, was the mastermind behind the mob's deepening involvement in sex and drugs on West 42nd Street. (Corbis-Bettman)

Enforcement Project, if something wasn't done about the proliferation of pornography and the availability of hard drugs on the city's streets.

Because of it, and an incident in which a Times Square cop's life was threatened, in October 1987 the long-standing policy of passive tolerance toward street crime on 42nd Street underwent a fundamental change.

The mobilizing event took place in the Paradise Alley Peep on Eighth Avenue between 43rd and 44th Streets, where a low-level Gambino street dealer by the name of Raymond Washington, aka Aussie "Beaver" Chandler, was hawking nickel and dime bags of pot and individually wrapped hits of coke, speed, and heroin to the club's customers. For some reason Chandler liked to carry a black water pistol with him whenever he was dealing. That day, while conducting his business, he was approached by a tall man in an overcoat who said he was looking to score some crack. Chandler sold him a few dollars' worth, then noticed that on the way out, the fellow stopped, leaned over, and said something to three similarly dressed men at a table near the door. A few seconds later they all stood up. Two covered the exit, two headed for Chandler. The one who'd bought the crack shoved a badge in his face. Chandler reached for his toy pistol, and the undercover officer pulled his service revolver and opened fire. Beaver Chandler was dead before his body hit the ground.

The shooting brought cries of outrage from the police. A gun, drawn against a cop, even a toy one, was taken as a declaration of war. There had been an essentially unspoken agreement between both sides of the street to leave weapons out of it. Now the enemy had crossed that line, bringing an end to the era of passive tolerance. According to the MEP, this time the dealer had died; the next time it could be one of their own.

The new policy on the street became one of strict enforcement. If someone so much as threw a wrapper of gum into the gutter, the police were ordered to go for the collar. This was welcome news for a force that for years had taken heat from every candidate who ran for public office, from the mayor to the president, for the proliferation of sex, drugs, and violent crime on 42nd Street. Now the time had finally come to try to take it back.

The police hit the Seven/Eight with force. They worked in teams, ripping into the pimps, the porno shops, the peeps, and the parlors. Hookers were arrested in bunches, taken downtown, booked and held without bail. Nickel bag dealers were rounded up by the busload and thrown into Rikers, left to rot. To show not only that they meant business but how much business they meant, the police started to bust the civilians they normally left alone, the young men who bought the joints and hung out at the peeps, the husbands coming home from work looking for a quick lay. They even stopped John Qs just for being down the block, taking them into buildings and frisking them. If they didn't find anything, instead of apologizing, they warned their "suspects" not to come back to 42nd Street if they knew what was good for them.

This campaign was supervised by Bill Daly, the head of MEP: "I can tell you, by 1987 the street had degenerated even further than anyone thought it could go, into a place where everything and anything went down twenty-four seven. Prostitution, muggings, drugs, pedophilia, white slavery, bestiality, the more disgusting and degrading, the more prevalent. After the Chandler shooting, we were finally able to make some moves. That incident allowed us to shift our energies away from prostitution and pornography and squarely onto drugs, where it belonged. The first thing we did was close the Paradise Alley club down for drug dealing. Eventually we were able to get additional funding for a separate, new narcotics division, the Tactical Narcotics Team, or TNT."

Although the TNT hit hard and often, it had less of an overall effect on the drug situation on 42nd Street than the relentlessly deadly nature of the product itself, especially heroin and crack. While unit sales remained high, the number of buyers actually began to go down, simply because users were dying in ever-greater numbers from overdoses, self-starvation, AIDS, and what was known on the street as junkie old age (twenty real-life years). Ironically, although the police and the TNT were never able to effectively control the crack epidemic, the problem slowly began to resolve itself. Although everyone from Reagan to Koch would try to take credit for the gradual decline in the numbers of New York's street crack addicts, the hard truth was, most of the drug's heaviest users simply couldn't keep themselves alive. According to Lieutenant John F. Ryan, whose beat was the Port Authority Bus Terminal in the 1980s, "We'd find bodies every morning in the terminal, either dead or so close to death that we didn't know if they could be saved."

Then in '88, Ed Koch found himself surrounded by political scandal, and 42nd Street was necessarily relegated to low-priority status, replaced in urgency by the growing struggle the mayor faced for his own political survival. Meanwhile, that fall, the Republicans retained the White House in the person of George Bush, and the so-called moral crisis in America evaporated overnight from the front pages, from the political white papers, and from the public consciousness. Not long after the TNT was quietly disbanded, the police began to pull back from their confrontational stance, and the drug and crime problem on the street rebounded, worse than ever. In defiance of the mayor, the Meese Commission, the U.S. Supreme Court, the police force, the MEP, and the TNT, by the end of the eighties the Seven/Eight corridor remained in the iron grip of Gotti's Gambinos. Eventually, the dip that had taken place in the numbers of crack users flattened, then began to climb as new and younger users came to 42nd Street to discover for themselves how easy it was to buy whatever thrill they wanted.

I N THE FALL OF 1989, having finally had enough of Ed Koch, the voters elected David N. Dinkins to be their new mayor, the first African American ever to hold that office in New York City. A functionary-style Democrat with sizable strength among the black and Puerto Rican populace, Dinkins had based his campaign on what he called the city's "beautiful mosaic" of races and nationalities. His pledge to help bring everyone together while keeping "big government off the backs" of New York's working-class men and women sounded right, and gave Dinkins a historic victory, won with the narrowest margin of votes in the city's history.

His opponent was hotshot U.S. Attorney Rudolph Giuliani, a young, tough RICO-backed hardnose who'd made his bones battling Gotti's Gambinos.* If the press had made Gotti a Billy the Kid in thousand-dollar suits, they also made Giuliani his Pat Garrett. In 1989 Giuliani, riding a crest of popularity, ran for mayor. Although he lost this try at City Hall's brass ring, New Yorkers knew they had not heard the last of or from him.

David Dinkins inherited the economic mess left behind by the Koch administration, and throughout his single four-year term in office, as Abe Beame had to in the seventies after taking over from Lindsay, he struggled to keep the city economically viable, and, like Beame, was, at best, only partially successful. Unfortunately for him and the city, it soon became clear that the new mayor's worst handicap was his overall incompetence in the area of race relations.

Only a few months after he took office, a boycott by blacks in Harlem of a Korean grocer gave the mosaic mayor an opportunity to demonstrate his ability to fit together the city's beautiful individual pieces. Reluctant to criticize the bullying actions of the

---

*"RICO" is the federal Racketeer Influenced and Corrupt Organizations Act created during the Reagan administration to reinforce its war on organized crime.

blacks, he waffled, and the city's ethnic working-class populace once more felt the effects of neighborhood race polarization.

Things got worse in August 1991, when, less than two hours after a local Jewish leader's car went out of control in Brooklyn and accidentally killed a black boy, a rabbinical student was killed by a black street mob seeking vengeance. The incident set off four days of near riots in the borough, during which Dinkins's failure to show as much sympathy for the second victim as he had the first infuriated the city's white community, especially its powerful Jewish liberal contingency.

From that point on, no matter what the mayor did, he was cast in the role of racist by an outraged, at times pandering, tabloid press, which pointed to his behavior following the incidents in Brooklyn as "proof" of his failure to keep his campaign promise to bring racial harmony to the city. Both the *New York Post* and the *Daily News* continually published unflattering pictures of the mayor playing tennis, suggesting he was fiddling, as it were, while New York burned with racist hate. Dinkins's personal idiosyncrasies also became juicy tabloid press and local TV news fodder as details of his habit of taking multiple daily showers and obsessively changing clothes leaked out.

Better days for Dinkins came in the summer of 1992, when he managed to attract the Democratic convention back to the city for the first time in sixteen years. New York had not played political host to either of the major parties since 1976. The mayor counted on an economic boost to help lift the city out of its lingering recession. For the few days it was in town, the convention did elevate the city's spirits and helped fill cash registers, but neither result proved long-lasting, and by the fall, New York was once more in the grip of a down economy. Office buildings continued to suffer from huge vacancies, and retail business continued to either go under or flee to the tax-friendlier confines of the nearby suburban malls of New Jersey and Connecticut. That year, Alexander's, one of the city's oldest and best-known discount department stores, became the latest in a list of longtime New York retail establishments to go out of business under Dinkins's watch.

Then, six and a half months after the convention, on February

26, 1993, the World Trade Center was bombed by Mideast terrorists. The incident filled the people of the city with a new type of fear that drove them off the streets at night and into their homes, behind the safety of their own locked doors. Restaurants, theaters, and clubs all suffered further heavy financial losses, a downturn that hit the city's food and entertainment community especially hard.

While Dinkins was washing his way through his mayoralty, and despite Klein's and Prudential's repeated attempts to convince him to become involved with the now more than sixty active lawsuits from landowners fighting eminent domain on West 42nd Street, the mayor expressed little interest in doing something about the stalled redevelopment project. Some thought his priorities were understandable in the wake of the economically tumultuous first three years of his administration. Others had a different view, and interpreted Dinkins's resistance as further proof of his racially motivated politics. According to what one close to the situation recalled, "A lot of black and Puerto Rican people still felt, perhaps rightly so, that the Seven/Eight strip was one of the few blocks outside of Harlem they could more or less call their own. Going down to 42nd Street, going to the movies and getting a bite to eat had been a tradition among their people for decades."*

In truth, any talk of City Hall's involvement with 42nd Street immediately raised flags for the so-called ethnic community spokespersons who had Dinkins's ear, including the omnipresent Harlem-based Reverend Al Sharpton, the city's most self-righteous opportunist, who often confused militant iconoclasm with a malignant desire to become an icon. His unhealthy dash of anti-Semitism in the midst of the largest Jewish community west of Israel only added to Sharpton's already unpopular stature among nonblacks. His was one of the most consistent voices speaking out against the idea of 42nd Street being turned into one more white-owned, white-occupied zone.

*An unpublished 1978 group study of West 42nd Street by the Graduate School and University Center of the City University of New York entitled "The Bright Light Zone," based on a statistical analysis of pedestrian street traffic throughout the seventies, concluded that "the use of the street is not racially segregated although Blacks and Hispanics are more numerous there than would seem to be true for other midtown corridors." Similar studies taken during the eighties and nineties show the situation did not substantially change.

And yet, in an odd way, Dinkins's distance from 42nd Street actually helped the situation more than it hurt, as his laissez-faire attitude passively allowed for a series of events to take place without any real interference from City Hall.

As early as 1990 a new cast of characters had entered the redevelopment picture, beginning with Carl Weisbrod, who'd served in one official capacity or another all twelve years of the Koch administration, including a stint as the head of the MEP before replacing Sturz as president of the mayor's 42nd Street Redevelopment Project. He then left that position when Dinkins, in his first year of office, chose him to be the president of the city's newly established Economic Development Corporation, a municipal branch of the state-based Urban Development Corporation. One of the first things Weisbrod focused on was finding a way to use his new position to jump-start the 42nd Street project, something he had not been able to accomplish during his time with Koch.

Weisbrod's replacement as president of the 42nd Street project was his longtime City Hall protégée, Rebecca Robertson, a lively and sophisticated young woman with the easy smile, hearty giggle, and natural charisma of a classic Broadway leading lady. Robertson, as it turned out, would become a key player in the attempt to revive 42nd Street's redevelopment. Born in Canada, she gained an early strong background in planning and development, served as a consultant on major restoration projects in Toronto, Mexico City, and Caracas, and had lectured at the Harvard Graduate School of Design before landing in New York City. After a year or two spent learning how to untie the knots in the city's political ropes, she gained a seat on the City Planning Commission. Those who remember her time there recall how she brought something to the table even more valuable than her sharp eye for creative development: the essential and, until now, missing ingredient of the revolving team of macho wanna-bes who had always managed to turn 42nd Street into one more political pissing contest.

"Rebecca was priceless, an invaluable key to the whole redevelopment," one associate remembered. "The one woman who not only got invited to the all-male cigar and steak-house bashes but wound up leading the whole pack by the tips of her high-heeled

Rebecca Robertson (left), president of "The New 42," seen here with Vince Tese, former chairman of the Urban Development ment Corporation. (Photo courtesy of Rebecca Robertson)

brains. She was a beauty with a first-class way of thinking who could run with the boys. And the prospect of having to deal with the topless bars and massage parlors on 42nd Street didn't make her automatically blush. In truth, she found the idea amusingly absurd. Going face-to-face with the operators of commercial venues that dealt in pornography actually made her laugh."

Robertson's joining the committee brought a renewed energy to the project. "Times Square had always been about entertainment," she told an interviewer for the *New York Times*. "The office market had died in the '90s, but all the elements of urban entertainment were still there."

Robertson worked to redirect the project's emphasis from corporate development, where it had stalled, back to entertainment, where it had originated and, she believed, still belonged. To that end, with Klein's and Prudential's approval, she supervised the issuance of a general RFU (request for use) to professional acting companies in the city that might be willing to relocate to one of the theaters on 42nd Street.

Robertson sent out a total of eight hundred RFUs, from which she received only forty-four responses, and of those, only three met the criterion as eligible, active theater companies—the Knitting Factory, the Manhattan Theater Club, and the Roundabout. Among these, the best known was the Roundabout, an off-Broadway theater group with a public reputation for outstanding productions and an industry reputation for perpetual financial disarray, due primarily to its inability to find a permanent home. The rest were either amateur groups or nontheatrical speculators looking to cut some deal that might allow them to share in the future profits of the air rights above the theaters. All of these were summarily rejected.

In the end, however, none of the three went for the deal. At least part of the problem was an old and familiar one: how to convince any legitimate operation to set up shop on the same block where a giant marquee promoted the less-than-Pulitzer live-sex-act-extravaganza *Eat My Pussy Now!*

Undaunted, Robertson continued to shop for theatrical tenants, all of whom ultimately passed. The producers of the off-Broadway *Rent* wanted to more their East Village–based production "uptown," considered one of the 42nd Street theaters, but eventually chose the long-neglected but immediately available and fully functional Nederlander Theater one block south on West 41st. Joseph Papp considered an offer from Robertson before deciding he wanted to remain in his downtown Astor Place location. Rocco Landesman, the president of Jujamcyn, the third largest Broadway theater conglomerate (after the Shuberts and the Nederlanders), had also expressed interest, but in the end he, too, decided against moving to 42nd Street.

By late 1991 Robertson was getting nowhere until Herb Sturz, an old friend of hers who, since resigning in 1986 from the collapsing house of cards that was the Koch administration, had served on the editorial board of the *New York Times,* suggested she start all over with 42nd Street by shedding the baggage of the previous mayor and finding a new, scandal-free blue-blood board of directors with greater social power and influence than the present members of her team.

Which is exactly what Robertson did. She renamed the project's committee the New 42 and put together a board that included Frederick Papert and Sturz, who in turn used his position at the *Times* to recruit an absolutely crucial addition to the team— the newspaper's publisher, Arthur Ochs "Punch" Sulzberger, a weathered, streetwise veteran of 42nd Street redevelopment via his participation in the surprisingly successful decade-long restoration of Bryant Park.

Plans for restoring the park had been in place since 1974, when it was officially declared a landmark. At that time, the Bryant Park Restoration Corporation (BPRC) was formed to raise funds for its rehabilitation, only to be cut short two years later when a drug-related murder took place in the park (incredibly, the first there in nearly fifty years), which was followed by another a year later. Attendance, spotty ever since the end of World War II, then dropped to as few as seven hundred New Yorkers passing through it in a day.

In 1979 the BPRC turned to respected urban analyst William H. "Holly" White, who delivered a thirteen-page report with some surprising conclusions. In it he wrote that "Bryant Park is now dominated by dope dealers, but they are not the cause of the problem. The basic problem is under-use. It has been for a long time. It antedated the invasion of the dope dealers and in part induced it. Access is the nub of the solution."

It was an extremely important document, strong enough to allow the BPRC to convince the Rockefeller Foundation that the park was rescuable. Together the Economic Development Corporation and the Foundation developed a philosophy startlingly different from the city's official war on midtown crime. More carrot (park improvements) and less stick (police force) was the formula they chose to bring the public back to Bryant Park. In 1980 Sulzberger's committee was able to persuade the city to officially lease the park to the BPRC for a dollar a year, while passing along with it the responsibility for its redesign and management and $6 million in capital funds (to be matched by $3.2 million in privately raised money). Working from the original Carrère and Hastings blueprints for the library and adjoining park grounds, the BPRC hired the architectural firm of Lew Brody Associates and the noted team of Hanna/Olin to restore the interior of the library and Bryant Park to their original layout in the hope of creating a modern midtown oasis for the area's day workers and resident elderly.

To help rid the park of any remaining undesirables, Sulzberger used a bit more stick than he'd originally intended when he enlisted the help of Bill Daly and the MEP. As Daly later remembered, "We moved in and took a stand to rid the park of the dealers who'd drifted over from Eighth Avenue in an attempt to expand their realm and sell drugs to the young men who worked in the nearby office buildings. We put a van along 42nd Street to serve as a portable police station, out of which we processed dozens of drug busts every day. We even started arresting the buyers who were going to the park on their lunch hours looking to score. That seemed to do the trick, and Sulzberger's people were able to take it from there."

Encouraged by his success with Bryant Park, in 1992 Sulzberger decided to expand his vision and asked Dinkins to sign into law a proposal that ceded certain of the city's responsibilities for all of Times Square, including additional sanitation, private security, and public relations, to a privately financed, semiautonomous district board. Dinkins quickly agreed, as it gave him a way to officially pass off the "problem" of 42nd Street to a highly influential and wealthy group of players whose political and financial (and, if possible, editorial) support he would need in the coming reelection campaign. At the same time, it made it easier for him to tell Sharpton that there was nothing he could do about the redevelopment since the street no longer came under the exclusive auspices of City Hall.

S ULZBERGER'S AGREEING to join Robertson's team led to the creation in 1992 of the Business Improvement District of Times Square, or BID. The BID's stated mandate was to "provide a mechanism by which property owners in Times Square could pool their resources to make the 'Crossroads of the World' clean, safe and friendly."

That same year, Robertson received $4.5 million in seed money from eight hundred private property owners in the Times Square area from 41st Street and the Avenue of the Americas north to 49th and Eighth, all eager to see something done about the decade-long standoff. Most of the money came from fund-raising drives led by the local merchants working with the major theater owners, including the Shuberts, Nederlander, and Jujamcyn. Under Sulzberger's close supervision, the BID hired its own private sanitation crew, outfitted them in bright red jumpsuits, and provided forty public-safety officers, unarmed but linked by walkie-talkie directly to the police. It also opened a visitor center for tourists, created a homeless outreach team, and initiated an annual "Broadway on Broadway" free outdoor Times Square show featuring songs from current musicals as a way to advertise shows and increase ticket sales.

Robertson's committee gained even more clout when Sulzberger then suggested that his sister, Marian Effie Sulzberger Dryfoos Heiskell, a member of the board of directors of the *New York Times* (daughter of the legendary Iphigene Sulzberger and wife of Andrew Heiskell, the publisher of *Time* magazine), be brought on board. New York City blood didn't get any bluer than that.

However, Heiskell initially declined the offer. Like everyone else involved with Midtown, she considered 42nd Street the one boulevard that could not be redeemed. Having recently chaired the committee to save Westbeth, a troubled housing project designed to provide low-income residences for artists that had resulted in nothing but animosity and anarchy among its members, Heiskell felt she had had enough of the city's bureaucratic merry-go-round. But Sturz and Sulzberger wouldn't take no for an answer, and after repeated requests, she finally and reluctantly agreed to join the New 42 if and when the committee found the right person, meaning not her, to take its chair.

That turned out to be Cora Cahan. Cahan was a veteran of the long and difficult sixties Lincoln Center development and had gotten several non-profit theater companies refunded and rehoused and knew how to work through the most convoluted bureaucratic mazes, as her experience with the celebrated West Side entertainment complex had well taught her. When offered the position she accepted. The choice of her good friend Cahan both surprised and pleased Heiskell, and at that point she officially signed on.

B Y THE END OF 1992 the city's economy had started to show signs of a real turnaround. That same year, the federal government finally won a conviction against John Gotti for the murder of Paul Castellano and several other mob figures (including Thomas Bilotti, "Big Gus" Sclafani, and Frankie De Cicco). He was sentenced to life without parole, a victory that, more than anything else, helped break the Gambino hegemony of West 42nd Street. Not long after Gotti was sent away, the family splintered and lost much of its power. At the same time, the sex and drug business in Times Square began to noticeably decrease and for the first time in forty-seven years, the number of murders that took place on 42nd Street actually declined.

The case against Gotti had been made by the testimony of one of his former hit men, Sammy "the Bull" Gravano, who implicated Gotti in the 1985 murder of Castellano, gunned down outside of Sparks, a traditional New York steak house on Manhattan's East Side. Gravano's testimony also for the first time established a direct and traceable link between the Gambinos and 42nd Street by, among other things, solving the long-standing mystery of the murder of Robert Di Bernardo, a small-time hood who, as it turned out, had been a part owner of the Show World.

The Gambinos, wary of RICO, had always been very careful to try to keep the names of all family members off any documents that could link the mob to 42nd Street. However, public records in Nassau County Court revealed that Di Bernardo was part owner of at least two of Richard Basciano's porn-related properties (Basciano, the proprietor of Show World, was one of the few sex store operators who actually owned his own property). Basciano had, in fact, built a small Midtown West real estate show business empire of sorts, which included a nonporn movieplex on West 42nd Street that catered to the kung fu crowd, several office buildings, a parking lot on West 41st Street, and at least five additional Midtown West porn outlets—Show Center, Show Follies, Peep Land, Peep World, and Peepalive Stage.

Di Bernardo was also a made member of the Gambino family. He was murdered in 1986 at the order of John Gotti, according to Gravano, for having put his name on those papers and to eliminate the potentially damaging connection between the Gambinos and 42nd Street, one that could open the floodgates to what surely would have been an intensive investigation by both the IRS and the FBI into the mob's involvement on the street.

As crucial as Gravano's testimony was in helping to send John Gotti away, in truth, even before his conviction the business of crime had taken a precipitous dip on 42nd Street, mostly because porn sales were down. This was not the result of any great social, economic, or political advances, or any major gains by law enforcement or sudden moral turnaround, but rather the invention of new technology. The widespread use of home videotape recorders had all but put out of business the lumbering porn theaters, not just on 42nd Street but in every major city. Sex tapes, easily made, duplicated, and sold through the mail by and for amateurs or small-time independents, gave viewers the one thing mob porn of the eighties couldn't—the ability to watch the stuff in the privacy of their own homes. As a result, by the early nineties the era of mob-controlled big-screen porn came to an end as the street action moved to the mostly mob-free, independent video storefronts. Whatever big-money action was left in porn, most of which by now was shot on video and coming out of Los Angeles' Simi Valley, would have to wait for the next generation's fascination with Internet sex.

Without the traffic lured to 42nd Street by porn, the sale of drugs dramatically dropped. While still maintaining a few midtown porn peeps, the Gambinos, led by John Gotti, Jr., chose to spread their drug dealers to where the customers lived: the relatively safe and still-fertile confines of upper Manhattan (Washington Heights), Brooklyn, the Bronx, and Queens. The Gambino

Family had finally lost its iron grip on 42nd Street, after thirty fabulously lucrative, murderously violent, and socially repugnant years.

What was bad news for the Gambinos was, of course, good news for the rest of New York City where even as the pinky-ring rats were being driven out of the western end of the street, the wheels had already been set into motion to bring a new leader of the gang to the crossroads of the world; a rodent of the lovable variety, with hollow eyes, white gloves, a high-pitched voice, and a billion-dollar smile.

I N 1992, NOT LONG AFTER Marian Heiskell agreed to join the board of the New 42, she and her husband, Andrew, were on a commercial jet bound for Los Angeles when an extraordinary coincidence took place with far-reaching consequences for the future of 42nd Street. On that flight, the Heiskells found themselves sitting near, of all people, Disney studio head Michael Eisner. As Heiskell later recalled, "Well, it was just pure luck. My husband is on the American Academy in Rome, and we were going out to California on Academy-related business. Michael, whom I've known since he was four years old, happened to be on the flight. We all talked awhile and he wound up inviting us out to dinner in Los Angeles that night.

"At one point I realized I had a map of the layout for the New 42 in my pocket, which I decided to pull out and show him. Then, without having planned it, I said, 'You know, Michael, this would be a great place for Disney to be. There are about eleven acres still available. You could do a lot of creative things with that property.'

"'Oh, I don't think so,' he said after taking a quick look, more out of courtesy than anything else, 'but let me think about it.' A few weeks later he sent two or three people to check out the street. He then wrote a lovely letter to me saying he was sorry but 42nd Street just wasn't in Disney's cards."

Disney Chairman Michael Eisner (center) *meets with newly elected Mayor Rudy Giuliani* (left) *and Governor Mario Cuomo in February 1994 to discuss Disney's potential role in the redevelopment of 42nd Street.* (Mayor Giulani's Press Photo Unit/provided by Tony Coles)

Heiskell had not been the first to approach Eisner about the possibility of bringing Disney to New York City. Carl Weisbrod, her predecessor, had pursued a deal with him for years without having anything to show for it, not even the cursory visit by the relatively low-level studio representatives Heiskell's coincidental meeting with Eisner produced. "We had approached Disney several times in the late eighties," Weisbrod recalled, "and they were totally unresponsive. Eisner said he wasn't interested in bringing his company to New York and that his decision was final.

"Then three events changed everything. The first was Marian Heiskell's chance meeting with Eisner on that plane. The next was something that happened during their dinner that night in L.A. The third involved Robert Stern, an architect with a solid background and deep knowledge of New York's physical history whom Rebecca Robertson, with George Klein's strong input, had chosen to help design what turned out to be an interim plan for short-term rentals on 42nd Street in anticipation of the restoration and construction period. If we ever got that far. As it happened, Stern was also on the board of directors at Disney and had Eisner's ear. Later on, when *Beauty and the Beast* opened in Houston and did well, it was Stern who suggested the studio move the show intact to Broadway."

Heiskell: "In March of 1993 Eisner called Cora Cahan, our chairperson, and, out of nowhere, said he'd like to personally come and see the New Amsterdam. He brought his wife and child with him and toured the theater, which by then was absolutely on the verge of collapse. There was a hole in the roof and gigantic rats were roaming about, the result of someone having carelessly left the roof hatch open. I must say, the theater's once-glamorous and exotic interior was in abominable condition."

However, that day when Heiskell, Stern, and Robertson accompanied Eisner on his inspection, to their surprise and relief, he appeared charmed and fascinated by the New Amsterdam's ghostly glamour and appeared to thoroughly enjoy Robertson's spirited tour, filled with tales of the New Amsterdam's storied past. Along the way she pointed out the visible remains of the once-beautiful and, she was certain, still-salvageable architecture. She stopped to admire the eminently practical, partially exposed steel structure that supported the enormous sixty-foot-deep, hundred-foot-wide stage, still able to be raised and lowered to a differential of thirty-three feet in either direction. She marveled at the gorgeous oval auditorium as she vividly recounted the theater's cultural legacy of legends, the Ziegfelds, Cohans, Cantors, and Berlins, all of whom had begun their Broadway careers "right in this building, Michael." She took them onto the stage, and couldn't he almost smell the makeup powder and perfume the Ziegfeld girls kept on the tables in their dressing rooms in the smaller theater upstairs where the great Flo had them put on his more private, by-invitation-only shows?

As they were leaving, Robertson explained to Eisner how, in 1937, the theater had been unceremoniously shuttered, only to have pornographic movies eventually take over. How wonderful a chance this was, she told him, to redeem those memories by sharing in the restoration of the theater to its former glory.

It was an expensive, sophisticated, and thoroughly professional wine-and-dine, well worth the time and effort, Robertson knew, because if Eisner went for it, as she put it, "Disney could bring something to the table nobody else could match. The mere presence of the name on the street could instantly change everyone's perception of what we could be done."

Of course, Eisner knew it, too, and he also knew that he held all the high cards in this poker game. More than once during the meetings that took place in the days and weeks that followed the tour, he folded his cards, got up, and walked out, only to return when the house was ready to deal him a better hand. That didn't happen until several months later, in the fall of 1993, when, having gotten Robertson's committee to agree to everything he wanted, including going to the city and getting additional tax incentives, Eisner made a preliminary nonbinding offer to have Disney take over the restoration of the New Amsterdam.

Back in L.A., Eisner handpicked David Malmuth to oversee the theater's restoration. Malmuth was a native Californian who'd come to Disney from Stanford University's Graduate School of Business. He was young, magna cum laude, and loaded with talent. He had

David Malmuth, Eisner's personal choice to head the restoration of the New Amsterdam Theater. (Photo courtesy of David Malmuth)

the work ethic of a priest and the clean-cut look of a choirboy, Eisner's image of the perfect Disney employee.

Malmuth's specialty was architectural restoration, and he'd quickly risen through the ranks of the corporation to the level of vice president and general manager of the Disney Development Corporation. At the time Eisner chose him to head the New Amsterdam restoration, Malmuth was working out of the studio's Burbank headquarters developing plans for a new Disney theme park.

As Malmuth later recalled, "Eisner wanted the New Amsterdam but only if the right deal could be made. For example, he was interested in buying it outright rather than long-term leasing, which was what the New 42 had offered, and if and when that could be worked out, he was still very concerned about what to do regarding all the pornography on the rest of the street."

That fall, Malmuth went to New York to see for himself what the situation was, take the tour of the New Amsterdam and meet with Robertson and the committee. When he returned to L.A., he called Peter Rummel, the president of the Disney Development Company, to say it appeared the city was willing to offer the moon to get Disney, and because of it the studio might be able to get a few planets thrown in to sweeten the deal. A week later Malmuth flew back to Manhattan to work out more details for Disney's possible acquisition of the New Amsterdam and to take a much closer look at the theater.

Malmuth: "We went to 42nd Street to go through the theater inch by inch, and as we did so a lot of things started to become clearer to me. The first and most obvious was that it was going to take a ton of money to turn this place around. The second was that even if we could somehow restore it to this beautiful and fantastic palace it once was, the rest of the street would still be a disaster. To me, it didn't make a hell of a lot of sense to spend $30 or $40 million to restore a palace that was going to sit nestled between a couple of dozen pornographic shitholes."

After returning to L.A. to confer with Eisner, Malmuth went back to New York again and met with the board of the New 42, ready to explain in detail Disney's position. First, Malmuth said, there was the street problem. He explained that Eisner was always reluctant to do anything that would endanger the company's name and reputation, and 42nd Street, in its present condition, seemed far too risky. Second, Eisner couldn't imagine Disney putting up the kind of capital the committee required to bring him into the project. "Don't misunderstand us. We love the idea, on paper, of bringing this theater back to life," Malmuth told the board, "as long as it doesn't somehow tarnish the Disney name and doesn't cost the company anything to do it." A lot of heads shook slowly up and down, pages of pads were written on and flipped over, water was sipped, breaths were taken, and nobody spoke a word. Their reaction was closer to a yes than a no, Malmuth thought to himself.

The next day Malmuth again flew back to L.A. to tell Eisner and Rummel it was his feeling they might actually be able to get the theater for nothing. Malmuth, like Eisner, had definitely seen the bones of the skeleton and felt the spirit of the theater on his tours of it, and believed Disney had exactly the right kind of magic to bring it back to life. Eisner agreed that from here on out everything would depend on how strong a commitment the city would be willing to make Disney, and not the other way around.

The next day Malmuth returned to New York for another round of meetings with the committee, this time to negotiate the specifics of the restoration. Talks dragged on for three more months until, on December 30, 1993, which happened to be the next to the last day of the lame-duck Dinkins administration—the mayor had lost his bid for reelection—Eisner finally signed a second, but still heavily conditional, letter of intent. From here on in, he would be dealing with the next mayor of New York, the man Dinkins had defeated in '89, Rudolph Giuliani.

In the fall of 1993 Giuliani ran his second campaign for mayor like something out of a modern spaghetti western, presenting himself as a good-guy Italian gunslinger-with-a-badge who'd successfully taken on the bad-guy Italian Gambinos, and who now promised to once and for all clean up the streets of his town. After the election, even before he was officially sworn in, Giuliani let Disney's people know that he intended to make the deal happen to bring Disney to 42nd Street and, by the way, felt he, not Dinkins, should get all the credit because he was prepared to close the deal on his watch. That was fine with Eisner, who saw no advantage in aligning himself with a lame-duck mayor.

Dinkins, however, made some noise, insisting Disney had to at least acknowledge his involvement with the deal as well, something John Dyson, Giuliani's deputy mayor, insisted he just didn't deserve. "No deal of any kind existed when the newly elected mayor took office January 1, 1994," he later recalled. "The only thing we inherited from Dinkins was a very long letter from Eisner stating his *intention* to sign a formal letter of intent. He wanted credit for that?"*

According to Kent Barwick, the haggling that went on over who was really responsible for bringing Disney to 42nd Street was both petty and pathetic. "Suddenly you have Giuliani and Dinkins

---

*Malmuth says Eisner considered that letter nothing more than a memo, titled "memorandum with indicative terms." Still, Dinkins was so anxious to be able to claim it as part of his administration's record, he signed it on top of a metal detector on his way out of City Hall for the last time.

fighting over who *really* brought Disney to the city, when the truth of it was that credit belonged more to Marian Heiskell than either of them. The really sad thing was that once again, as with Portman, it had taken an outsider, a carpetbagger, to finally make those in charge of the city sit up and say, 'Ah, Times Square, oh yes, what a great place to do business.'"

According to Malmuth, this was the financial breakdown of the deal: "The estimated cost of renovating the New Amsterdam came to $32 million, of which $24 million was to come from the committee, with Disney contributing the remaining $8 million. The $24 million was to be structured as a low-interest loan to Disney at 3 percent, with thirty years' interest-only, no recourse. In other words a loan that wouldn't have to begin to be paid back until well into the twenty-first century. It was about as attractive a deal as anyone could ever imagine, especially for a multibillion-dollar corporation that really didn't need the financial assistance."

Eisner also wanted the committee to convince the city to guarantee that Disney's financial commitment would not exceed that $8 million figure, and a promise to find two additional mainstream entertainment companies, both requiring Disney's approval, to bring to the street, and, finally, the elimination of any existing sex shops on 42nd between Broadway and Eighth Avenue. To get all of this done, Eisner gave the committee and the mayor exactly one year— until December 30, 1994—or there was no deal.

Although that deadline appeared to everyone on the committee to be, and in truth was, an arbitrary one, from Disney's perspective there was a certain logic to the schedule. For one thing, Cuomo was facing a difficult reelection in the fall of '94 and Eisner wanted an out-clause, the right to walk away if Cuomo's opponent, George Pataki, won the election and appeared to be in any way hostile to the deal. As for the other two entertainment companies, they represented Eisner's litmus test for the power of the Disney name in a previously untried New York City. If they failed to materialize, that would be a strong signal to pull out of the deal.

For Giuliani, meanwhile, it meant having to have everything in position by the end of his first year in office, including, at Eisner's urging, getting the City Planning Commission to push through a special rezoning amendment for 42nd Street, which he believed was the fastest way to eliminate the remaining porno-related storefronts and ensure they would never have the opportunity to come back.*

Less than a month after taking over City Hall, on February 2, 1994, Giuliani called a press conference to officially announce Disney's coming to New York City. It was, however, a press conference that almost didn't take place, this time for reasons having nothing to do with Disney, and everything to do with the egos of New York politicians. When Governor Cuomo was informed the meeting was to be held at City Hall and not in the governor's Manhattan office, he exploded. Having been connected to the 42nd Street redevelopment project for nearly thirteen years, Cuomo felt strongly that he deserved at least some of the credit, and was now being purposely snubbed by a Republican mayor who'd been in office less than four weeks.

According to Rebecca Robertson, Cuomo's reaction was justified. "There's a certain protocol when you have a joint announcement between a governor and a mayor, which is you generally have it either at the governor's office or at a neutral place. Giuliani insisted that it be held at the Blue Room of City Hall. Cuomo had been working on this project since he'd first become governor and felt it had to rank as one of his greatest gubernatorial accomplishments. It was incredibly important to him. Furthermore, the truth is, Giuliani had exactly zilch to do with bringing Disney to 42nd Street. Regardless, Giuliani made it clear there would be no press conference if it weren't held in the Blue Room. It was a demonstration of a lack of grace, to say the least."

An infuriated Cuomo finally acquiesced, believing any internal political differences between the state and the city played out in public might kill any chance of getting the always tentative Eisner to finally commit his corporation to the project.

Robertson: "Cuomo seemed out of sorts that day, really pissed,

---

*The amended zoning guidelines for 42nd Street were eventually expanded by the commission to include the entire city. The new rules stated that sex-related businesses had to be at least five hundred feet from one another, and from schools, day-care centers, and places of worship. These specifications had, in fact, first been suggested to Giuliani by Eisner, who believed them to be the most constitutionally expedient method for the city to once and for all legally zone pornography, for all practical purposes, out of existence.

but it was Disney and he didn't want to be the one to blame for screwing the whole thing up. His prepared remarks at the press conference were unusually dull, even for him, after which Giuliani made his comments, followed by Eisner, who made a *really* stultifying speech. When they all finished, someone from the press asked only half-jokingly if this whole 42nd Street deal was really an attempt on Disney's part to divert attention from EuroDisney, which up until then had been considered by many to be something of a social and financial disaster. Giuliani's face turned beet-red, and he looked as if he was about to lose his composure, but fortunately the rest of the reporters laughed, and Eisner managed to brush the question aside. Another reporter then asked the governor, and not the mayor, 'How can you justify this kind of subsidy to a superrich corporation like Disney?'

"Cuomo, already simmering, took this as a chance to focus his anger and leveled the guy with a diatribe during which he talked about the soul of the city, the hearts of all those involved being ripped from their breasts these past fifteen years, and how here was finally the chance to re-create a fabulous, spiritual part of historical and legendary New York. It was Cuomo at his absolute rhetorical best. Even the most hardened member of the press in the place that day totally bought it, and we knew we were in business."

During all of this, George Klein had continued to work with Robertson and Stern on the interim commercial development plan for the Seven/Eight. To fund it, Klein and Robertson petitioned the court to release $10 million of the portion of the escrow fund earmarked for theater restoration for construction of several temporary retail storefronts, in return for a ten-year protected extension of Klein's and Prudential's building rights to the four corner highrises. Klein also asked as part of the deal to be let out of the long-standing obligation to refurbish the Times Square subway stations on Broadway and Eighth. The court granted both these requests.

As a result, by the spring of 1994 Robertson's committee had become the new landlord for a series of standard-fare fast-food outlets, camera, postcard, and souvenir shops, and brand-name clothing outlets. At the same time, Giuliani opened negotiations with the lawyers who represented the landlords, to try to settle out of court the last of the outstanding lawsuits. The lawyers agreed to talks, on condition their tenants not be harassed in any way during the interim period, and that each one be allowed to remain for as long as he wanted until all the property collection cases were resolved, either out of court or by judgment.

As a result, because of a few quick settlements, the New 42 also became the landlord for about a dozen porno bookstores and peep shows, which created some bizarrely comic situations. The maintenance, upkeep, and collection of rent on these venues fell to Robertson. Every day, with spiral notebook in one hand and a pen in the other, she blithely made her rounds, which included a fair number of the existing porno emporiums. She briskly whizzed by men in overcoats studying each porno tape box as if it were an object from another planet, to check on a faulty heating pipe or dripping faucet or to collect rent.

"There was this one place called the Times Square Adult Shopping Center, near Eighth Avenue on the north side of the street. It actually had carts, like a supermarket, complete with aisles, overhead fluorescence, and they had as many tourists as 'regulars.' The place became a kind of tourist attraction all its own for people who came to the city wanting to see the 'real,' 'notorious' 42nd Street they'd read and heard so much about.

"The committee were now property managers and therefore had to maintain the buildings. I had to go into some pretty sleazy places and didn't dare go without a security person, a fellow named Cliff who'd shined shoes on the corner of Eighth Avenue and 42nd Street for about thirty years. The peeps had these rows of booths framed with red lights, and I'd see all these young naked boys sitting on stools outside them, waiting for customers. When they'd see Cliff, they'd get all excited, and then they'd see me and quickly cover themselves with towels."

That summer, with the drop in street crime continuing and a gradual increase in tourist traffic on West 42nd Street, Fred Papert and his 42nd Street development committee decided to promote a summer-long outdoor "Art Project." Papert managed to get the participation of such celebrated New York City–based artists as Nam June Paik, Dick Elliott, and Ken Chu. From Memorial Day to Labor Day, the entire two-block stretch between Broadway and Eighth was "redecorated" into one gigantic, continuing creative

Fred Papert's 1994 summer 42nd Street Art Project temporarily invigorated the stalled redevelopment of Seventh and Eighth Avenues. (Brochure provided by Fred Papert)

expression. The front windows of a Kentucky Fried Chicken storefront were covered with eighteen thousand reflectors. Similar expressionistic exhibits were put on display in the windows of the venerable Tad's Steaks and the interim Bill's Gyros. Even the few holdout independent porno theater operators took part, allowing the names of their movies to be replaced on the marquees with street-savvy sex-related aphorisms ("Men Don't Protect You Anymore"). For the entire summer, at one end of Seventh Avenue and 42nd Street an enormous "Cat in the Hat" rendering of Dr. Seuss's famous character replaced the corner patrolman as the twenty-four-hour guard over everyone and everything.

The exhibit was surprisingly successful. By the end of the summer, the influx of new, interim retail establishments and the art exhibit had drawn more than 13 million people to 42nd Street between Broadway and Eighth, six times the number of visitors of the year before. Even west of Ninth, progress could be seen. Restaurants like Chez Josephine, opened by the son of the legendary chanteuse, managed to attract large crowds to the street.

In the fall, new billboards began to appear everywhere in Times Square. A giant TV screen was installed on the north side of the old Times Tower above the news zipper and proved so popular that before long the entire area was bathed in TV screens, animated billboards, and neon signs.* As Barwick had correctly predicted, the signage not only added a historic sense to Times Square but became a popular tourist attraction.

Some, like the giant Midwest vista that sat astride the Marriott Marquis, brought a sense of home-sweet-home to tourists. Others didn't offer quite so Kodak a moment. "One of the first big billboards to back up 42nd Street," Rebecca Robertson recalled with a chuckle, "was a fifty-foot blowup of Marky Mark in his tight Calvin Klein underwear. Here on one hand we had condemned all these porno businesses that had catered to every sexual perversion imaginable, including pedophilia, making such a big deal about 'cleaning up' Times Square, and on the other was this huge billboard in Times Square of an all-but-naked teenage boy, surrounded by a dozen others advertising brand-name products with practically naked young women. It made me wonder how far we'd actually come."

Unfortunately, when the summer ended, so did the sudden burst of tourism. The forward progress then took another, giant

---

*The zipper, first used in 1928 to report the results of the Hoover-Smith election, has remained continuously in operation, except for three dim-outs during World War II at the direction of the government. The news is still supplied by the *New York Times*.

step backward when the Durst Organization, which had by now passed into the control of Seymour's three sons, Kristoffer, Jonathan, and Douglas, instituted a new lawsuit to halt any future ground-breaking on the elephant legs. The Dursts, who still owned land on the Avenue of the Americas and 42nd Street (the as-yet-undeveloped site of the former Stern's department store), because of the success of the first stage of the interim business plan, now wanted the city to reevaluate all the development properties on 42nd Street, after which they should all be auctioned off to the highest private bidder. The goal of the lawsuit was twofold. First, it was an attempt by Durst to increase the value of the four corners, and, if for any reason anyone wanted out, to be in a prime position to buy in. Even if that failed, the result of the forced reassessment would no doubt increase the value of the considerable Durst holdings on 42nd Street.

That fall Cora Cahan's New 42 began refurbishing still another theater, the Victory, the oldest of the legitimate houses on the Seven/Eight. Built by Hammerstein in 1899, it sat on the northern, once-independent side of the street, directly across from the New Amsterdam. It was, in fact, a brilliant countermove to the Durst lawsuit, which threatened Klein's and Prudential's air-rights deal to the four corners, and with it Disney's participation. Under the present agreement, it was the escrow money that was to pay for the assemblage of the street's properties. By moving ahead on a project that didn't involve Disney, the committee was affirming Klein's and Prudential's right to build, as the $19-million budget for the restoration of the Victory came from the escrow account by mutual agreement of Klein, Prudential, and the court.

Less than a year later, the "New Victory" Theater opened as a not-for-profit children's theater with the highest-priced ticket in the house a modest twenty-five dollars, discountable to two dollars, and in some cases where money was tight, admission was free. "We took the opening of the New Victory as a very positive sign," Malmuth said later, "but still it was the only sign that things were moving ahead on the street. There were rumblings of other interests, and disgruntled landowners, and the Durst lawsuit, which we knew about, but what concerned us most were the porn theaters and shops that were still operating. When the 1994 deadline passed, to show that we were still in, we acquired the rights to build [in partnership with Tishman-Speyers Realty] a forty-seven-story hotel with time-shares, retail outlets, and other entertainment-related uses, at the southeast corner of 42nd Street and Eighth Avenue.*

Nevertheless, Eisner remained uneasy. Despite Robertson's best efforts, no other major entertainment company had agreed to come aboard, leaving Disney the only new game in town. Madame Tussaud's Wax Museum had looked at space in an abandoned building between the Harris and Empire Theaters. The AMC movie chain had considered building a multiplex film house on the site of the old Liberty Theater, but as yet no private, for-profit corporations had actually committed to paper. Nevertheless, Robertson reassured Malmuth and Eisner that progress on the street was continuing.

Then, early in 1995, a major hurdle was passed when the final amount of the payments for the remaining property owners' lawsuits on the street was agreed to and paid. The total cost of the buy-outs, which had all been settled, in theory, if not amount, by 1992, came to a little more than a quarter of a billion dollars. The City at 42nd Street, anxious to get rid of the last of the holdouts, made very generous settlements. Richard Basciano, for instance, got a reported $11.3 million for three of his 42nd Street porn palace properties. (Because the Show World was on the other side of Eighth, outside Disney's prescribed demarcation, he was able to keep his flagship venue.)† And yet, for all this, by October 1995 Eisner still hadn't signed the final draft of what had turned into a 250-page lease agreement for the New Amsterdam.

That same month, the city's new zoning rules went into effect.

---

*This purchase particularly rankled Fred Papert, whose organization had once held an option on the parking lot for $5 million, which for one reason or another they let lapse. Those rights eventually found their way to the Milstein Brothers, who bought it and then offered it to Disney for $30 million, leading Papert to describe (to his friend Brendan Gill) all the developers on the street as "pirates and savages." (Gilmartin pp. 449–50)

†By the end of 1999, the Alamo of 42nd Street porn announced it was throwing in the towel and "going legit." It intended presenting a group of one-act plays by Chekhov in its "new" ninety-nine-seat theater that was, in reality, the same old venue where the likes of porno legend "Aunt Peg" had done their thing. One sailor from England on leave in New York City for the first time, anxious to see the sex emporium he'd heard so much about from friends, studied the new marquee, turned to his mate, and asked, "'Ey, does this 'ere Chekhov bitch 'ave nice tits?" Despite that brief experiment, the Show World still sells adult materials, although it no longer provides live sex shows.

Not surprisingly, and with great fanfare, the first of the remaining porno shops to go were the ones the committee had taken over on 42nd Street between Broadway and Eighth. Giuliani, in what had become something of a ritual among New York mayors, had them publicly police-padlocked, a front-page gesture meant to show Disney as much as the citizens of New York that he meant business.

In the face of the new regulations, many of the remaining purveyors in the area had simply sold the remaining time on the leases on their rented storefronts, peeps, and topless bars to the city. Although some still chose to fight the new zoning by filling the front of their stores with "traditional" videotapes to conform to the new definition of what constituted a porno store—40 percent or more of the inventory being adult videos prominently displayed—for most, the battle was over, the city had won, and West 42nd Street's signature sleaze all but disappeared. That it remained (and in abundance) to the north, south, east, and west of the Seven/Eight, the mayor insisted, was a situation that would soon be "corrected."

Eisner, satisfied that porn was finally off Disney's block, and while still fine-tuning the agreement for the New Amsterdam, struck a separate deal with the New 42 to open a Disney retail store on the southwest corner of 42nd and Seventh, directly adjacent to the theater, a move that greatly encouraged the committee.

Such was the power of the Disney name that even before the Mickey Mouse souvenir shop opened its doors for business, just knowing it was going to do so caused a sudden rush by a whole series of new, upscale interim retail stores. Warner opened a Studio Store on the ground floor of the old Times Tower, the Gap opened across the street, several new restaurants and a host of mall-type establishments took whatever storefronts they could get, for as long as they could have them and for however much they cost, understanding they would have to vacate at what amounted to a moment's notice.

The name-brand establishments that replaced the old coffee shops, fried chicken franchises, Statue of Liberty stands, army and navy stores, porno outlets, and kung fu shops were willing to pay top dollar to attract the new and huge numbers of cash-carrying customers, the great majority of them tourists eager to visit the once-notorious street that now looked as familiar and nonthreatening as, if a lot more expensive than, the rural shopping mall back home. Paying high prices for a stuffed Donald Duck purchased in Times Square became the newest tourist treat in town, with as much prestige attached to the toy as a diamond bracelet bought at Tiffany.

As for the residents of the city, they remained, for the most part, unimpressed. To many who'd grown up in the days of the old 42nd Street, nothing had really changed. Sex and drugs were still easily and plentifully available around the corner of 42nd and Eighth. Everything else, like food, clothing and souvenirs, had just gotten more expensive.

I N DECEMBER 1995 the New 42 handed a revised budget proposal for the New Amsterdam to Eisner, who still hadn't signed the old one. To his dismay, Disney's end had now escalated to $14 million, $6 million more than the amount he'd originally agreed to pay. Once again, he threatened to walk, until Rebecca Robertson, in anticipation of Eisner's reaction, produced signed letters of intent from Tussaud's and the AMC movie theater chain. At that point, Eisner, realizing the value of the street had already increased dramatically and would probably go a lot higher, stopped haggling and agreed to put up the additional $6 million. (The final cost came to almost fifty million dollars, which the city and the state paid.)

Not long after, Eisner ran into Schoenfeld at a social function, took him aside and asked, "Gerry, what kind of business are you in? Can anyone make any money in live theater?" Schoenfeld smiled and replied that it was even harder when the money came from private investors.

Although everything seemed finally in place, Eisner was still not able to completely shake a lingering uneasiness he felt about bringing his fabled franchise to New York. A souvenir store was one thing; a $14-million investment in a theater was quite another. Eisner still worried that 42nd Street was not the smartest choice for Mickey Mouse to store his cheese.

Indeed, from the moment Disney had been formally approached by the New 42, there had been loud industry opposition to the Hollywood-based movie studio getting a huge tax break from the city to invade the turf of and compete with the legitimate New York theater establishment. James Nederlander, Rocco Landesman of the Jujamcyn organization, and Gerald Schoenfeld expressed their concern about the deal at a meeting with the mayor. *They* were the ones, they complained, who'd established New York theater as a private, profit-making industry, with little or no financial help from the city. Giving away so much potentially valuable property, to an out-of-towner no less, was, they insisted, a slap in the face not just to the Broadway community but to the citizens of New York City. Giuliani quickly reminded the Nederlanders that not very long ago they had walked away from a chance to take over the New Amsterdam.

Schoenfeld then went to the city asking if they would consider some sort of parity deal, perhaps suspending the real estate taxes on all Broadway theaters that went dark. Giuliani, fearing Schoenfeld might use that as an excuse to keep some of his more expensive theaters empty, countered with a promise to restructure taxes for those Broadway theaters that managed to stay open. Neither proposal went anywhere. Several additional meetings were held, a lot of shouting took place, before Giuliani agreed to consider enlisting the governor's help in establishing an indirect tax-incentive program in the form of state-financed low-interest loans to help with the upkeep of Times Square's legitimate venues. The deal never went anywhere, beyond sale tax exemption for costumes and sets, as the film industry already had. According to Schoenfeld, "We really got nothing."

Nevertheless, Eisner feared the theater industry's strong ties to the press would result in the Disney organization's being portrayed as carpetbaggers. Until now, Eisner's biggest supporter, besides the mayor and the committee, had been the *New York Times*. However, as connected as he was to Sulzberger and Heiskell, Eisner knew he couldn't control the newspaper's editorial board. He decided to approach the *Times* directly and ask for guarantees—*guarantees*—that he would be warmly welcomed in the editorial pages of the newspaper whose general policy was not to tell the subject of a story whether to take an umbrella to the interview until two days after it rained.

At a private meeting with Arthur Sulzberger in his office at the *New York Times,* attended by Marian Heiskell, Eisner made it a deal-breaker, signed agreement or no signed agreement. Sulzberger then reassured Eisner that the city and the newspaper would indeed greet the arrival of Disney with open arms. "Getting Eisner to commit to 42nd Street was in our best interests," said Marian Heiskell. "It was explained to Eisner once again at that meeting, as it had been so many times before, that anyone who could help the situation on 42nd Street would always be welcome, and Disney was certainly the kind of image anyone in his right mind would prefer to be associated with than the streetwalkers, the drug pushers, and the petty thieves we had all been plagued with the past thirty-five years every time we stepped outside."

That was good enough for Eisner. In June 1995, two years after his first exploratory trip to 42nd Street, with great ceremonial fanfare, the restoration of the New Amsterdam theater began.

I F DISNEY'S TEMPORARY retail store had attracted a stream of other merchants to the block, the studio's occupancy of the New Amsterdam opened the corporate floodgates. In 1996 Cora Cahan opened negotiations with the Livent Organization, a Canadian-based theatrical company headed by magnate Garth Drabinsky that had produced a string of Broadway hits, and the Ford Foundation to combine the Apollo and the Lyric Theaters on the northern side of the street into one grand playhouse. In 1997 Livent and Ford christened their new complex the Ford Center for the Performing Arts. In January 1998 its premiere offering, *Ragtime,* opened to rave reviews. (A year later, Grabinsky went bankrupt as the result of separate dealings having to do with his Canadian-based operation, and the Ford Foundation took sole control of the new Victory, successfully completing its decades-long quest to establish a viable theatrical presence on West 42nd Street. That same year, the surviving elements of Livent's various operations were bought out by SFX, a live-entertainment conglomerate considered by many to be the country's premier concert booking agency, composed of such well-known companies as Delsener/Slater, Bill Graham Presents, and the Pace Entertainment Corporation, which produces everything from Broadway shows to rock concerts to monster-truck events. SFX moved into the Candler, which had sat empty since the Lazar scandal.)

Also in 1996 the long-standing problem of what to do with the still-vacant Selwyn, one of the last of the available theaters, was finally resolved. At the memorial service for Bernard B. Jacobs, the president of the Shubert Organization and Gerald Schoenfeld's longtime friend, who had passed away at the age of eighty, Rebecca Robertson found herself sitting next to Todd Haines, the artistic director of the Roundabout Theater Company. Although the timing was awkward, Robertson once more brought up the possibility of his theater company taking over the Selwyn. This time, Haines, whose company had since been ousted from its 45th Street and Broadway location as the result of the real estate frenzy sparked by Disney's presence in Times Square, was far more receptive to the idea. "I noticed everything going on around me," Haines later told the *New York Times*. "I said, 'Let's do something.'" A deal was struck, and shortly thereafter fund-raising began for restorations, with a budget projection of $21 million for the New 42–owned 740-seat theater. Not long after the theater company signed on, the Selwyn found a corporate underwriter for the Roundabout, American Airlines, which struck a ten-year, $8.5 million sponsorship deal Haines described as "wonderful." As part of the agreement, the restored Selwyn became the American Airlines Theater, with the airlines' name prominently displayed on the marquee, prompting *New York Observer* theater critic John Heilpern to declare, "There goes the neighborhood (again)."

While it was easy to see why Haines loved the idea of what in effect was a guarantee of his company's continued existence, it was also hard to miss Heilpern's point. What had once been a mark of Broadway honor and distinction, the naming of a theater (the Helen Hayes, the O'Neill, the Henry Miller, the Walter Kerr), had become a purchasable commodity. Ford, Disney, AMC, Loew's, a multilevel, multimedia HMV Records store, and a host of others were now joined by American Airlines' trademark shingle. Not long after, the Shuberts began discussions with General Motors, about renaming the Winter Garden, Jolson's Broadway "home," on 50th and 51st on Broadway, the Cadillac Winter Garden.

O N MAY 18, 1997, the New Amsterdam celebrated its official reopening with the "World Premiere Concert Event," five-performance-run of *King David.* For the occasion, Eisner was met at the airport and driven directly to the theater with a full-siren, flashing-lights NYPD escort, courtesy of the mayor's office. In November the live version of an animated Disney film, *The Lion King,* opened at the theater, received ecstatic reviews, including one from the *Times,* and immediately became the hottest ticket in town.

Disney's success on 42nd Street helped solve the Durst situation. Not long after *The Lion King* opened, Douglas Durst suddenly reversed his long-standing position and sought a way to get in on the action, at the same time Prudential decided it wanted out.

An internal struggle over leadership and direction and a desire to build its cash reserves caused Prudential to exercise its option and leave 42nd Street. This meant that Klein was out as well. Each sold its share in all the holdings, including the escrow fund, to a series of high-end buyers who eagerly lined up with cash in hand (Klein held on to what he described later as a "minuscule" portion), and the newest gold rush east of San Francisco kicked into overdrive.* *Daily News* publisher Mort Zuckerman snapped up the rights to the southwest corner of 42nd and Seventh, where Disney's temporary retail store had been, for a hotel. Developer Lew Rudin got the northwest corner of 42nd and Seventh and immediately signed up Reuters, the international news agency, as his primary tenant (a deal sweetened by an additional $26-million tax abatement granted to the media organization by the city). The Milstein Brothers, in the hunt for yet another piece of the boulevard pie (they'd already acquired the parking lot across from the Port Authority Bus Terminal), submitted the winning bid for the southeast corner of 42nd and Broadway where the shell of the landmarked Knickerbocker Hotel still stood, and announced plans to completely refurbish it. Finally, in a move that surprised everybody, the Durst Organization was virtually handed the rights to the

---

*Prudential was ultimately unable to resist the lure of Times Square. Late in 2000 the company announced a joint venture with KW Partners, an Internet marketing company which promotes rock stars, to purchase the twenty-story building at 230 West 42nd Street, built in the mid-twenties to house the *New York Herald Tribune.*

(Left to right) *George Pataki, the governor of New York, Mayor Giuliani, and Michael Eisner at the long-awaited and highly anticipated grand reopening of the New Amsterdam Theater in May 1997.* (Mayor Giuliani's Press Photo Unit/provided by Tony Coles)

northeast corner of 42nd and Broadway, the original site of Hammerstein's Music Hall (whose northern end in the seventies was the Manhattan home of Nathan's Famous hot dogs).

It was one of the most unexpected and highly ironic twists to the continuing saga of 42nd Street. As soon as Prudential announced it was giving up its right to the "four corners," Durst offered to drop its long-standing lawsuit in return for one of the suddenly available sites, for what one close to the deal called "a very cheap price." Prudential and Klein quickly agreed (both were parties to the suit), and Durst acquired the land, along with Prudential's twenty years of city and state guaranteed tax abatements from the original Koch plan. Shortly after, Durst announced he had two primary tenants for his building, the Condé Nast publishing organization and Wall Street's NASDAQ exchange. "We're proud that this project is moving ahead so well," Durst announced in a press release, "and that our presence here will add to the grandeur of the New Times Square, New York's newest and most thriving community."

The long-awaited groundbreaking on the four towers ignited yet another new and intense round of corporate buyouts in and

The northwest corner of Seventh Avenue at 42nd Street in 1998. The interim Disney store adjacent to the New Amsterdam Theater would soon come down, but the Disney presence on the street would remain. (Rebel Road, Inc.)

The Victory, which had screened porno films for a quarter century, was restored and combined with the adjacent Apollo by Ford Foundation money and renamed the New Victory, the show palace for the "Ford Center for the Performing Arts." (Rebel Road, Inc.)

around Times Square. The investment firm of Morgan Stanley bought out the previous owners of a high-rise on 49th and Broadway, put up a flashy hundred-foot-high stock market zipper sign, and then immediately announced plans for yet another new tower at the site of what was for many years an open-air parking lot on 50th and Seventh Avenue. In addition to the Marriott Marquis, a high-rise luxury Holiday Inn, a Renaissance, and at least a dozen other either new or refurbished independent hotels opened around Times Square. The Hilton Corporation then announced it was building a luxury hotel on 41st and Broadway, with an entrance on 42nd Street. Hilton's entry signaled the start of the southern expansion of the 42nd Street/Times Square real estate boom.

In 1999 Tussaud's announced plans to combine the sites of the former Empire and Harris Theaters to create a showcase wax museum. And AMC completed negotiations for a twenty-five-screen cinema complex to replace the old Empire, with a seating capacity of five thousand. Ironically Loew's then announced it, too, was going to open a multiplex on the Seven/Eight. These two movie theater complexes not only brought mainstream film back to the street whose theaters had been ruined by the emergence of talkies sixty years earlier (and whose restoration had been made possible by a Hollywood movie studio) but also helped close the door on the last of Broadway's glory-day film palaces. The Criterion (original site of Hammerstein's turn-of-the-twentieth-century Olympia) had become the sole survivor of a group of theaters from the era of reserved, or road-show, presentations that included the Roxy, the Palace, the Paramount, and Radio City Music Hall (the latter still in existence only as a live concert venue), proved unable to compete with 42nd Street's forty new first-run screens and said good-bye forever to Broadway. The property was immediately sold to a developer who planned to build a high-rise on it.

In 1999 international media giant Bertelsmann, Inc., opened its new Times Square headquarters. Not long after, the Disney-owned American Broadcasting Company rebuilt the Times Square theater it acquired during the Livent sell-off and converted it to a multiple-level glass-enclosed TV broadcast studio. Viacom, the media conglomerate that owns MTV, opened its new hi-tech glass-walled studios across the street and one story up in the Minskoff building. The rock studio immediately began drawing daily hordes of teenagers onto the streets of Broadway, hoping to catch a glimpse of their favorite groups or be caught themselves on TV by one of MTV's most popular daily programs, *TRL* (*Total Request Live*), whose constantly roving camera teams used Times Square as the show's backdrop. Condé Nast, Reuters, ABC, Viacom, SFX, ESPN

A corporate theater on a corporate street. The former Selwyn Theater was restored and renamed in honor of its prime benefactor. The American Airlines Theater is the new home for the Roundabout Theater Company. (Rebel Road, Inc.)

Times Square billboards in a "cleaned-up" midtown in 1999. Near nudity and sexual come-ons remain the primary eye-catching advertising attraction. (Rebel Road, Inc.)

(yet another Disney-owned enterprise, a 42,000-square-foot sports-theme dining and entertainment complex on 42nd Street and Broadway), and NASDAQ's ten-story animated facade, "the giant tin can," as it is often called, joining the dozens of other Times Square TV screens, laser signs, and neon billboards. As for the "quaint little bowl," it had all but vanished, hidden from the sun by the newest and glitziest corporate media center in America.

AND SO AS THE CITY PREPARED for its final New Year's Eve of the millennium, the "new" Times Square braced itself for the celebration to end all celebrations. It was an unusually warm day for late December, and it brought the crowds out. As darkness fell, some looked up to the sky to make sure it wasn't falling, and that they weren't all about to be Y2KO'd. By 11:59, 2.5 million people, more than 70 percent of them tourists, stood in the mayor's heavily policed pedestrian grids waiting for the day, the month, the year, the decade, the century, and the millennium to turn. From around the world, as midnight struck each country, a great wave of celebration rolled its way west.

At precisely 12:00, the glistening crystal ball began to descend from its perch atop the old Times Tower, delivering New York City into the future. On some silent and unseen cue, the tourist-filled dry and dreamless boulevard was showered with styrofoam snowflakes. And so it was that Ed Koch's long-ago warning had finally come to pass. Down 42nd Street there was artificially flavored juice everywhere and not a single drop of seltzer left to drink.

Epilogue

THE NEW CROSSROADS, with its electronic marquees, magical billboards, and come-hither storefronts that endlessly winked, twitched, and rolled, was to native New Yorkers, kitschy, catchy, and cold. A small neo-arcade opened on the north side of 42nd Street just east of Eighth Avenue, next to the new Loew's E-Walk movie complex. Above the entranceway to the pinball parlor a plain, large sign declared, "You can still have fun here with a handful of quarters." It was a revisionist punch line to a joke most people, if they got it at all, didn't think was all that funny. For tourists it offered a wink-wink to a historic strip that had simply ceased to exist. In its place was anywhere else, USA, familiar to every American except those who'd been born and raised in New York City.

Any complaints regarding the aesthetics of the new 42nd Street were all but buried by the sound of jackhammers and cash registers, at a time when the quality of product was measured, not by its historical worth, but by the quantity sold.

Broadway as an industry (rather than an art form) made the case. Since the mid-1960s, a full third of the twentieth century, no great new, original American voice had emerged from the New York stage. Increasingly the street's glorious playhouses were filled with musicals, imports, and revivals. For the last decade of the last century and the first year of the new one, the most memorable drama to be found on the Great White Way was in the regurgitated

Welcoming the millennium in the "new" Times Square. (Rebel Road, Inc.)

works of the Big Four—Eugene O'Neill *(The Iceman Cometh, A Moon for the Misbegotten)*, Tennessee Williams *(A Streetcar Named Desire)*, Arthur Miller *(Death of a Salesman, The Price)*, and Edward Albee *(A Delicate Balance)*. New-millennium Broadway had become less a New York theatrical experience than a tourist attraction.

Nevertheless (or perhaps because of it), all box-office records were broken during the 1999–2000 Broadway season, with a total gross reaching $603 million (three of the biggest hits were *Aida*, *The Lion King*, and *Beauty and the Beast*, all Disney productions). By comparison, in 1994, the last year before Disney took over the New Amsterdam Theater, Broadway's total take was $406 million. The ancillary value of this 30 percent, $200-million increase to the economy of New York City is best measured by the success of *Cats*, the British-import musical based on T. S. Eliot's *Old Possum's Book of Practical Cats*, which closed in September 2000 after eighteen years and a record-breaking 7,485 performances, more than seventy percent of which were attended by tourists, at the Shuberts' Winter Garden Theater.

During its run, *Cats* grossed nearly $400 million, which, according to the *New York Times*, factoring in the money spent by all those theatergoers on taxis, hotels, drinks, meals, souvenirs, and sundries, added a total of $6 *billion* to the city's economy. Allowing for the fluctuation in the price of tickets through the years and maintaining the ratio of approximately fifteen dollars spent on items and services for every dollar paid for tickets, the value of the two-year increase in post-Disney Broadway box-office revenues translated into 3 billion taxable dollars.

Elsewhere on the street, the Ford Center continued to flourish, with its multiple Tony Award–winning revival of the musical *42nd Street*, a remake of a 1980s David Merrick remake of the 1933 movie remake that was, essentially, a remake of every Broadway musical of the theater's early twentieth-century heyday.

And finally, Fred Papert's dream of reviving Off Broadway west of Ninth Avenue was realized with the completion of the Playwrights Horizons new headquarters, located between Ninth and Dyer (the split-block exit between Ninth and Tenth where cars emerge into Manhattan from the Lincoln Tunnel). Playwrights Horizons, founded in 1971, had somehow survived the onslaught of porn and peep shows, taking up residence for a while in the old Maidman Playhouse, while the rest of the street and neighborhood succumbed to midtown's social blight. During its long struggle to survive, it offered an outlet to such notable stage voices as Wendy Wasserstein, James Lapine, Stephen Sondheim, Albert Innaurato, A. R. Gurney Jr. and Christopher Durang. As Papert had envisioned, the theater followed the redevelopment plan of the Seven/Eight restoration by coming under the auspices of the non-profit 42nd Street Development Corporation. It was then able to benefit from the sale of its air rights to the Brodsky Organization for $1.5 million, which planned to build a high-rise apartment tower over the theater, and another in the complex, a new 499-seat Shubert House. The $24 million was raised in part by grants from Ford ($2.2 million), the estate of Edith K. Ehrman ($10 million), and a number of other benefactors. Combining the best of the West Side, it marked another strong step in the ongoing renaissance of 42nd Street.

I N 1976, THE YEAR Abe Beame raided the Show World, less than $6 million in city taxes had been collected from the Seven/Eight. In 1999, the city had collected nearly $1 billion in revenues from retail operators, hotels, advertisers, sales taxes, occupancy taxes, and a hundred other financial hooks it had attached to this revamped stretch of real estate.

Without question, Michael Eisner deserved the lion king's share of the credit for lending Disney's prestige and credibility to 42nd Street at a time when its commercial life had all but bottomed out. But it should also be remembered that Disney wouldn't have come to the street without the benefit of enormous tax breaks, and a fair amount of credit must go to the man at the starting end of the three-decade saga, John Lindsay, who believed that tax abatements were the key to generating huge amounts of new income for the city.

Attention should also be paid to Gerald Schoenfeld. He is the only player who was and is there from the beginning, when Lindsay first contemplated upzoning and redevelopment for Midtown West. Schoenfeld and the mayor's Midtown Committee (which he still chairs) helped organize the district, helped define quality-of-

42nd Street in the twenty-first century, at the northeast corner of Seventh Avenue. The cigar store is finally gone, replaced by a new and sleek corporate high-rise, the headquarters of Reuters, the international news service (3 Times Square), one of the corner's four long-awaited "elephant legs." (Rebel Road, Inc.)

The northeast corner of Broadway at 42nd Street. The new Condé Nast high-rise (4 Times Square), which replaced a series of low-rises and a porno movie theater, is the midtown headquarters of the ESPN Zone. (Rebel Road, Inc.)

The southwest corner of Seventh Avenue and 42nd Street (5 Times Square). Boston Properties is the latest in a long line of investors to take control of this "elephant leg" and the first to break ground. Gone are the fabled Nedick's and the interim Disney store. (Rebel Road, Inc.)

A tourist favorite. Referred to as "the can" by native New Yorkers, the new NASDAQ billboard at the southwest corner of 43rd Street and Broadway is a spectacular nine-story active TV screen attached to the front of the Condé Nast building, whose street-level tenant is the media headquarters for the exchange. (Rebel Road, Inc.)

The southeast corner of Broadway at 42nd Street. The Knickerbocker Hotel is seen undergoing preservation. In the foreground, a restaurant occupies the site, directly south of the original New York Times headquarters, which once housed a porno bookstore replaced by the fourth elephant leg, the new "Times Square Tower." Gone without a trace are any of the elaborate plans for the corners designed by Philip Johnson and John Burgee and commissioned by George Klein with Prudential funding. (Rebel Road, Inc.)

The facade of the Allied Chemical Tower. The famed zipper, the Warner Bros. studio store, and a giant billboard. The interior of the building remains largely unoccupied, with extensive interior renovation still in the planning stage. (Rebel Road, Inc.)

life crimes, took part in the fight to keep Broadway a viable, if progressive, industry, and held the theater district together through five mayors, a mob war, developers, interlopers, rebellions, Johnny-Come Latelys and federal consent decrees. He is a fighter, a warrior, a diplomat, and a survivor. After thirty years Broadway had once more become the number one tourist attraction in New York City, well ahead of any of its sports franchises, with a combined ticket income for 1999 that outgrossed the attendance dollars of the Yankees, the Mets, the Knicks, the Rangers, the Giants, and the Jets *combined.*

As for Ed Koch, the middle man in the street's long road to rejuvenation, he never reentered politics. Instead, he joined a major law firm and succumbed to his desire to entertain by taking a job as a "judge" on a daytime courtroom series (he was never appointed or elected to such a post in real life) where, in a bit of inspired typecasting, he played an Old Testament–type God to an endless flow of petty plaintiffs and defendants arguing over who should pay for the dent in the rear fender.

I N THE FIRST YEAR OF the new millennium, a nasty cluster of porn shops, several of which still offered women performing sex acts on themselves and one another, continued to do business on either side of a parking garage, on the north side of 42nd Street between Avenue of the Americas and Broadway. The odd distribution of this parcel of land had allowed it to remain the last unassembled strip of West 42nd Street, the lone outpost for what now appeared to be an almost quaint walk-in video and magazine emporium.

Also, farther over to the west, porn stubbornly proliferated along Eighth Avenue, from 34th Street up to 48th. More than a dozen brightly lit independently owned video outlets, run mostly by first-generation Indian immigrants, stayed open for business twenty-four hours a day, seven days a week. In addition, video and DVD porn remained easily available for a couple of dollars in virtually every corner bodega and Korean grocery in town, sold in explicitly illustrated boxes stacked alongside the chilled fresh fruit or steam tables. Everywhere, it seemed, *except* on the Seven/Eight, that tourist-friendly street of gold-plated souvenirs unofficially designated as the city's moral high road. As a California-based industry, porn had become an apparently legal major American industry, with an annual gross in 2000 of eleven billion dollars, more than either Broadway, mainstream Hollywood, or the music industries each grossed that year.

Ironically, the loudest complaint in the year 2000 came not from those trying to prevent the further demolition of old and beloved buildings, but from those desperately trying to build new ones. Whole sections of the city, including Greenwich Village, the Upper West Side, and Brooklyn Heights, had become in part or in whole designated "historic" by the Landmarks Commission and therefore protected from any development in the foreseeable future. Those who opposed this insisted that progress had been halted and that in fifty years the city will resemble a giant museum, a place people visit when they want to see the relics of the past. The result of a policy has been the unbelievable markup in the price of whatever few land parcels there are that qualify for development. Those who favored the current landmarking criteria called that a victory, claiming nothing being built today could compete architecturally, aesthetically, in terms of pure functionality or presentation.

Both sides of this issue have used 42nd Street to make their case. On the one hand, the buildings and theaters that have gone up during its redevelopment cannot aesthetically compare with those that came down. The street's restored theaters, especially, have an artificiality that makes them look more historical than historic, more Hollywood than Hammerstein, fine for those wishing to bring their kids to them, tragic for those who believe the real experience of performed drama begins the moment one steps inside a theater.

For the rest, 42nd Street had become a horizontal statue of Liberty, a place native New Yorkers avoid like Yellow Fever. As one observer put it, "The old 42nd Street was considered too garish. The new 42nd Street celebrates that garishness as if it were a saleable commodity. Which, of course, it is. In the old days I feared for my life if I had to go to 42nd Street. Today, I wouldn't be caught dead there."

The first new midtown statues since George M. Cohan's were being prepared to honor Frank Sinatra and Jackie Gleason. Ol' Blue

Eyes, the New Jersey–bred saloon singer who loved/hated women from bobby-soxers to hookers to movie stars, who gave Italian mobsters a sharkskin gilt by association, and who had been banned from playing nightclubs in New York City for most of his career after he failed to qualify for the required cabaret license (another left-over law from the La Guardia era), was slated to have his image cast in life-size bronze outside the entrance of what had once been the Paramount Theater (which no longer exists), where, in the forties, he had broken all box-office records. As for Gleason, his statue was announced by the Port Authority Bus Terminal, to be erected in the likeness of his character, Ralph Kramden, the fifties TV-sitcom bus driver, who not only didn't work for the Port Authority—he was a city bus driver working for the Transit Authority—he never actually *existed*.

Finally, in the fall of 2000, the Giuliani administration announced a new plan to cure the growing congestion caused by the great numbers of tourists in Times Square by turning it into one giant pedestrian walk.

Not to worry, all was not won or lost. On the way is a giant Ferris wheel, courtesy of Toys-R-Us, scheduled to start going around in circles, smack in the middle of Times Square. All that will be missing is a giant walk-through apple.

Rebel Road, Inc.

BIBLIOGRAPHY

Parts of this book were researched at the Central Research Library, also known as the main branch of the New York Public Library on Fifth Avenue and 42nd Street; the Information Exchange of the Municipal Art Society; the International Center for Photography; the New York Public Library for the Performing Arts; the Municipal Research Library; the Museum of the City of New York; the J. P. Morgan Library; the New-York Historical Society; and the Old York Library, created and administered by the Durst family.

MISCELLANEOUS SOURCES AND SOURCE MATERIALS

The Mayor's Midtown Citizens' Committee.
"Yesterday and Today on 42nd Street," by F. W. Schoonmaker, Sr. Undated pamphlet.
"42nd Street River to River," by Gerald R. Wolfe. Pamphlet. 1984.
New York Law School, Center for New York City Law. Various newsletters.
Education Theater Culture, Inc.
Public transcripts of the Knapp Commission.
Rent Guidelines Board of New York City.

PEOPLE INTERVIEWED BY THE AUTHOR FOR THIS BOOK

Kent Barwick, president of the Municipal Art Society; former mayor Abe Beame; Tony Coles, senior adviser to Mayor Giuliani; William H. Daly, director of the Office of Midtown Enforcement, Office of the Mayor; Douglas Durst, Durst Real Estate Organization; John Dyson, former deputy mayor for Economic Development, Planning and Administration under Mayor Giuliani; Don Elliot, former head of the City Planning Commission; Deputy Chief Thomas Fahey, NYPD Commission for Public Information; John Feinblatt, director of the Center for Court Innovation of the Midtown North Community Court; Lawrence Field, police inspector, Port Authority Bus Terminal; Joe Franklin, TV and radio host; Ralph Ginzberg, publisher; Gary Goldstein, editor and pop culture historian; Jack Goldstein, Theater Development Fund; Marian Sulzberger Heiskell, chair of the New 42nd; Alan Hicks, information officer for media relations at Port Authority Bus Terminal; Alan Hoehl, chief of patrol, Borough of Manhattan South; Celeste Holm, film and theater actress; George Klein, president of Park Tower Realty; former mayor Ed Koch; Tom Leahy, entertainment executive, former head of CBS-TV Local News, New York City; Barry Lewis, architectural historian; David Malmuth, developer and restoration project organizer; Frederic Papert, president of 42nd Street Development Corporation/42nd Street Fund; Rebecca Robertson, vice-president in charge of real estate and special projects for the Shubert Organization; John F. Ryan, police lieutenant, Port Authority Bus Terminal; Andrew Sarris, film historian and film critic for the *New York Observer;* Gerald Schoenfeld, chairman of the Shubert Organization; Brendan Sexton, president of Times Square Business Improvement District; Herb Sturz, deputy mayor under Mayor Koch; Richard Weinstein, member of the Lindsay administration, one of the architects for the City at 42nd Street; Carl Weisbrod, president of the Alliance for Downtown New York.

The following also assisted, either as primary sources or as links to other primary and secondary sources: Ray Fisher, photographer; Vivienne Maricevic, photographer; Harvey Sabenstein, Abby Schroeder, George Wachtel, and Madelyn Kent, assistant curator of the Old York Library.

BOOK SOURCES

Asbury, Herbert. *The Gangs of New York.* Alfred A. Knopf, New York, 1928.

Barrett, Wayne, and Newfield, Jack. *City for Sale: Ed Koch and the Betrayal of New York.* Harper & Row, Perennial Library, New York, 1989.

Bayor, Ronald H., and Meagher, Timothy J. *The New York Irish.* Johns Hopkins University Press, Baltimore, 1997.

Belle, John, and Leighton, Maxinne R. *Grand Central: Gateway to a Million Lives.* W. W. Norton, New York and London, 2000.

Binkowski, Carol J. *Musical New York.* Camino Books, Philadelphia, 1999.

Blumenthal, Ralph. *Stork Club.* Little, Brown, New York, 2000.

Bosselman, Peter. *Times Square, 1985.* Videotape. Narrated by Jason Robards. Produced by Municipal Art Society. Not available for general release.

Burrows, Edwin G., and Wallace, Mike. *Gotham*. Oxford University Press, New York, 1999.

Colter, Ephen Glenn, et al. *Policing Public Sex*. South End Press, Boston, 1996.

Diamondstein, Barbaralee. *The Landmarks of New York II*. Harry Abrams, New York, 1993.

The Dictionary of American Biography. Scribner's, New York.

Doherty, Thomas. *Pre-Code Hollywood*. Columbia University Press, New York, 1999.

Dupré, Judith. *Skyscrapers*. Black Dog & Leventhal, New York, 1996.

The Durst Organization. Privately printed by the Durst family.

Federal Writers' Project. *The WPA Guide to New York City*. The Guilds Committee for Federal Writers' Publications. Random House, New York, 1992.

Friedman, Josh Alan. *Tales of Times Square*. Ferel House, Portland, Ore., 1993.

Gilmartin, Gregory F. *Shaping the City: New York and the Municipal Art Society*. Clarkson Potter, New York, 1995.

Henderson, Mary C. *The City and the Theatre*. James T. White, Clifton, N. J., 1973.

Hirsch, Foster. *The Boys from Syracuse: The Shuberts' Theatrical Empire*. Southern Illinois University Press, Carbondale, Ill., 1998.

Hoberman, J. *42nd Street*. Trinity Press, Worcester and London, 1993.

Hood, Clifton. *722 Miles: The Building of the Subways and How They Transformed New York*. Johns Hopkins, Baltimore, 1993.

Hope, Bob, and Thomas, Bob. *The Road to Hollywood*. Doubleday, New York, 1977.

Jackson, ed., *The Encyclopedia of New York City*. Yale University Press and the New York Historical Society, 1995.

Jones, Alex S., and Tifft, Susan E. *The Trust*. Little, Brown, New York, 1999.

Knapp, Margaret May. "Historical Study of the Legitimate Playhouses on West 42nd Street Between Seventh and Eighth Avenues in New York City." Ph.D. diss. City University of New York, 1982.

Koch, Ed, *Mayor*. Warner Books, paperback edition, New York, 1986.

Lankevich, George J. *American Metropolis: A History of New York City*. New York University Press, New York, 1998.

Maeder, Jay. *Big Town Biography*. Daily News, New York, 2000.

McNamara, Robert P. *Sex, Scams, and Street Life: The Sociology of New York City's Times Square*. Praeger, Westport, Conn., 1995.

Mitgang, Herbert. *Once Upon a Time in New York*. Free Press, New York, 2000.

Moorhouse, Geoffrey. *Imperial City New York*. Henry Holt, New York, 1988.

Morris, Lloyd. *Incredible New York*. Syracuse University Press, Syracuse, N.Y., 1951.

Moscow, Henry. *The Street Book.* Fordham University Press, New York, 1978.

New York Times Archives. *The Century in Times Square. New York Times,* New York, 1999.

Reichl, Alexander J. *Reconstructing Times Square.* University of Kansas Press, Lawrence, Kans., 1999.

Rhodehamel, John. "The Great Experiment: George Washington and the American Republic." Catalog of an exhibition organized by the Huntington Library with additional material from the Golder Lehrman Collection and the Pierpont Morgan Library. Yale University Press, New Haven and London; Huntington Library, San Marino, Calif., 1998.

Rogers, W. G., and Weston, Mildred. *Carnival Crossroads: The Story of Times Square.* Doubleday, New York, 1960.

Stern, Robert A. M.; Mellins, Thomas; and Fishman, David. *New York 1960.* Monacelli Press, New York, 1995.

Taylor, B. Kim. *The Great New York City Trivia and Fact Book.* Cumberland House, Nashville, 1998.

Thompson, J. William. *The Rebirth of New York City's Bryant Park.* Spacemaker Press, Washington, D.C., 1997.

Tournac, J., and Little, Christopher. *Elegant New York.* Abbeville Press, 1989.

"West 42nd Street: The Bright Light Zone." Unpublished report. The Graduate School and University Center of the City University of New York, © 1978. Project Director, William Kornblum, Associate Professor of Sociology.

Ziga, Charles J. *New York City Landmarks.* Dovetail Books, 1999.

ONE

[p. 8] "42nd Street and the Statue of Liberty": Ed Koch, interviewed by David Hartman on "A Walk Down 42nd Street with David Hartman," WNET-NY, produced by PBS, Reuters. First air date August 22, 1998. The quotation regarding his mother is from this program, which recreates one of Koch's trademarks—his New York City walks. The scene depicted here is taken from several reports of various 42nd Street walks, in addition to the one he made especially for Hartman.

[p. 14] Additional information on the subterranean composition of Manhattan: Much of 42nd Street is built atop Manhattan schist, which, when properly excavated, provides incredible foundation strength, and, once hollowed, the core of the modern subway system's outer layers. It was the unstable nature of schist that, at the time, made the placement of Ochs's underground presses unable to coexist with Belmont's Times Square subway station. From Hood, *722 Miles: The Building of the Subways and How They Transformed New York:* "Manhattan is shaped like an irregular rectangle. Seven miles long from the Battery to the Harlem River, the island has a width of roughly two miles up to 125th Street, and then it tapers into an elongated neck that ends at Inwood." With the exception of a few specific regions where the bedrock has been softened by the seepage of water, the island of Manhattan is covered by a type of rock known as Manhattan schist. According to Hood: "Schist is a well-foliated rock that . . . can thwart subterranean construction. A metamorphic rock forged deep within the earth's crust under intense pressure and great heat, Manhattan schist is a very hard rock that is murder to cut through . . . [and] susceptible to decay and can fracture or collapse without warning."

[p. 17] "The best organization mayor": Riis, quoted in Lankevich, p. 144.

[p. 17] Additional information on the early history of the *New York Times:* The "paper of record" was founded in 1851 as the *New-York Daily Times* by two Republicans, Henry J. Raymond, Speaker of the New York State Assembly, and George Jones, a banker, to compete with Horace Greeley's *Tribune.* The *Times* made its journalistic reputation by exposing the widespread corruption of Boss Tweed and Tammany Hall. Nevertheless, by 1893 the paper was nearly insolvent, kept open by funds from the Democratic Party, which needed a liberal voice in a city overrun with the "yellow journalism" of William Randolph Hearst. In 1896 Adolph Ochs, a newspaper publisher from the Midwest near bankruptcy himself, raised an initial $75,000 (how and from where has never been fully explained) to buy out the *Times* twenty-four hours before its being put on the auction block. Jacob Schiff and Isidor Straus, the latter the co-owner of R. H. Macy & Company, believed Ochs could be of "great service" to the Jewish community and provided much of the additional financial backing that made it possible for Ochs to acquire the paper. Eight years later, in league with August Belmont, who secretly controlled a huge block of the newspaper's stock, the New York Times building—the Times Tower—opened in the newly renamed Times Square, in conjunction with the building of the world's largest subway stop, Belmont's IRT Times Square station. The *Times* had tended to downplay this connection until quite recently, when a supplement called "Inside the New York Times," "a newsletter exclusively for New York Times Home Delivery Subscribers," dated winter 1999–2000 and entitled "The True Story of Times Square," gave this colorful, if somewhat qualified, explanation of the origin of Times Square: "Construction of the Times Tower, as it was to be called, began in 1903. While the new landmark was reaching for the heavens, a second Long Acre Square construction project was heading in another, darker direction. This was the new IRT subway station, burrowing directly beneath the newspaper building. And just as Ochs wanted a visible symbol of the Times's stature, August Belmont, the president of the IRT Company (and, according to some reports, a secret shareholder in the paper), wanted a snappy name for his new station. Therefore he petitioned the New York City Board of Alderman, which granted his request on April 8, 1904, by renaming Long Acre Square . . . TIMES SQUARE." Some additional information regarding the connection between Belmont and Ochs comes from Jones and Tifft, *The Trust.*

[p. 25] Some information regarding the Walker administration is from Mitgang. Additional information is from Terry Golway's review of Mitgang in the *Observer,* January 10, 2000.

[p. 30] Some information on the Chrysler Building is from Dupré, pp. 36–37, and from "A Walk Down 42nd Street with David Hartman." Additional information is from Robert D. McFadden, "Chrysler May Be in Chrysler Building's Future," *New York Times,* July 7, 2000, and Diamondstein, p. 360.

[p. 32] "Shit on Henry Ford": anonymous.

[p. 35] La Guardia was a fanatic about the heroics of the fire department and often rode along on one of the engines on their way to a four- or five-alarmer. The story is told that one time the truck he was on was delayed by a crossing trolley, which was the most popular surface transportation along 42nd Street, and he became so angry he outlawed trolleys as a viable means of public transportation.

[p. 38] Times Square homosexual lifestyle in the 1940s: Gregory D. Squires, "Public-Private Partnerships: Who Gets What and Why," *Unequal Partnerships* (New Brunswick, N.J.: Rutgers University Press, 1989).

[p. 42] "The rich get richer": anonymous.

[p. 45] The proper name of the great landmark is Grand Central Terminal. It is often mistakenly referred to as Grand Central Station.

TWO

[p. 49] Some background and additional information on George Washington and his 42nd Street battle with the British army is from John Rhodehamel's "The Great Experiment: George Washington and the American Republic," catalog of an exhibition organized by the Huntington Library, 1998, the Golder Lehrman Collection, the Pierpoint Morgan Library, and the Huntington Library, San Marino, California.

[p. 50] "Death and we shook hands": Burrows and Wallace, p. 358.

[p. 51] "When the British finally abandoned the city in 1783, after having held it throughout the war, it still was a small place extending north only to the site of the present City Hall. But at the turn of the century, it began to burst at its seams. On January 20, 1806, the city council felt it necessary to resolve that 'it is highly important that a correct survey and map be made of the Island of New York'—which meant, of course, only Manhattan. And on April 3, 1807 . . . the commissioners [supervised by De Witt Clinton] considered a plan of curves and circles like that which characterizes Washington, D.C., but decided that 'straight-sided and right-angled houses are the most cheap to build and the most convenient to live in.' So what they came up with in 1811, in a map drawn by John Randel, Jr., was a so-called grid plan of rectangular, symmetrical avenues 100 feet wide and streets mostly 60 feet wide, interspersed with occasional public squares. Avenues that could be extended some day north to Harlem were numbered from First to Twelfth (reading from right to left if one faced uptown). East of First, the avenues that geography would keep short were designated A, B, C, and D." (Henry Moscow, *The Street Book: An Encyclopedia of Manhattan's Street Names and Their Origins.*)

By the mid-1830s sixteen streets had become main thoroughfares and either already were, or were reconstructed to be, one hundred feet wide rather than sixty. Forty-second Street officially became a main river-to-river thoroughfare in 1837. As early as 1658 local notaries used names, many of which remained, in one form or another, after the 1811 mapping. For instance, a major and uninterrupted trade route ran through the entire length of Manhattan, to what was then the upper forestland. The path was known by its Indian name of Beaver Path. When it was eventually widened and leveled, it was called Breede Wegh by the Dutch, which eventually became "Broadway." This north-south boulevard has never been officially numbered.

[p. 53] Some information on Paddy Corcoran and Corcoran's Roost comes from Barry Lewis's PBS production "A Walking Tour of 42nd Street" and the New York City Landmarks Preservation Commission. Additional information is from Asbury, pp. 358–59.

[p. 55] "a cancer eating away": Ronald H. Bayor and Timothy Meagher, *The New York Irish* (Baltimore: Johns Hopkins University Press, 1996).

[p. 60] Description of the facade of Grand Central Depot and the quotation are from Burns. Additional information on Vanderbilt and the depot is from Belle and Leighton, Lankevitch, and Gilmartin.

[p. 64] Some information on the history of the New York Public Library is from *The WPA Guide to New York City* and from Tournac and Little.

THREE

[p. 71] Some information concerning turn-of-the-century prostitution is from an essay by Timothy G. Gilfoyle in Colter, p. 271.

[p. 72] Some information regarding the Tenderloin is from Reichl, p. 50.

[p. 72] Quotation is from Morris, pp. 260–61.

[p. 74] Some information on the Syndicate is from Knapp and from Henry Hope Reed, Jr., "Greater New York: Beneath the Squalor, Yesterday's Glamor," *New York Herald Tribune Sunday Magazine,* October 28, 1962.

[p. 75] Hammerstein owned hundreds of patents, including at least four involving cigar-making; a leg-baker, which applied heat to an injury; and an automatically closing inkwell.

[p. 81] "What I did": Colter, p. 271.

[p. 82] An all-time high of 150,000: ibid., p. 272.

[p. 84] Information about Heatherbloom's electric sign is from Gilmartin, p. 442.

[p. 87] "The best-lit stage": Hoberman, p. 9.

[p. 88] "42nd Street is a prime chunk": ibid.

[p. 88] Background on the opening of *42nd Street* is from Knapp, p. 369.

[p. 92] *Hair* opened on Broadway April 29, 1968, at the Biltmore Theater. It was revived for a limited run in 1977 and again in 2001. *Oh! Calcutta!* opened off-Broadway June 17, 1969, and soon moved to a Broadway house, where it ran to full houses for several years.

FOUR

[p. 95] "Not what it used to be": *Business Week,* January 9, 1954.

[p. 96] Some information on brothels, nightclubs, massage parlors, and street drugs, on this page and throughout the rest of the chapter is from Rogers and Weston, pp. 158–63.

[p. 97] "A decrepit walk-up": Edward Sorel, "Missing Pieces," *New Yorker,* December 6, 1999.

[p. 97] When Huberts first appeared in the 1920s on 42nd Street between Seventh and Eighth Avenues, Brooks Atkinson, the sophisticated drama critic for the *New York Times,* seemed annoyed by its presence, complaining that it was too raucous and uncouth for the theater block. However, as the level of entertainment declined, Huberts's reputation as a legitimate freak show continued to rise to the point where often fringe celebrities, mainly from the world of sports, "played" there, including boxing champion Jack Johnson and pitching phenomenon Grover Cleveland Alexander. The place was a favorite of Lenny Bruce's, who often referred to it in his comedy routines. Huberts lasted until the mid-sixties, when the site became "Peepland." The building has since been torn down.

[p. 98] Joe Franklin's reminiscences and all other commentary by Joe Franklin, unless otherwise noted, are from an interview with Eliot.

[p. 98] "There were never any 'good old days'" and all other comments by Andrew Sarris, unless otherwise noted, are from interviews with Eliot.

[p. 100] "I used to rush down there": Phillip Lopate, "42nd Street, You Ain't No Sodom," *New York Times,* March 8, 1979.

[p. 104] In 1933, the same year Prohibition ended, *The United States v. "Ulysses" and Random House, Inc.* marked the beginning of several key anti-censorship victories that included successful defenses of *Mademoiselle de Maupin, Casanova's Homecoming, Frankie and Johnnie,* and *God's Little Acre.* The *Ulysses* case was a turning point, as it offered the first definition of what would eventually come to be known as "redeeming social value" to defend the publication of so-called obscene literature. This decision came more than a hundred years after what is generally regarded as the first recorded suppression of a literary work on grounds of obscenity in the United States—the 1821 indictment of Boston-based Peter Holmes and Stillman Howe for their publishing *Memoirs of a Woman of Pleasure,* otherwise known as *Fanny Hill.* The case was responsible for the popularizing of the phrase "banned in Boston." 162 years later, following the book's 1963 publication by Putnam, it was deemed to be publishable under the Supreme Court's 1957 landmark *Roth v. United States.* The standards established in *Roth* said a work is patently obscene if its predominant appeal is to "prurient interest," it goes "substantially beyond customary limits of candor in description or representations of such matters," and it is "so offensive on [its] face as to affront current community standards." This was followed by the successful publication of such previously banned books as Vladimir Nabokov's *Lolita,* D. H. Lawrence's *Lady Chatterley's Lover,* Henry Miller's *Tropic of Cancer* (first American edition), William Burroughs's *Naked Lunch,* and Jean Genet's *Our Lady of the Flowers.* Although several challenges were later made to the production, exhibition, and distribution of pornographic movies, with few exceptions they were most often defined as filmed versions of printed material (scripts or books) and therefore entitled to the same protection, as defined by the above cases, of the First Amendment. In 1973 the Burger Court tried, without apparent success, to narrow the definition when it declared in a 5–4 ruling that local juries would have the right to decide what offended standards of community taste and be able to convict if they found a work "taken as a whole, lacks serious literary, artistic, political or scientific value."

[p. 104] "Languishes in this *quartier Latin*": Andrew Sarris, *Village Voice,* May 30, 1977.

[p. 108] "Show me a man": quoted in Chris Erikson, "Naked City," *New York Daily News,* New York, 1999.

[p. 109] "The street was already": interview with Eliot. Mr. X wishes to remain anonymous.

FIVE

[p. 115] *USA v. Lee Shubert et al.* The roots of this 1950 lawsuit were planted at the turn of the century with the creation of the Theater Syndicate or Trust. Although the Shuberts were initially independents, over the years their national touring operation brought charges of monopoly against them, particularly in the area of booking, as non-Shubert productions had difficulty acquiring a chance to fairly bid for the use of major theaters throughout the country. This was an era when show business was being looked at very closely by a federal government concerned not just with the distribution of politically subversive material but also with unfair competition, both taken as threats to "the American way" that was thought to be rampant among the so-called liberal entertainment media.

Hollywood studios had suffered a similar fate two years earlier in 1950 when a decision of the Supreme Court forced them to sell off one of their three branches of what was considered monopolistic operations: the production, distribution, and exhibition of motion pictures. The Schoenfeld suit and the Block-Booking suit both occurred during what is now referred to as the Cold War, between the first HUAC entertainment industry investigations of the forties and the height of McCarthyism in the fifties.

[p. 116] Information on Shubert Alley is from Diamonstein, p. 311. "The two facades [of the Shubert and the Booth] are joined by a projecting curved pavilion, which contains the central doorway, and decorated with Venetian Renaissance details, including low-relief sgraffito decoration below the cornice. The Booth and the Shubert contain the only known surviving examples of sgraffito in New York City." Information on the financial operations of the Shubert empire in 1971–72 comes from Hirsch, p. 276.

[p. 118] "The single worst block": Milton Bracker, "Life on 42nd Street: A Study," *New York Times,* March 14, 1960.

[p. 122] "In fact, for all the self-kudos": Barwick interview with Eliot. Unless otherwise noted, all quotations from Barwick in this chapter are from interviews with Eliot. Additional information on Barwick and the MAS is from Gilmartin, pp. 380–81.

[p. 124] "Very soon": "Movie Theatre on 42nd Street May House Stage Plays," *New York Times,* December 1966.

[p. 125] "Jerry Minskoff, the developer": Weinstein interview with Eliot. Unless otherwise noted, all quotations from Weinstein in this chapter are from interviews with Eliot.

[p. 128] "There was a movie theater": Franklin interview with Eliot.

SIX

[p. 136] "The black Hole of Calcutta": Schoenfeld, interview with Eliot.

[p. 136] Some of the information on the proposed Portman and Durst development deals is from Alan S. Oser, "About Real Estate: Times Square Site Undergoes a Gradual Conversion," *New York Times,* September 10, 1975.

[p. 139] "These were hard times": Beame interview with Eliot. Unless otherwise noted, all quotations from Beame in this chapter are from interviews with Eliot.

[p. 142] "By the mid-seventies": Daly, interview with Eliot. Unless otherwise noted all quotations from Daly are from interviews with Eliot.

[p. 143] "I was the executive captain": Hoele, interview with Eliot. Unless otherwise noted all quotations from Daly are from interviews with Eliot.

[p. 147] "The crime problem": Ryan, interview with Eliot. Unless otherwise noted, all quotations are from interviews with Eliot.

[p. 150] "Crowning glory": Dupré, p. 51.

[p. 151] "Seven-league monster," "fatal blow": Dupré, p. 57.

[p. 154] "The decision is . . . a dreadful blow": Huxtable, *New York Times,* January 31, 1975.

[p. 155] "My involvement in saving the terminal": Papert interview with Eliot. Unless otherwise noted, all quotations from Papert in this chapter are from interviews with Eliot.

[p. 157] "Not only was it still the most beautiful": Papert, quoted in the *London Sunday Times,* April 11, 1977.

[p. 157] Even before she became actively involved in the Committee to Save Grand Central Terminal, Jackie Kennedy Onassis had publicly complained against the construction of the Pan Am Building, warning it would completely obliterate Grand Central Terminal.

[p. 162] "There are more ways to destroy a building": *New York Times,* April 27, 1977.

SEVEN

[p. 167] "I had never": Schoenfeld interview with Eliot. Unless otherwise noted, all quotations from Schoenfeld in this chapter are from interviews with Eliot.

[p. 168] "Seymour Durst was a dear friend": Papert interview with Eliot. Unless otherwise noted, all quotations from Papert in this chapter are from interviews with Eliot.

[p. 171] "What the community" and "Tennessee doesn't care": David Bird, "For Some Theater People, Home Is Low-Cost Luxury," *New York Times,* November 18, 1978, sec. B, p. 18.

[p. 172] "The Portman Hotel": Davidson, quoted in Gilmartin, p. 449.

[p. 174] "Schoenfeld didn't care": Holm interview with Eliot. Unless otherwise noted, all quotations from Holm in this chapter are from interviews with Eliot.

EIGHT

[p. 177] The McGraw-Hill Building: Described by architectural historian Vincent Scully as "proto-jukebox modern," and by Lewis Mumford as one of the buildings that shaped the future of New York. Erected in the hopes of stimulating commercial investment in the West Side, when it failed to create a Depression-era boom, it remained for many years the only high-rise on 42nd Street west of Sixth Avenue. Commonly known as the Green Building, the one-time home of McGraw-Hill publishing, it was put on the market for $15 million in 1973 when the publisher relocated to Rockefeller Center, and failed to find a buyer (CRF Equity agreed to buy it in 1970 for $15 million but withdrew after paying a $4-million down payment). When Papert's organization took over the building to save it from being demolished, the so-called white elephant of 42nd Street was completely empty, losing about $450,000 annually in taxes and maintenance. In the late seventies the building was designated a landmark and reclaimed by the city as headquarters for several official New York City agencies. Papert's 42nd Street Development Corporation also relocated there and later on, after the Crossroads was turned into a restaurant, so did Bill Daly's Midtown Enforcement Project offices. (Some background information from the *New York Times,* November 3, 1973. Additional information from Fred Papert interview with Eliot.)

[p. 178] Some of the information on Roger Kennedy is from Wolf Von Eckhardt, "High on Tech," *Washington Post,* March 1, 1980.

[p. 182] "My office was on the fifty-fourth floor": Weinstein interviews with Eliot. Unless otherwise noted, all quotations from Weinstein in this chapter are from interview with Eliot.

[p. 184] "A celebration and investigation": from a proposal for the City at 42nd Street.

[p. 185] "By the end of": Elliot interview with Eliot. Unless otherwise noted, all quotations from Elliot in this chapter are from interview with Eliot.

[p. 188] "A thinly disguised land grab": Brandt, *Wall Street Journal,* August 20, 1980.

[p. 190] "Cut through the red tape": Sturz, *New York Times,* April 28, 1980.

[p. 190] "It wasn't so much": Sturz, interview with Eliot. Unless otherwise noted, all quotations from Sturz in this chapter are from interviews with Eliot.

[p. 190] "We'd made up a model": Papert interview with Eliot. Unless otherwise noted, all quotations from Papert in this chapter are from interviews with Eliot.

[p. 192] "Too much orange juice": Quotation recalled by Koch during interview with Eliot. Unless otherwise noted all quotations from Koch are from interviews with Eliot.

[p. 193] "What nonsense": Sturz interview with Eliot. Unless otherwise noted, all quotations from Sturz in this chapter are from interviews with Eliot.

[p. 194] "They got what was coming": interview with Eliot. Subject wishes to remain anonymous.

[p. 194] "Weinstein and Elliot": Barwick interview with Eliot. All quotations from Barwick in this chapter are from interviews with Eliot.

[p. 197] "Broadway is currently casting the Portman Hotel": *New York Times,* March 8, 1980.

[p. 199] "The goddamn corny image": Portman, quoted in "Portman, Thinking Big, Is Unfazed by New York," *New York Times,* October 7, 1981.

[p. 200] "Either a funeral or a rebirth": Arthur Miller and the others are quoted in "Broadway Stages a Drama to Save 2 Theaters," *New York Times,* March 5, 1982.

[p. 200] "As I was standing": Celeste Holm, interview with Eliot. Unless otherwise noted, all quotations from Holm in this chapter are from interviews with Eliot.

[p. 200] "Koch may have come across": interview with Eliot. Subject wishes to remain anonymous.

NINE

[p. 207] Koch's request for proposals was prepared by the architecture and design firm of Cooper Eckstut Associates, whose proposal for Battery Park City had just been accepted by the city and resembled to a remarkable degree the concept and physical layout of the now-defunct City at 42nd Street. The RFPs were done in cooperation with the City Planning Commission (CPC), the Department of City Planning (DCP), and the state Urban Development Corporation (UDC, which in 1995 became the Empire State Development Corporation). The original purpose of the UDC was to promote the development of low-income housing in the sixties, but gradually its focus shifted to construction of urban-based office space and middle-to-upper-income housing. When the RFP was issued, Koch employed yet another city agency, the New York City Public Development Corporation (PDC, later renamed the Economic Development Corporation, or EDC), whose primary purpose was the same as the UDC, only functioning at the city level. This move clearly demonstrated Koch's intention to have Times Square developed in a joint partnership of the public and private sectors. The primary difference between Koch's plan and Elliot's was the level of intended corporate involvement. Koch's plan favored less nonprofit sponsorship and more profit-incentive private investment.

[p. 207] "Had landed one of the great real-estate plums": Jonathan Greenberg, "How to Make It Big in New York Real Estate," *Forbes,* October 8, 1984.

[p. 210] "George Klein was a brilliant choice": Barwick interview with Eliot. All quotations from Barwick in this chapter are from interview with Eliot.

[p. 212] "The greatest single private real estate development": Cuomo, quoted in Reichl, p. 103.

[p. 214] "By 1983": Barwick, interview with Eliot. Unless otherwise noted, all quotations in this chapter from Barwick are from interviews with Eliot.

[p. 215] "A toilet bowl": Schoenfeld interview with Eliot. Unless otherwise noted, all quotations from Schoenfeld in this chapter are from interviews with Eliot.

TEN

[p. 224] The *Time* poll is from *Time,* July 21, 1986.

[p. 225] "The coming theme for the liberal society": Michael Novack, quoted in *Time,* July 21, 1986.

[p. 225] The reference to the mob's Waterloo is from Alan Feuer's obituary of Anthony Corallo in the *New York Times,* September 1, 2000.

[p. 228] "I can tell you": Daly interview with Eliot. Unless otherwise noted, all quotations from Daly in this chapter are from interviews with Eliot.

[p. 229] "We'd find bodies every morning": Ryan interview with Eliot. Unless otherwise noted, all quotations from Ryan are from interviews with Eliot.

[p. 232] "A lot of black and Puerto Rican people": interview with Eliot. Subject wishes to remain anonymous.

[p. 233] "Rebecca was priceless": interview with Eliot. Subject wishes to remain anonymous.

[p. 236] "Bryant Park is now dominated by dope dealers": from White's 1979 report to the Bryant Park Committee, quoted in Thompson, p. 23.

[p. 239] Some information on Basciano and Di Bernardo comes from Nassau County Court records and William Bastone's article "The Porn Broker," *Village Voice,* July 12, 1995, p. 13. According to Bastone, the origin of the link between Di Bernardo and Basciano is unknown. Bastone cites Salvatore "Sammy the Bull" Gravano's testimony against John Gotti, which helped convict the Gambino don, wherein Gravano made no mention of Di Bernardo's connection to Show World. Instead, he "testified that Gotti ordered Di Bernardo murdered because he believed the mob soldier had supposedly bad-mouthed him to other Gambino family members. Lured to a meeting at Gravano's Brooklyn office one night, Di Bernardo was stuffed into a body bag, loaded into the trunk of a Cadillac and disposed of somewhere. Di Bernardo's body has never been found."

ELEVEN

[p. 243] "Well, it was just pure luck": Heiskell interview with Eliot. Unless otherwise noted, all quotations from Heiskell in this chapter are from interviews with Eliot.

[p. 244] "We had approached Disney several times": Weisbrod interview with Eliot. Unless otherwise noted, all quotations from Weisbrod in this chapter are from interviews with Eliot.

[p. 245] "Disney could bring": Robertson, interview with Eliot. Unless otherwise indicated, all quotations from Robertson in this chapter are from interviews with Eliot.

[p. 246] "Eisner wanted the New Amsterdam": Malmuth interview with Eliot. Unless otherwise noted, all quotations from Malmuth in this chapter are from interviews with Eliot.

[p. 248] "No deal of any kind existed": Dyson interview with Eliot. All quotations from Dyson in this chapter are from interviews with Eliot.

[p. 248] "Suddenly you have Giuliani and Dinkins": Barwick interview with Eliot.

[p. 256] The figures regarding the buyout of Richard Basciano by the Empire State Development Corporation (formerly the Urban Development Corporation) are from William Bastone, "The Porn Broker," *Village Voice,* July 12, 1995.

[p. 258] "Gerry, what kind of business": Eisner quoted by Schoenfeld, interview with Eliot.

[p. 261] Some of the background information on the Roundabout's involvement with the Selwyn and the New 42 is from Ralph Blumenthal, "New Theater: Your Name Here," *New York Times,* November 23, 1999.

ACKNOWLEDGMENTS

PART ONE: THE STREET AND ME

Although I was born in the Bronx and spent most of my childhood there, I have always considered Manhattan my true spiritual and creative birthplace. In the early years of my life, whenever I was lucky enough to venture out of the dreary gray streets of my neighborhood "to go downtown," I felt as if I were taking a journey into another century. The next one. By the age of ten I was certain that when I grew up, Manhattan—how I adored the lush, caramel, triple-syllable sound of that name—with its sleek, tall buildings, gorgeous movie and stage theaters, hallowed libraries, and cool-looking kids (the coolest of which, I was certain, looked just like me), would be the only place I could ever truly call my home.

My first physical exposure to 42nd Street came at the height of the fifties, during a school trip to the Secretariat Building of the United Nations. I remember we were told to put earphones on and listen to seven or eight different languages of a session in progress, and how amazed I was at the speed of the translators.

The next time I encountered the street came later in the fifties when my father took me to work with him one day. He worked in the garment industry and his showroom was on 39th Street and Broadway. For lunch he took me to the Horn and Hardart Automat on 42nd and Third Avenue, gave me a dollar, and told me to slip it through the opening at the bottom of the glass window to the woman dressed in what looked to me like my Aunt Dottie's nursing outfit, only pink, sitting in a booth in the middle of the restaurant. She had yellow-lightbulb hair captured in a thick black spiderweb, skin like sand, cherry-red lipstick, and an enormous smile. She looked a hundred. She took my dollar and slid back twenty nickels to me in four sets of five for use in the restaurant's famous automated windows.

One night just before my eleventh birthday I heard my older brother, Jeffrey, explaining to a friend of his in graphic, vivid, unforgettable detail how he had taken a neighborhood girl, Sandy, downtown to a "dirty movie" on 42nd Street, where they'd sat in the balcony while he slipped his hand underneath her bra. I can still remember the nuclear mushroom that went off inside of me. It was the first time in my life I had connected the dots between girls and movies. My world would never be flat again.

At the age of twelve I became a professional child actor and appeared on several live television dramas. That same year I made my off-Broadway debut at the Carnegie Hall Playhouse, a legitimate theater in the basement of the great music hall (a few years later it became the Carnegie Cinema). Just before my thirteenth birthday I auditioned for and was accepted to the High School of Performing Arts, then located in a Romanesque Revival building at 120 West 46th Street, between Sixth Avenue and Broadway (specifically chosen by the city in 1948 for its proximity to the theatrically rich Times Square). The school's building is still standing, having been designated a landmark in 1981.

P.A. offered a split day—half academic classes, half "arts" training. Whenever I could get away with it, I'd cut my afternoon academic classes, walk down to 42nd Street and over to the strip between Seventh and Eighth Avenues where all the old movies played, alongside new ones and some foreign films. This was where I saw for the first time many of what would become my favorite films—*On the Waterfront, Rebel Without a Cause, The Man Who Shot Liberty Valance, L'Avventura, Smiles of a Summer Night, Invasion of the Body Snatchers, World Without End, This Island Earth, Dial M for Murder, Psycho*—and, later on, what I would conservatively estimate to be about 2 million pornos (none of which, much to my disappointment, ever matched the Jeff and Sandy saga from the big screen of my childhood memories).

At the age of seventeen, after graduating from P.A., I costarred in an off-Broadway play called *The Goings On at Little Wishful* at the Maidman Playhouse on West 42nd Street.

One day when I was twenty, I found myself on 42nd Street looking to catch a movie, any movie, and discovered, to my utter horror and endless fascination, the "black sheep" of the family, my father's brother, selling hot dogs behind the outdoor aluminum and tile eatery adjacent to what I think was the Selwyn Theater's entrance. I hadn't seen him in years. I said hello. It took him a couple of seconds to recognize me, after which he asked me how I was doing, how my mom and dad were, bought me one "on the house," then leaned over, grabbed me by my collar—I can still remember the smell of mustard coming off his hairy knuckles—and told me he'd kick my ass straight into Queens on a fly if he ever caught me on the street again. I don't remember the movie, but I'll never forget that day.

My theatrical swan song proved to be a 1969 production of *Macbeth*, produced by the Roundabout Theater, whose venue at the time was a 150-seater in the basement of a supermarket on, I believe, West 25th Street. It was a not-for-profit, non-Equity production, meaning no one got paid. I almost didn't take the "job" until I discovered that, in keeping with the spirit and style of the times, this version of the Shakespeare classic was going to have the three witches be topless. I joined the cast, watched every rehearsal, and became involved with one of the actresses giving her all for show business. The Roundabout managed to survive that production and my performance through some pretty rough times, until finally in July 2000, it moved into the old Selwyn, the same theater where my uncle had once worked, renamed the American Airlines Theater, restored in 2000 at a cost of $25 million. The repertory company that couldn't afford to pay its actors when I was a part of it was now the second most successful not-for-profit theater in the country, one of the new crown jewels of the "new" 42nd Street.

Still in the sixties, out of work and trying to pay my hundred-dollars-a-month rent, I did some time as a typing temp for a variety of midtown companies, one of which was a major insurance underwriter whose offices occupied several floors in the Lincoln Building on East 42nd Street. I was so good at it that in the quarterly temp agency newsletter the following appeared, written by my employer: "Would that the girls I hired worked as hard as Mr. Eliot." My mother carried that clipping around for years to show all her friends what a great *typist* I was.

By 1972 I was a college graduate living full-time with my beautiful Irish girlfriend who was from the Midwest and who'd freaked out one day on 42nd Street where she'd stopped off on some errand for a cup of coffee, saw two Hasidim, and to her horror discovered for the first time that Jews were not an ancient race that had died out some time around the birth of Jesus. It was her introduction to the city and the street. One day that same year I stood in line for five hours on the second level of the by-then severely run-down and dreary Grand Central Terminal, where Ticketron had set up a booth to sell Rolling Stones tickets for an upcoming concert at Madison Square Garden. Also in '72 I taught part-time at a private school connected to the U.N. for "special" children. I worked for a man we were only allowed to refer to as "the Admiral." One of my students went on to become a famous movie star.

Having earned my master's degree in fine arts from Columbia University and still desperate to avoid real life, I was about to start work there on a Ph.D. in film history. The summer before classes were scheduled to begin, I killed a lot of time going to the movies, often with my good friend folksinger Phil Ochs. Like me, Phil was obsessed with American film. He loved John Wayne more than I did, especially in John Ford westerns such as *The Searchers*. We both agreed *The Long Voyage Home* was one of the greatest movies ever made. When, the following fall, I began classes again at Columbia, Phil often came along to sit in the back row and listen to

Andrew Sarris's already legendary lectures. In 1976, having completed my classwork, I was about to begin my dissertation (on films of the fifties) when, sadly, Phil committed suicide. That's when I decided to write his biography, *Death of a Rebel*. My writing career had officially begun and I never looked back, leaving my Ph.D. and the world of academia in the storage room of my past.

In the eighties I often went to the Show World on 42nd Street and Eighth Avenue with my best friend, Dennis, to see our favorite porn star, "Aunt Peg," who always put on an unforgettable show, complete with props (telephone), sound effects (phone ringing), and a confessional monologue that never failed to break my heart and raise my . . . hopes.

One day in 1990, having just returned to New York City after spending a year living and writing in Los Angeles (a whole other story), I took what I thought would be an easy and by now for me ritualistic return-to-Manhattan walk down 42nd Street and, out of curiosity, wandered into a store between Seventh and Eighth on the north side that sold kung fu paraphernalia. When I stepped back outside, I was immediately detained by two NYPD street cops who took me into a nearby hallway for an intense search-and-frisk. While they patted me down and checked the insides of my belt buckle and boots, they casually informed me they were looking for weapons and/or drugs, and that if I were carrying either I should tell them before it was "too late." I told them the truth, that I wasn't, and when they didn't find anything they apologized and explained how they were just doing their job, which this day was to be on the lookout for "suspicious characters." Ah. I told them I was a writer, which seemed to satisfy them, we shook hands, they wished me luck, and I got the hell out of there.

Not long after, I returned to Los Angeles, where I spent a good part of the first half of the nineties writing a big fat biography of Walt Disney. While there I barely survived the '94 earthquake, only to dive out of that particular frying pan to find myself somehow subpoenaed to testify in the O. J. criminal trial. To avoid having to do that, I escaped back to New York City and lived under an assumed name in a Times Square hotel where I wrote the initial draft of what became a best-selling book about that experience.

I first thought of writing about 42nd Street one summer afternoon in 1996 while taking a stroll on a street I now considered an old friend. To my surprise, although the signs on the corners insisted that's where I was— 42nd Street—I experienced a vertigo-like sensation when I found I didn't recognize *a single thing*. No Nedick's, no cigar store, no porno, no old movies. On top of that, a Disney store's sidewalk Mickey Mouse stood like a giant nightmare, scaring the bejesus out of the kids. And me.

What, I wondered, had happened? Why did I feel like a tourist in my hometown on a street filled with tourists who seemed much more at home than I did? Why wasn't what had always been there *there* anymore? Where had it all gone? And why? It was the day I decided to write this book.

The first thing I did was to take an apartment in a brand-new luxury high-rise in Midtown West, what used to be known as Hell's Kitchen, although the only thing hellish about it now was the unbelievably high rent. It wasn't until I wandered down the stairs of a subway station near Times Square, where I was able to get a haircut and my shoes shined for a total of twenty dollars, and a shot of vodka at a literal hole in the subway passage walk called Siberia, that I began to feel a little better. Later that day I had a Nathan's hot dog at the corner outlet and had such strong indigestion everything for the moment finally felt right again.

But only for the moment. No sooner had I settled into my new nabe than Nathan's suddenly shuttered and Siberia had to close. The entire corner of 49th and Broadway was owned by a Rockefeller consortium, and they had scheduled the corner for demolition, including the subway station, to be replaced by yet another Times Square high-rise, the *twelfth* in the area since 1998. That night I sat hunched over a nine-dollar martini in one of the fancy new restaurants on West 42nd Street, where everyone around me was smoking like a fiend and yelling to be heard until hoarse and paying for drinks with expense-account credit cards. I sat alone wondering if the city I had grown up in was indeed gone forever, when out of nowhere a beautiful, young, very well-dressed woman sat next to me and ordered a Jameson, no less, straight up. She clutched a pair of expensive-looking brown suede gloves in one hand, a folded copy of the *Wall Street Journal* in the other. When her drink came, she put her gloves down and just before she shot it back, oblivious to everyone and everything—the deepening crush, the deafening roar, the Knicks play-off game on the TVs that hung at each end of the bar, the middle-aged men eyeing her as if they'd never seen a female up-close before, the not-so-middle-aged women doing the same, the bartender with one foot up on the metal beer refrigerator letting the rest of his customers wait while he slowly dried his hands on his apron and mentally undressed her—she buried her perfect nose deep into the paper, studying the Dow like a scholar deciphering Sanskrit. I sent over a drink. She looked up. The bartender nodded in my direction. She turned and smiled at me. That's when I knew I was home at last.

PART TWO: GRATITUDES

I wish to thank everyone whose information and insights helped make this book possible. They are listed elsewhere. Without them I simply could not have written *Down 42nd Street* as I conceived it. I remain grateful for the generous cooperation I received.

I wish to especially thank Gerald Schoenfeld, the chairman of the Shubert Organization, who, after granting me a single five-minute interview, allowed it to somehow stretch over a five-month period. He always made himself available to me, answered all my questions frankly and with great detail, and opened dozens of doors that likely would have remained otherwise closed. He is a charming and gracious man.

Rebecca Robertson readily shared many illuminating stories, provided an extensive list of leads for me to track down, and turned me on to several people and publications I otherwise might not have discovered.

Also generous with their time and information were Frederic Papert, Kent Barwick, William Daly, Don Elliot, Richard Weinstein, and Andrew Sarris.

I also wish to thank Laurence Kirshbaum, chairman of Time Warner Trade Publishing, a class act and one of the good guys; Bob Castillo, Managing Editor of Warner Books; my editor, Les Pockell; his able assistant, Karen Melnyk; copyeditor Bill Betts; and my agent and friend, Mel Berger.

My personal assistant and researcher, Carol Rabadan, was helpful making contacts, finding documents, organizing material, and generally getting me through the professional day.

The Palm West is one of New York City's classic midtown steak houses with a great front bar. It often served as my second office during the writing of this book. Thanks to all the fine young boys and girls there.

And finally, as ever, tips of the Hatlo to my best friend and Chairman of the Board, Dennis Klein, Uncle Duane, and finally Chi-Li Wong, who was, for most of the time *Down 42nd Street* took, my partner in time.